THE STRENUOUS YEARS 1948-55

Cecil Beaton's Diaries
Volume Four

SAPERE BOOKS

THE
STRENUOUS
YEARS
1948-55

Published by Sapere Books.

11 Bank Chambers, Hornsey, London, N8 7NN,
United Kingdom

saperebooks.com

ISBN: 978-1-912546-39-8

Foreword to the New Edition

I welcome the republication of the six volumes of Cecil Beaton's diaries, which so delighted readers between 1961 and 1978. I don't know if Cecil himself re-read every word of his manuscript diaries when selecting entries, but I suspect he probably did over a period of time. Some of the handwritten diaries were marked with the bits he wanted transcribed and when it came to the extracts about Greta Garbo, some of the pages were sellotaped closed. Even today, in the library of St John's College, Cambridge, some of the original diaries are closed from public examination, though to be honest, most of the contents are now out in the open.

The only other person who has read all the manuscript diaries is me. It took me a long time to get through them, partly because his handwriting was so hard to read. I found that if I read one book a day, I had not done enough. If I did two in a day, then I ended up with a splitting headache! This in no way deflected from the enormous enjoyment in reading them.

Altogether there are 145 original manuscript diaries dating from Cecil going up to Cambridge in 1922 until he suffered a serious stroke in 1974. A few fragments of an earlier Harrow diary survive, and there is a final volume between 1978 and 1980, written in his left hand. 56 of these cover his time at Cambridge, some of which appear in *The Wandering Years* (1961). 22 books cover the war years, and were used for *The Years Between* (1965), and nine books record his *My Fair Lady* experiences, some of which appear in *The Restless Years* (1976) and were the basis for *Cecil Beaton's Fair Lady* (1964). These six volumes probably represent about ten per cent of what Cecil Beaton actually wrote.

The diaries attracted a great deal of attention when first published. James Pope-Hennessy wrote of Cecil's 'thirst for self-revelation', adding that the unpublished volumes were surely 'the chronicle of our age'. Referring to Cecil's diaries, and those of Eddy Sackville-West, he also commented: 'We could not be hoisted to posterity on two spikier spikes.'

I have to tell the reader that these volumes were not always quite the same as the originals. Some extracts were rewritten with hindsight, some entries kaleidoscoped and so forth. Certain extracts in these six volumes were slightly retouched in places, in order that Cecil could present his world to the reader exactly as he wished it presented. And none the worse for that.

Hugo Vickers
January 2018

Part I: London and Broadchalke, 1948-9

INDECISIONS ON RETURN TO ENGLAND

April, 1948

For most of us — if we are fortunate — each day seems to help us, even a little, along the road we have chosen to take. Often the 'going' is pleasant, and so beguiled are we by the interest on the wayside that we hardly notice that we are travelling. Only at certain junctures are we faced with decisions and have to take stock of our situation. Have we come along the path we intended? And if so, do we go straight on? Or do we now decide to alter course?

On arrival back in England, after so long and momentous a stay in America, I felt that I had come to such a juncture. In what direction should I now go? For some considerable time after my return I felt in a bit of a quandary. What was my aim? What did I really want to do? Was it worthwhile continuing with all the doings that had occupied me for so long? Some decision must be made. But, as often happens, I made no decision. Force of habit resulted in my continuing along the same road.

At first progress was slow. There seemed to be less than the usual variety of distractions — certainly less excitement. But, after a quiet beginning, I came to accept a certain loneliness, to make the best of it, and to rely more upon my old, familiar friends. They did not appear hurt or resentful that I had ignored them, or paid less attention to them than before: they were glad that I should pick up and mend the threads that had been temporarily broken. After being away for such a while, I found that they reappeared with a delightful freshness; I had forgotten that they were so bright, understanding and wise. They gave one a sense of stability merely by the fact that one felt one had their backing. I enjoyed even more than I remembered their wit and their art of conversation. They seemed more brilliant at argument, courageously holding unpopular views, filling the air with conflicting opinions without losing their tempers. In the worlds of art and entertainment so much was being created. There were many exciting things happening around me. London life seemed extraordinarily invigorating.

And then I rediscovered the joys of the English countryside. It was particularly wonderful now that I had a new house to cherish and a garden to develop. Already there were signs of the beginnings of spring: a line of snowdrops flanked the wall each side of the front door at Reddish, and soon other parts of the garden were beginning to respond to the reorganization already started. The apple trees were forming new growth, and the Victorian rosebeds disappeared almost without trace from the lawn. Inside the house, which I was growing to love, there was a lot to be done. The Charles II wallpapers were just as suitable as I had hoped for the library and my bedroom. Of furniture I had only the minimum, but excellent things could be found if one went often enough to Mr Percy Bates's and other Salisbury antique shops.

For almost two years I have been free-wheeling along quite pleasantly without thinking much about making any money or giving thought to my career. Now I really must consider what most it is that I want to do. The war had given me an incentive to step out towards new photographic horizons, and to point my camera at more rugged aspects of life; but that incentive was now removed. Yet I did not want to go back to my old vomit. Enough of taking fashions on young models who survived just as long as their faces showed no sign of character, or of elderly, but rich harpies appearing as if butter would not melt in their terrible mouths. But I would not give up photography: it was an important part of my life. Perhaps I could be strong enough to turn down photographic offers that were no longer a challenge, and concentrate on people and subjects of real interest to me. I must also allow myself time to start painting seriously. Perhaps I would have more confidence if I took a course at some art college; I would see if this could be arranged. And there was always, at the back of my mind, the biting desire to write a play. Already I had three or four comedies relegated to the chest of drawers in my bedroom at Reddish; each represented much concentrated work, application and endeavour, besides months of expensive retyping. I knew they were not stage-worthy; they were merely repositories of hopes unfulfilled. However, I had long since an idea of writing a play about Gainsborough, an artist with whom I had a close rapport, and whom I felt was, in his dislike of pretentiousness and in other ways, not unlike my father. That would be of great help in developing the character. Perhaps this present lull provided the opportunity to start writing it.

But before the memories were any the less acute, I must write about my fifteen happy years at Ashcombe — that house in the downs so little distance from my new home, but which I could never visit again. Soon all other activities became secondary. Even the diary entries were spasmodic: when writing on some specific subject, my journal jottings, which I enjoy, go by the board. With *Ashcombe*[1] at the printers, normal

---

[1] My book about my fifteen-year lease of my other house in Wiltshire,

9

existence began. Several tempting jobs were offered. Would I care to decorate a theatre? The Duke of York's was in a sorry state of disrepair, and despite post-war conditions Marianne Davis, the delightful, sporting young owner, considered it could be made to look pretty again. It could.

Would I design *The Second Mrs Tanqueray* for the Haymarket? I had never quite recovered from the beauty of Gladys Cooper whom I had seen when the Victorian play was revived in the twenties. At a time when fluffy bobbed hair was fashionable, she had parted hers in the centre and scraped it back into a large, pale honey-coloured, silken bun. Her white marble face with the noble forehead and deep-set blue eyes of a deer were of a haunting loveliness. She had worn a fashionable Molyneux dress, shapeless as a sack but as heavily encrusted with jewels as a Byzantine empress. It was as this *demi-mondaine* out of her social depths, a part that had previously belonged to Mrs Patrick Campbell, that Gladys was first considered seriously as a fine actress; the trace of a slight cockney accent gave added poignancy to her performance. Another good actress, Eileen Herlie, who had created a furore in Cocteau's *Eagle with Two Heads*, was now to be the wanton Paula.

It is a fallacy to pretend that most people look better on the stage than off. The overhead lights add ten years to create havoc with all but the most bun-like of faces. My only difficulty with the delightful Eileen Herlie was to make her as beautiful on the lit stage as she was under the one harsh 'working light' of rehearsals. Eventually we discovered that her classical features were seen at their best when — like Duse — she appeared without any make-up. It was agreed that the costumes and scenery should be done in the styles of the original, though for the second act drawing-room I went for

published by Batsford, 1949.

my source to the tapestry of haymaking scenes in the library at the Dashwoods' West Wycombe Park. Although Eileen Herlie gave a performance of tremendous power, the difficulty of finding contemporary male actors with the necessary 'Edwardian' style was responsible for the revival carving no niche in theatrical history.

Other designing jobs kept me in London. Now that Sadlers Wells Ballet, with Margot Fonteyn, had become so grand and successful in its new quarters at Covent Garden, it was natural that they should revive their early success *Apparitions*, Freddie Ashton's romantic Liszt ballet, which had originally been produced on one of Dame Lilian Bayliss's thinnest shoestrings. (The fifty pound fee I received for designing the work went back into the kitty to pay for the costumes.) But to accommodate the giant stage the sets now had to be enlarged and reproportioned. Since most of the original costumes were worn to rags they, too, had to be redesigned in a bolder conception. Having previously had the unique talent of the Russian Karinska, who had made from my original sketches confections of lightness and delicacy, it was now like being at the mercy of a plain, but wholesome English cook to have, in the wardrobe of Covent Garden, Miss Crammer's heavy hand on the spun-sugared dresses of the ball scenes. Somehow this most exquisite of Freddie's ballets lost much of the haunting quality that made it unique on the smaller stage.

Soon my secretary, Maud Nelson, was busy putting down too many dates in the appointments book. They consisted of sittings to photograph brides, theatre people, and even members of the Royal Family. I did advertising photographs for America, often using my new house and garden as background. Although sometimes the arrangements were almost as elaborate as if for a theatrical production, and might necessitate several visits to Paris fashion houses, I made a small fortune photographing for my good friends at Johnson & Johnson.

But, most important of my projects, was the jotting down on paper of the ideas, going around restlessly in my head that, in turn, revolved about the character of Gainsborough. The more I read about the painter the more I loved him, and the jigsaw pieces of his lifetime seemed to create a picture that seemed, at least to me, to make a play. I went to Broadchalke to work, and soon became absorbed. Maud Nelson, between bouts of asthma, would call me from London only if there was urgent need to distract me from my intended masterpiece.

Most writers discipline themselves to working certain hours, then knock off for relaxation until the morrow. Charles Morgan writes for a limited time each day, after which he goes out to cut wood; Willie Maugham has a stopwatch by his side and, on completion of the day's quota, goes to the terrace and prepares for the elaborate ritual of the dry martini. When I am deep into my subject it is only when overcome by the extremity of fatigue, resulting in eye-strain and headache, that I am able, of my own free will, to call it quits. Of course to work all day, then late into the night as well, is a short-term policy; but perhaps it is the fear of never being able to put down my thoughts on paper which causes me to flog myself beyond endurance. Perhaps, also, it is the terror of the blank page that makes me scribble something, no matter of how little interest it may later prove to be. Sometimes, when painting, my high hopes are suddenly dashed by the ruin in front of me of what I had thought would be a tower of achievement. It is then that the disappointment and frustration are almost beyond endurance; I have lain on my bed in the acutest agony, every bone aching as if run over by a tank.

Mercifully one does not suffer in this way when writing. If one sees later that one was tired and uninspired and the work rotten, at least a word or two can be salvaged from the mess and one has some sort of foundation on which to continue. There are playwrights who can spend a whole morning inventing an exit line. Amateur that I am, I barge ahead ruthlessly, hoping to get the general shape of a scene and that, perhaps many moons later, the dialogue will receive the necessary buffing. Maybe this is an extravagant and wasteful way of working. Certainly the bulk of typescript keeps the dustman busy.

In order to keep myself green in the memory of Greta Garbo in New York I wrote to her two or three times a week. I loved writing to her, for it brought her closer to me. It was a pleasant surprise — since she had often told me that she did not know how to write, and hated sending letters to anyone — to see envelopes written in pencil in her strong block-lettering arriving quite frequently. They were delightful — addressed to 'Beat', 'Master Beatie' or 'Beatie boy'. She had put up her Californian house for sale, but suddenly got 'panicki' and could call it off again. She might be able to come to Europe again this late summer, if it were the will of Allah, or whoever knows the ways of the Lord in heaven. Once she wrote that she had gone to the trouble of flying to an island to get rid of a three-months-old cold. After a day or two she had left; it was too windy.

Sometimes the letters were funny, sad or morbid. All alone in the wilderness, running around on the hard asphalt in the filthy air of Manhattan, she was 'out of order', but continued fighting it out with her perturbed soul. She felt that she had messed up her life. She trusted that, with the will of the Lord, we might meet soon; but added that, as time flies so fast, 'soon' is practically 'now'.

BROADCHALKE NEIGHBOURS

Since I have come to live in the Chalke valley, some unexpected delights have almost compensated for the pain of being uprooted from Ashcombe. No doubt but this Broadchalke landscape is less wild and romantic than the wooded valleys and downland nearer the Dorset border, and there is not the variety of walks that I used to enjoy. But it is pleasant to feel one is part of a rustic community. At Ashcombe the nearest villages of Tollard Royal and Ludwell were too distant to drop in on, and I knew few of their inhabitants who seemed to me, in my ignorance, to be unwelcoming, even unfriendly; an inter-marrying, straggling little population without newspapers or radios, they were quite remote from the world outside.

My new house is only eight miles away from Ashcombe, so I am still fortunate in having such interesting neighbours as the David Cecils at Cranborne, Raymond Mortimer, Desmond Shawe-Taylor, and Eddie Sackville-West at Crichel, and I am even nearer to dear Juliet Duff and other close friends at Wilton. But, on arrival at Broadchalke, I discovered that village life along the River Ebble is friendly and welcoming, and that much of it passes in a pageant along the small street below my bedroom windows.

The 'lord of the manor', taking his front-row pew in the church, is picturesque Dr Burroughs, long since retired from his London practice in Hertford Street, who occupies what is known as the King's Old Rectory. Not that it ever was a vicarage; from the year 950 it was a farm belonging to the

Rectors, later to become the property of the Abbess of Wilton before she swapped the Wilton estate for King's College, Cambridge, to whom most of us in Broadchalke still pay our dues. The grey stone archway to the rambling house is the village's chief landmark, and there is an Italianate water garden with cypresses and rare species of primulas, fritillaries, and plants brought from all quarters of the world. This was created originally by Maurice Hewlett, whose mock medieval novel, *The Forest Lovers*, earned him a fortune before the 1914 war. But — and let this be a warning to me — Hewlett overspent on his ever-expanding garden schemes, and had to retire to a nearby cottage. Henry Burroughs is a little, rosy crab-apple of a man, with brilliant turquoise eyes that sparkle with amusement — even when he was suffering from having fallen from an apple loft.

That strange apparition, bicycling along at great speed with a stream of fluttering drapery behind her, is Sister Agnes and she enjoys her sobriquet 'the lady in grey'. The widow of a clergyman in Dar-es-Salaam, she arrived from New Zealand to dig herself deep into the viewless and damp 'Walnut Cottage' below the village street. She is too strange and unreliable to be popular, and her neighbours say she is not entitled to wear the Franciscan nun's habit; but the fact that her life is shrouded in mystery gives her added interest. She has tiny beads for eyes, white wayward strands of hair, and a long, magenta nose as pointed, if not barbed, as her conversation. She does not mince her words in her hatred of the vicar. But the love of her life for many years has been a cat named Happy. Often pet animals take on the character of their owners, and perhaps because its mistress takes so little pride in her own appearance, Happy allowed her long Persian fur to become matted, lustreless and smelly. When Happy died and guinea pigs took her place, the stench at Sister Agnes's made a visit an ordeal rather than an entertainment.

Wearing an old-fashioned Girl Guides' uniform, complete with whistle and 1914 khaki-brimmed hat, Mrs Rhoda Templemore-Richardson, long past the age of retirement, is nearly always to be seen at the crossroads in the village hearing the news of all who live within a wide radius. She is the confidante of everybody. No farmer has a more encouraging audience than Mrs Templemore-Richardson, who is appalled to hear about the latest disaster to the crops, and she will walk five miles to Bowerchalke to take a bundle of watercress to an invalid in a wheelchair. Her gaunt, but once pretty face, with its wishing-bone-thin nose, nail-pointed teeth and wild, dark eyes, will be lit, like a Georges de la Tour, by a lantern as she sings Christmas hymns with the children in the snow. She takes the local wolf cubs under her wing for a day's outing, and returns at night, her hair streaming, in time to serve on a local committee in the village hall. The Templemore-Richardsons' house is the ugliest and most uncomfortable in the village, built eighty years ago of bright red brick and flint. It is entirely without heating, but Rhoda feels that, if she thaws for long enough in a hot morning bath, she will accumulate enough warmth to see her through to bedtime. How Rhoda Templemore-Richardson manages to survive on such small amounts of food is a miracle: her diet consists of a peck at a few crumbs and a rare cup of village hall tea. She is a squirrel-hoarder; she never throws away a newspaper — the result is chaos.

Major Charles Prest is still sadly crippled by his wounds from the First World War; but, in spite of them, he and his pretty wife Marguerite — with long, wire-thin limbs and old-fashioned loops of hair like an etching by Shepperson in an early *Punch* — are active in the welfare of the community while keeping up appearances in a style that is becoming sadly obsolete.

A more exaggerated military type is Captain Sebastian Dalrymple — a true Edwardian and the personification of the Yeomanry Regiment to which he proudly belonged during the 1914 war; Captain Dalrymple, as he liked to be known, had always had dash and style since the early days when he danced with my mother before her marriage. Now, with his puce face a mass of broken blood-vessels, and hair sprouting wildly from every orifice, with his aquiline conk and glassy eyes, he presents a quixotic appearance in his antiquated tweeds as he drives around in a very old Daimler with his imperious wife by his side.

Another highly-hued complexion belongs to Simon Maxton who lives in the Little Lunnon valley, but manages, in his 'old bone-shaker', to make the distance between us non-existent. Simon, immensely tall and lanky, white-haired with lots of wrinkles, is eternally young. He is extremely well-read and a mine of information on diversified subjects but he enjoys being racy, bawdy, and lewd. He is also extremely kind, though he seldom seems to be given his rewards, or even be shown normal gratitude. One evening he told me about how his sister got married.

'I've never been very close to Ida; we were brought up in different households, and we seldom see one another today. But I did get her off the shelf — though she never thanked me for it.'

'Why? Wasn't it a success?'

'Oh, a great success! It's another instance of a *mariage de convenance* being more lasting than a love match. All my other sisters married for love and have been divorced. But Ida seemed as if she was going to be left high and dry. I went to her one day and said: "Now look — old Admiral so-and-so's been hanging around after you for a very long time. Hadn't you better make a go of it and marry him?" My sister said oh, she didn't know about that. Was it necessary? Was it really a good idea? And, in any case, the Admiral had never mentioned the subject, and would he be willing to marry her?

"'Well, if he would, would you be willing to marry him?"

"'Oh, I suppose so."

'I went to Admiral so-and-so and put the proposition to him, and he scratched his head a bit and said well yes, if she wanted to marry him that would be all right by him. So back I went to my sister, and the whole thing was fixed by me — even the date of the wedding. And I had to get all her clothes. Ida's the worst-dressed woman in the world — looks a perfect fright if she possibly can — so I thought I'd play safe and I bought everything for her trousseau in navy blue. (I got the shock of my life when I discovered it all went black at night — but no matter!) The day of the wedding came, and it was the most revolting November day in London with thick fog — so depressing — you could hardly see a yard in front of you. Well, the old girl and I motored together to the church, and I don't know whether it was the fog or not, but she suddenly became most terribly depressed and started to cry, and just as we were slowly nearing the church she said she didn't want to be married — couldn't face it and wouldn't go through with it! Imagine my feelings! I'd arranged the whole clam-jamphrie, and all the guests were in the church. So I just quietly told the driver to go on driving round the square in the fog until I gave him other instructions.

'Then I started on at her as she sat blubbing in all her finery. I said: "Now, old girl, you don't want to get married to this man? Right! What alternative have you in mind? Has anyone else ever paid you any attention? Have you got anyone else who'll keep you? If not, how are you going to live? You haven't any money: I haven't a penny — I can't spare you a farthing. You're thirty-five already. And you have the kind of appearance that won't last more than a year or two. What's to happen then? You're not trained for any job — you've got no talents: what are you going to do? You say you don't want to marry this man who's willing to look after you, but what else is in store?"

'Thereupon, amidst more tears, she told me to tell the chauffeur to drive to the church. So we made our way through the fog, and the progress was so slow I was terrified she'd change her mind again. She went on sobbing, and I thought what a freak her husband will think her when he sees her coming up the aisle on my arm. We got out of the motor and she put her arm through mine, and I was about to take her up the aisle when the verger came rushing up to us saying we were in the wrong positions — she must be on my other arm. This set her off — not crying but laughing — she couldn't stop! All the way up the aisle she giggled and laughed; I don't know what the congregation must have thought of her — let alone her husband! Anyway, they were married, and the marriage has been a very happy one blessed by four children. But I thought it a little ungrateful — stupid of me, I suppose, ever to expect recompense — however, I was a little hurt that she never thanked me for my help in providing for her happiness. Of course Ida's now very well off, but she never even thinks of sending me a card at Christmas.'

EMERALD CUNARD

July 10th, 1948

Emerald ceased to live on Saturday.

She had started to fail last winter, yet she refused to take a bronchial bout seriously enough to curtail her activities. Eventually doctors took charge and pronounced her to be in a 'serious condition'. Her spirits pulled her through until the spring, when again, she was stricken. Emerald, very angry, told the doctors of every concert, play and party that she was missing. 'You stay right here; you've got an infected lung and a weak heart.' Again she recovered, and described her heart attack to Diana Cooper as 'extremely pleasant — one was floating among the clouds!'

One afternoon I had arranged to visit her among the ormolu decorations of her Dorchester Hotel suite. On arrival, Gordon, her nice, homespun, Scots maid, explained in fluting terms that her ladyship was asleep and must not be disturbed. I was slightly vexed, having made an effort to be there on time.

Next day Emerald telephoned to say it was a most extraordinary thing, but she had gone out that afternoon to do some shopping, and returned so utterly exhausted that she had had to ask a young visitor, the painter Robin Ironside, to go away as she could not talk or listen to what he was saying. She had slept till lunchtime today.

A few days later I again went along to see her. She had forgotten that I was due, and when Gordon showed me into her bedroom, Emerald — a very white china doll — sat looking at me quite dazedly, with her piercingly kohl-rimmed eyes, from her small French bed. She explained later that, since her illness, she had felt quite dizzy and that it was some little time before she could see who people were. She seemed peevish at feeling ill and weak. 'I've never been ill in my life before; this is something I'm not accustomed to. It's really most objectionable.'

Emerald soon rallied to talk with much of her accustomed tenderness, which is the quality that I like most of all in her. She is witty; yes, one laughs more in her company than in that of others. She is brilliant, and often profound in a worldly, cynical way. But it is her sense of melting sympathy in the presence of beauty, poetry, and the people she loves, that appeals to my heart.

Unfortunately, it was not long before several other visitors arrived in her hotel bedroom. Emerald was even more put out by the invasion than I was. Although she did not scruple to show her feelings to the unannounced guests, they did not take the hint to leave; so she made a superhuman effort and started to conduct the conversation.

Never for an instant did I suspect that this was to be the last time I should see Emerald alive.

As a young man I used to warm myself in my friendships with older people; they often seemed to be such excellent value, and their experience of the world gave them an added brightness. Emerald was a dazzling, but distant star. From the newspapers I knew that originally she came from San Francisco, had married a fox-hunting squire, Sir Bache Cunard of the shipping line, but soon found that she preferred the company of writers and musicians and arrived in London to become hostess in a large house in Grosvenor Square. From the sidelines I watched her in Venice, or at the Covent Garden opera. I thought I had never seen a more amusing-looking little parakeet in her pastel-coloured plumage. Emerald's clothes were witty confections and retained, with her perfumed Edwardian aura, the romantic aspects of the turn of the century — yet Emerald's mind could never be bound by Edwardian conventions. Her cheeks were always rouged with carnation pink, her lips cerise, her hair as pale yellow and fluffy as the feathers of a day-old chick; her legs and feet were more like a wagtail's, so staccato and expressive. Yet, in spite of features that on others might be considered ridiculous, she presented herself with such artistry that she succeeded in appearing to be the embodiment of her own wit and gaiety. No one else remotely resembled her.

When Emerald took notice of me, I felt I had not lived in vain; by degrees, she would invite me quite regularly to lunch parties. I was tremendously impressed — not only by the illustrious company, but by the manner in which she gave each guest his opportunity to do the best for himself. If, unfortunately, some performance was not as good as expected, or was running over length, Emerald had a deft way of pulling in the reins so that the runaway would be halted in order to give place to others; or she herself would take the centre of the stage — her histrionic gift was a brilliant and natural phenomenon. She could be wonderfully Wildean, no writer has been able to create on paper the quality or effect of Emerald's conversation. Not only were her observations apt, completely spontaneous and sometimes devastatingly frank, but they were delivered with the artistry of a great actress. She had perfected the art of inflection: the pause and timing were innate. Her hands — in later years twisted with rheumatism — weaved and swept or jabbed the air only when gestures were needed, for she also knew the value of repose.

Of course Emerald could be quite unreasonable if she took a dislike to someone, or if she considered they had failed her; but she was seldom unkind. At an early stage in my career she was aware that I wished to include her — as a Marie Laurencin type

— in my first publication, *The Book of Beauty*. She posed willingly, though somewhat self-consciously, for a photograph to be included. But when the book appeared she became highly embarrassed, as she always was when the subject of her appearance was broached. She took against my book. She reviled me: 'He calls me a "hostess" — a most objectionable word!' She was quite right: the book was full of journalistic clichés of the time. But perhaps Emerald gave the jejune effort too much importance when, in front of a group of luncheon guests, she threw it on the fire and put the poker through the burning pages. That particular storm took a long time to pass; but friendship was restored when I rescued her from a carousel horse that revolved too merrily in the grounds of Gerald Berner's house at Farringdon.

This friendship became very real: I felt Emerald had a unique sympathy for me and my problems. Without being told, she could gather what was passing through my mind; sometimes she knew my mood better than I myself. Courage, loyalty and friendship were embedded in her little frame; she gave a fresh life to everything, including the most obvious. Often, when listening to her talk, I have felt that 'This is what I enjoy most of all; at this moment I am happy'.

Emerald, for all her fantasies and foibles, was a woman who lived *dans le vrai*. Someone as rough and rowdy as Lady Astor could never appreciate Emerald's subtlety, and quite wrongly judged her 'a pushin' American'. She was far more than a social figure. The much richer hostess, Mrs Ronnie Greville, was a galumphing, greedy, snobbish old toad who watered at her chops at the sight of royalty and the Prince of Wales's set, and did nothing for anybody except the rich. Emerald cultivated important people if she could play with them as if they were notes on a harpsichord. She had a keen eye for spotting the merits of people in most unknown places; she was a true patron and pioneer.

Although she seldom ventured into the country any more, Emerald listened with such understanding to my enthusiasm for my new house in Wiltshire. 'What is it called?' she asked me, and I told her its name was 'Reddish'. She expostulated: 'But that's impossible! It must be called "Oriflamme!"' Emerald made a definite date on which to visit me: that visit will now never take place.

I particularly admired Emerald in America when, at the beginning of the war, cantankerous and in somewhat reduced circumstances, she was determined to maintain her high standards, and could not understand much that she saw all around her. Not only was she completely misunderstood and unappreciated by most of her fellow countrymen, but she realized she had become a foreigner. She preferred to come back to London for the bombing. Her Grosvenor Square house sold, she took rooms at the Dorchester, where she paid scant attention to the holocaust from the guns outside her windows; but the bombshell that shattered her was the news of Sir Thomas Beecham's surprise marriage. She confided that only two days before, when she asked him if the rumours of his love affair with Miss Betty Humby were true, Sir Thomas had leant back and laughed: 'Oh no, no! She's impossible! Do you know, she told me yesterday that she was descended from a long line of dentists!' When Emerald read of the wedding of the man to whom she had devoted so much of her life, and upon whose musical projects she had spent most of her fortune, she was never quite the same, although she rallied bravely, and never spoke ill of the man who had treated her so ruthlessly.

By degrees, she recovered her spirits enough to fabricate a little flutter of the heart with a delightful and brilliant young man, of great promise at the Foreign Office, named Nicholas Lawford. The 'romance' was in the nature of play-acting with amusement and delight on both sides. Nicholas would hang a bunch of early morning flowers on the handle of her bedroom door before going off to Whitehall, and Emerald would confide her tender feelings to her friends; but the romance was not serious and, in spite of her other varied interests, Emerald was a lonely Joan without her Darby Beecham.

Emerald's critics ask why she operated only in the world of privilege. It is true that she could only breathe in the rarefied atmosphere in which the arts often flourish. But her insistence on the encouragement of young painters and playwrights, and her organizing of the performance of the works of young musicians, have done more to help the masses appreciate and enjoy theatre, ballet and opera than all the reforms made since the war.

To me, Emerald was the quintessence of the civilization that is now in eclipse; she brought a sense of artistry, fantasy and charm to everything. Yet she emerged during those frustrating years of the war's aftermath to weather the changes and become part of the new scene. Although she lived in her ivory tower in Mayfair, immune from queueing and the more rigorous restrictions, she reacted like a barometer to certain developments that were taking place outside. She recognized as 'dated' other much younger people whose point of view was less adapted to change than her own, and she welcomed some of the free forms of expression.

In spite of illness, her joy in living continued, and she scolded a young man for being late for lunch when he excused himself by saying he had been to see a doctor. 'You're a young man. You don't need a doctor to keep you alive; you only need a doctor when you're old to help you to die.' At the last small dinner party she gave, it seemed as if her bodily aches and pains had conquered her spirit. She admitted she believed she could not survive another three months, but that since much of the world had become so ugly, and life unlike everything she believed it should represent, she was not sorry to go. Thereupon, she raised a glass of champagne and said: 'I drink to my death.'

When a friend told me of Emerald's death, I telephoned her maid, Gordon, to know if I could come and pay my last respects. Gordon, who had been at Emerald's side for almost eight weeks without more than an hour or two's sleep at a time, told me of the last scene. Emerald knew that she was dying but had no fear of death. She gave instructions that there was to be no memorial service, no publicity, and that she wished to be cremated with as little fuss as possible. For days she lay in a drugged state. Then, when they knew that the end was near, the doctor, nurse and Gordon stood by her bed. Emerald, incapable of lucid speech, kept whispering the word 'pain', 'pain', 'pain'. The doctor asked: 'Where is the pain?' Emerald shook her head. 'Pain — pain,' she repeated. Gordon gave her the new novel by Robin Maugham, which happened to be by her bedside, together with a pencil. On the fly leaf Emerald managed to scrawl the word 'champagne'. Gordon thought it curious that she should wish to drink now, since she was accustomed only to an occasional small glass of hock. Gordon produced a teaspoon and put a little on Emerald's lips. But she shook her head again, pointed to an unopened bottle of champagne, then nodded to the doctor, nurse and Gordon in turn. They understood. She seemed to smile as they drank to her.

Gordon beckoned me to the room where, on her small French bed, lay a strange object of art. A minute bird-like head, wrapped in a wimple-scarf, was for a moment quite unrecognizable as the person that I loved. And yet, as I studied it, the sharpness of the mouth and the beak were the same; but, without her colour, she had become as if carved in deep ivory: teeth, lips, eyelids and cheeks were all made of ivory. Death had changed her, but had shown her strength and ennobled her.

It is difficult to realize that Emerald, always so immediate and vital, is now something of the past. I cannot believe that somewhere her force and vitality will not again emerge. For me, her death is as if a certain music had gone from life. I cannot believe that the old German liftman at the hotel will not take me up automatically to the seventh floor (707), and that I shall not be overjoyed by the sight of a great array of gilt chairs, cherry-coloured brocade, ormolu figures and, standing bird-like among her remaining possessions, Emerald, the most exquisite object of all. Like a fantastic, twittering canary in a pinchbeck cage, she would be holding forth with great originality, authority, and a unique attitude of mind on some most unexpected topic, even her own death. When asked by a friend if she would not like to die in her sleep, her reply was immediate: 'No, I'd rather be shot.' Emerald, a worshipper of beauty until the end, made her life into a work of art.

PRINCE CHARLES

December 1948

Happily summoned to the Palace to take the first long-awaited photographs of the heir to the throne. Prince Charles, as he is to be named, was an obedient sitter. He interrupted a long, contented sleep to do my bidding and open his blue eyes to stare long and wonderingly into the camera lens, the beginning of a lifetime in the glare of public duty.

THE LAURENCE OLIVIERS

Thursday, January 24th, 1949

I was now about to see how my work on the Olivier production of *The School for Scandal* had materialized. The preliminary work had been extremely pleasant; in fact, everything had gone so smoothly from the moment I first showed my rough designs. Larry and Vivien had come to dinner after his day's shooting in *Hamlet*, and every proffered suggestion had been accepted with enthusiasm by him until, exhausted, Larry laid his head on the dining-table and went fast asleep.

I knew only too well what a risk it is if a designer cannot supervise the execution of his work throughout every step of the way until the last moment before the curtain goes up on the first night. Inevitably readjustments have to be made as one discovers that a certain notion does not materialize as expected, or that an actor is unsuited to a particular garment. Someone else's lighting can ruin the colours of a set, and a prop master can produce some anachronism that is so obvious that it is amazing that no one else has noticed it.

Due to Larry's *Hamlet* film having taken far longer to shoot than scheduled, and the subsequent postponement of his work on *The School for Scandal*, I had had to drag myself away towards the end of the preparations in order to fulfil a long since arranged photography contract in America. I was satisfied with the preliminary fittings for Lady Teazle's clothes which made

Vivien appear an exquisite figure of Chelsea china, and fortunately the scene painters seemed to have the time and talent to paint my sets to look exactly like enlargements of coloured engravings. But I knew I was leaving with the opportunities for so many cup and lip slips. Now, having finished the first stage of the work, I had to abandon it to others; it was like leaving a child to find its way alone.

It must have been hell at the dress rehearsal when the designer was absent, and Mrs Candour wanted to change her bonnet and Sir Benjamin Backbite would suddenly like to add a muff to his costume. It was also a bloody nightmare for me — taking each theatre job as seriously as I do — knowing that the Atlantic was between me and any alterations that others were now perfunctorily thinking fit to make.

The Olivier company went off to Australia and my contractual obligation was over. It was a great relief when clippings filtered back praising my work. It was an even greater relief when the company returned to open the play in London and Larry wired me (I was still in New York) that, in his first night 'curtain' speech my name had received the greatest applause of all.

It was, therefore, a hideous surprise when, a few nights after my return to London, a comparative stranger who works in films, Anatole, known as Tolly, de Grunewald, came up to me and said: 'My God, the Oliviers are gunning for you! What have you done to them?' I was too breathless to reply, and did not wish to let this man see how shocked I was. I had felt that Larry and Vivien — particularly Vivien — were real friends, and I could think of no reason why they should both have anything against me.

February 24th, 1949

John Gielgud came with me to see the Sheridan play the next time it was given in the repertory. Over an early dinner John and I had a great deal to talk about though I did not mention to him the qualms I was feeling since I had met the 'intolerable' de Grunewald. We arrived too late at the New Theatre to call on the Oliviers before curtain time, but as we crawled into our seats the lights dimmed in the auditorium and went up on stage to reveal a richly-coloured engraving of Lady Sneerwell's house with super-elegant footmen bowing, moving furniture and lighting candles. It was not surprising that I paid more attention to the decorative aspects of the evening than to the play and its performers; but I doubt if ever before have I, in the theatre, so unrestrainedly enjoyed the fruits of my own work. I was wreathed in rapturous smiles as one stage picture, and one delightful costume after another, appeared in the glow of a masterly lighting expert's effects. John, likewise, was in a condition of euphoria about the whole evening and, at the end of the performance, together we went backstage to congratulate all concerned. Rather than visit each room together we decided to go our separate ways, John starting off with Larry while I tapped on Vivien's door.

On going into the leading lady's dressing-room, in spite of the de Grunewald story, I expected the usual backstage superlatives, the 'darlings', the hugs and kisses. I met with a view of Vivien's back; she did not turn round to greet me. I kept up a hollow flow of flattery, filled with green room jargon, in praise of her performance and her appearance. Vivien's eyes of steel now stared at herself as she rubbed a slime of dirty cold cream, a blending of rouge, eyeblack, and white foundation over her face. Not one word did she say about my contribution to the evening. She broached no other subject, and answered any question with a monosyllable. Somehow, after a short while, I managed to extract myself from the room. Phew!

Now I must face Larry and, possibly — though why I knew not the reason — the same frigid reception. It was worse than I could have expected: no smiles, no back thumping, and no 'old mans' or 'old cocks'. Larry had some elder relation with him — a cleric to whom I was not introduced — who naturally monopolized his time and interest. I remained silently in the background, like a recalcitrant schoolboy waiting to be given a severe 'dressing down', by the 'governor'. As soon as the clergyman was the other side of the door, in a panic to avoid a silence, I let forth an avalanche of praise about the production: about how right he was in his portrayal of a middle-aged, not a senile Sir Peter; about the prettiness of Vivien, the polish of the teamwork, and the charm of so much 'business' that he had invented — such as the cascade of bandboxes arriving at the front door as an indication of Lady Teazle's extravagances. But no reaction: even the most fulsome compliments failed to thaw the temperature. I suppose I should have asked Larry quite bluntly why he and Vivien had suddenly adopted this extraordinary attitude — in fact, it must appear incomprehensible that I did not — but I am always anxious to avoid a row if it is possible to do so. I know, in the theatre, that great explosions of temperament take place on an impulse; appalling things are said in the heat of the moment. Wounding, vile insults are thrown around when the adrenalin rises. But everything is forgiven and forgotten on arrival at the theatre next day. Some people enjoy these blood-lettings: I do not. In fact, if I have to be subjected to an unpleasant scene, or someone is wounding to me, it is likely to be a very long time before the scars are healed.

Larry's dresser now became the focus of his attention: whispered instructions given about his clothes... Then the dresser left, and still Larry addressed no word to me. The silence was broken by John Gielgud coming into the room. I don't know if John noticed anything peculiarly cold about the atmosphere, and I did not mention it to him when, a few moments later, together we left the theatre. But once outside the confines of 'backstage' my indignation rose to the surface. I knew that, such is my unforgiving, unforgetting nature, no matter how hard the Oliviers might try, one day, to make up for this evening's affront, I would have no further interest in them — let alone feel that we were friends. They were both out of my life for ever.

Part II: Holidays and Visits, 1949

VILLA MAURESQUE AND SOMERSET MAUGHAM

Winter, 1949

A vicious attack of the prevalent 'flu felled me completely. For several weeks I tried from my bed to carry on with writing, but I knew I was working under an impossible disadvantage: I seemed to make no progress. When my kind neighbours, Juliet Duff and Simon Fleet, sent me a telegram from the south of France to say Willie Maugham would like me to join them and recuperate in the winter sun, I was soon on an airplane.

My friendship with Willie had only recently started. A few days before taking a ship in New York to return to England, I met another fellow-passenger, one of my oldest and most delightful New York friends, Monroe Wheeler, an erudite and entertaining director of the Museum of Modern Art. He told me: 'Willie wondered if you would care to have your meals on board with us?' Not only was I delighted to be with two such excellent conversationalists, but I was pleased to have this opportunity of perhaps getting to know Willie a little less formally.

My first acquaintance with him had been when, at the start of my professional career as a photographer, he came to my parents' drawing-room to be photographed for *Vanity Fair*. He was shy: I was shy. The sitting did not become alive. I gave him cursory instructions as to where to place his arms and hands. He obeyed: 'Thus?' or 'So?' As a result the photographs were completely static. Although we then became acquaintances over a long period of years, he never seemed to thaw — certainly not towards me. I doubt if this had anything to do with the fact that his wife, the effervescent Syrie, whom he detested, became a particular friend of mine.

On the first day of the Atlantic crossing Willie at dinner said: 'Sissel, I hear you've written a very good play. I would like to read it; have you a copy on board?' I lied. I wished to do a lot more rewriting on it. Couldn't I send him a copy later? Then, of course, I realized that there would surely never again be such an opportunity to benefit by his advice. I owned up to my lie, and sent the play to his cabin.

At luncheon next day Willie said: 'I have read your play, and I will tell you what I think of it at some more suitable time, and in private.' I was full of nervous anxiety at the prospect of the acid test. Of late I had been becoming increasingly dubious about the merits of this gigantic opus; but if I am to go ahead and put it, as I hoped, before the public, it would be asinine to flinch at hearing the opinion of a dramatist who really knows what he is talking about.

The following day I was pacing the deck with Monroe when he said: 'Willie was in wonderful form before luncheon. He came down feeling rather crotchety after a sleepless night. He asked me to take the air with him, and he told me he was worried about what he was going to say to you about the play. Then, proceeding to tell me what he thought of it, he warmed to the task, and when his thoughts were formulated and straight in his head, he said: "Now I think I'll sit down and have a drink." The relief of having got off his mind all he had to say to you was so great that his spirits then began to soar. He was unusually comic — never been in better form!'

At luncheon in the restaurant we talked about Willie's collection of Zoffanys and his other theatrical pictures, about the Old Vic company, a comparison of Noël's and Terry's dramatic talents — but never a word about my play. Eventually I asked when could I have the interview?

'This afternoon at three-thirty.'

Precisely on the moment he appeared: 'We had better go into the dining-room: it is quiet there.'

It was as if I were 'up to the head beak'; I was terrified.

'Well, Sissel, I've read your play with a great deal of interest. It is extremely well written and constructed, and the story is very moving. The characters are excellent, and it's dramatic.' (My heart beat with relief and joy!) 'But there is one thing that worries me very much indeed: you must explain it to me. Why do the characters of Gainsborough and the auctioneer, Christie, talk in a quasi-eighteenth-century manner but then address one another by their Christian names?' Willie recommended Jane Austen and Fielding and that I should read *Clarissa Harlowe* and Sheridan to give the play a far more authentic eighteenth-century flavour. Or perhaps I would prefer to use a contemporary dialect? Then it would be correct to use such phrases as "a place in the sun" which was said by Germans before the last war. "Giving someone a lift" is entirely modern. You must make up your mind which idiom you are going to use.'

I confessed to ignorance and slovenliness and an inattention to detail. Willie also told me he thought the ending could be strengthened. 'You want your final curtain to be something that will make your audience sit up: yours is too arbitrary.' He made the suggestion that I should bring back the dashing young Lord Angus to buy his own portrait, and when the two daughters, both of whom had so disastrously loved him, saw him again, neither could recognize him. Poor, dotty Mary, who has been seduced by him, might ask: 'Who was that man?'

I agreed gladly with everything Willie told me. The criticisms seemed so unimportant compared to my fears that he might say that my play was split down the middle, that it contained some irrevocable fault of construction. What a relief to feel that basically the workmanship was sound, and comparatively little wrong that could not be remedied. Willie stuttered: 'I d-don't know w-whether or not you are prepared to go to all this t-t-trouble; but if you don't, you'll have people laughing at you for these an-an-anachronisms.'

Willie does not realize the vast amount of seventeenth- and eighteenth-century plays I have read and the research I have done (all so very agreeable) in order to arrive at a style that does not smack the ear as being archaic, yet is not jarringly of today: he does not know the lengths to which I am determined to go to make even the smallest improvements. He has no idea how ambitious I am to succeed in any major project I undertake — but more than ever in this particular one.

I thawed towards Willie. The little vellum mask with its tired eyes and drawn mouth suddenly seemed to gain a lost youthfulness and vitality. The eyes twinkled, and the lips smiled albeit in a downward curve. I was amused to know that he was pleased at the way the interview had gone and at the success of his own performance. Quite suddenly he got up and said: 'Now, Sissel, I'm going to leave you for the cinema,' and he bolted out of the room having written 'finish' successfully to another everyday chore.

By the end of the trip I felt more sympathetic to Willie than ever before; but he still seemed too remote to consider as a friend.

Life at the Villa Mauresque is ideal for the semi-invalid: breakfast in bed; the garden below the balcony a sea of magenta and blue cinerarias; no need to put in an appearance before midday. The large salon, with french windows opening onto a terrace, is impressively decorated with a huge sunburst of gilt carving, much golden gesso, huge sofas, and eighteenth-century paintings in carved frames. On the terrace the lunch visitors assemble: maybe witty, delicious and slightly scatty Lady Kitty Lambton with piercing eyes and iron-grey curls, the raven beauty Muriel Wilson who had been part of King Edward's coterie, renowned for organizing amateur theatricals, and who owned the famous nearby 'Maryland' garden. One day that old silenus Marc Chagall appeared with an astonishingly young and pretty wife. For me the special treat was the arrival of Graham and Kathy Sutherland. He is still working on the drawings for a portrait of Willie, and those I've seen are brilliant. Graham does not spare any horses, and he has made Willie as sour as a quince — yet Willie seems delighted.

Occasionally we go off to the Château de Madrid or to the Hôtel de Paris in Monte Carlo to have some appallingly over-rich meal with Lady Bateman. Lady Bateman, a wealthy widow with very little brain under a magnificent head of snow-white hair, is pretty, snobbish and spoilt. No matter how late she returns from a dinner party to her hotel suite, her maid must wait up for her to brush her hair with starch. Her lunches are generally given in aid of some local celebrity such as Prince Pierre de Monaco, and this Edwardian hospitality is something from which Juliet, who suffered an excess of it in her youth and has since devoted her life to artists and intellectuals, longs to absent herself. But for Willie's guests this is one of the few obligations. Yet we wonder why Willie bothers himself with

37

such a group. It is odd that he seems to dislike the company of his fellow-writers, and finds people who have not been able to succeed with the difficulties of old age anathema to him. He was grateful to poor, dithering, bleating, stuttering Eddie Marsh for proof-reading some forthcoming publication of his, and felt he should be invited to stay for a fortnight. Juliet agreed that it would be a treat for Eddie, who was finding time going slowly for him. 'No,' decided Willie quite suddenly, 'I couldn't stand it! I'll send him a case of brandy.'

Perhaps we go to a picture gallery where Willie has bought many of his post-impressionist paintings which grace the walls of the dining-room. But although he professes to be a connoisseur, I am cad enough to feel that he has no real understanding or love for it. It is more in terms of an investment, or as a status symbol, that I see him as a collector.

The early evening is when the garden is at its most magical. The sound of the crickets in the olive trees drowns even the birdsong. For someone coming from the bleakness of winter in England it is incredible that here tuberoses and sweet peas are flourishing out of doors; at this hour of dusk their scent is all-pervading.

Willie prides himself on the variety of his menus. He says anyone can provide a good dinner, but his aim is never to repeat the fare during the length of his guests' visit. Juliet and Simon, who have been here longer than I, have not twice been offered the same dish. Meals are treated with the reverence they deserve.

Willie holds forth for a short time on a topic of his choosing: he selects his words with care. Then bridge, and an early night.

Willie Maugham, at the age of seventy-four, knows exactly what he wants to do with his remaining years. They are ordered with a mathematician's accuracy: so many months for travelling, six weeks for visits to England, and March to September in his Riviera house. At the Villa Mauresque everything is arranged with military precision. Woe betide anyone who puts a spanner in the running order so that an appointment is delayed; a guest who is late for a cocktail on the terrace learns not to be late a second time. My darling Lily Elsie, the original 'Merry Widow', now, like so many of us, past middle age, found the foreign currency restrictions made her holiday seem alarmingly expensive. Willie invited her to lunch at the Villa Mauresque, but omitted to send his motorcar for her, deciding that she could hire a taxicab from her Monte Carlo hotel. But Lily Elsie decided to save her precious francs by taking a bus which deposited her at the bottom of the Cap Ferrat hill. Unfortunately, the bus was late, and the great heroine of musical comedy who, in the phrase of the time, 'had all London at her feet', arrived, distraught, sweating and tired, twenty minutes late. Willie was furious that lunch was kept waiting. 'She was always a stupid woman,' he said.

Perhaps the atmosphere is never entirely relaxed, for Willie can be extremely capricious. He can turn violently against an old friend for some quite small reason: a guest who has upheld unpopular views, who has been argumentative or shown bad manners at the card table, has been told to pack his bags and leave forthwith. Willie admitted that his temper was so violent that he could quite well imagine, in a moment of rage, killing someone. If ever this should happen, he had quite decided that he would at once destroy himself. One day recently Willie was walking in the garden with his companion, Alan Searle, when they stopped in their tracks to watch the progress of a snail. Alan picked up a small bit of gravel and tossed it at the snail. Willie shouted: 'Don't do that!' Alan threw another little pebble. The next Alan knew was that he was lying with an unrecognizable face in a nearby hospital.

TANGIER HOLIDAY

August 5th, 1949

Now the summer's work is over, for the first time since the war I can abandon myself to the luxury of a long summer holiday — and what a luxury it is!

It would have been my first choice to share this holiday with Greta, but she wrote that she was uncertain about her plans, couldn't shake off her cold, and was in her usual state of cursing. (This consisted of using the word 'h—l'.) She went nowhere, saw no one — was obviously someone God forgot. '*C'est la vie.*' Could I get her some 'woollies' (long underclothes from Harrods)? 'Waistline 29 inches, dam it!'

So I am very pleased at the prospect of making a trip to Tangier with David Herbert, who is a master of the impromptu — a valuable asset in a travelling companion. We had, years ago, together taken a white-sugar house in the *kasbah*; it had been one of the greatest successes of all my ventures abroad. This time we have been lent a house on the Maidan belonging to a rich friend who never occupies it, but keeps it for tax-saving purposes.

Maud Nelson, my asthmatic secretary, has again been ill, this time very seriously. Her continued recuperation has made it impossible for me to leave at the appointed date but, after several crowded days with Maud on her return, explaining what things must be taken care of in my absence, I am now able to join David and his car in Paris.

We drank a glass of champagne in the street outside our small hotel in the Rue Cambon before setting off. Our first stop for luncheon was in the Forest of Fontainebleau. Here a roast chicken, fragrant with herbs, was the speciality in a restaurant whose decoration reminded us of Bavaria. The polished wood floor is a booby-trap. Our waitress made a spectacular fall with plates and cutlery — fortunately no injuries to herself or our chicken.

By evening we had driven through the heartbreaking beauty of agricultural landscape at its best — the corn stacked, the poplars dark horizontals among the pale grey trees — to arrive at Vézelay. In the twilight the straw-hatted labourers, the bullocks and bullock carts, all harmonized in a wonderful soothing cadence of buff colour. The Romanesque abbey church — the finest pattern there can be for a lofty place of worship and contemplation — is made in colourless harmony and light.

The widow-owner of the adjacent antique shop, and whose own rooms are filled with splendid furniture, has a singularly touching quality about her. She seemed surrounded by unknown sorrows, and sighed that since the war she has become too poor to build a little pavilion from which she had dreamed of spending her old age overlooking the panoramic view from her garden. This widow owns a *tulipière* of Delft which I long to possess — but how to pay for it with restricted allowance, or to get it back to England?

Later: we were foolish and greedy to try and arrive in time for luncheon at what is generally considered to be the best restaurant in France: La Pyramide at Vienne. The heat was almost too great for such a long dose of motoring. The result was that we wondered, as we opened the iron gate and walked up a curving gravel path, if we were not too late and exhausted to do justice to the famous cuisine. Monsieur Point had had the idea of naming a small, but superb, restaurant after the neighbouring eighteenth-century obelisk commemorating the retreat of the Egyptians in battle with the Romans. Soon after he opened, the word went round, and gourmets from over all France made their tracks to La Pyramide.

At the mere sight of the pyramids of butter, and the basket of breads, toasts and biscuits, our juices began to flow, and curiosity was feverish by the time the first course was presented on a silver tray decorated with a large vase of mixed anemones. The dish consisted of pale rose-colour *pâté*, truffle-dotted, embedded in a sponge cake. How could this miracle be achieved? But this mystery is only one of Monsieur Point's secrets, and the *Pâté Erioche* proved to be an unbelievable delicacy, the richness of the *pâté* contrasting with the dry lightness of the sponge. A turbot in champagne sauce was served on a tray decorated with other flowers; in fact, each item of our enormous meal was served to the accompaniment of new floral delights. The turbot, savoured to the accompaniment of an excellent dry white Bordeaux, evaporated lightly on the tongue in a haze of the most delicate scent. Now, on a dish displaying a small Roman chariot of tiny garden flowers with its wheels set in the sauce, came the *pièce de résistance* in the form of a duck cooked in sauerkraut: the dark sauce and the flesh of the bird was of an unimaginable richness. The accompanying wine was a Côtes du Rhône *rouge*.

When our oxygen seemed to be running low, the palate was titillated by a display of home-made ice-creams in different flavours. Alongside was another tray of doll-like pots, each containing a vanilla cream or chocolate mousse. As if Pelion had not long ago been piled upon Ossa, another treat of the day was presented: a special *gâteau* — today's being flavoured with a coffee cream, of a light, but richly succulent consistency. By now the meal could be considered at an end, yet here was the serious matter of the *petits fours* — a jewel-like selection of bright and shining colours. Then came the 'digestives', made on the premises. If you should acquiesce to the invitation of the wine waiter, wearing a green baize apron, his heavy hand pours with such prodigality and lavishness that you would imagine he was offering you a libation of water. Before you can cry 'Whoa!' your glass is filled from a vast bottle (labelled in pretty, faded handwriting) in which a whole golden William pear has been submerged to scent the liqueur.

As we left La Pyramide the final gesture of service was shown by a waiter opening, for our comfort, the door to the lavatory.

Later in the afternoon we began to smell the familiar, rather acrid scent of plane trees which formed impressive avenues with their interlocking arms, writhing and gesticulating in the green shade of the leafy ceiling. It is an exciting smell, sappy and healthy. Later the long, straight auto-routes along which we drove were lined with bleached, strong, knobbly limbs of trees like Renaissance sculpture.

To return to Provence, which I had learned to love in the early days of touring with my dear friend Peter Watson, for the first time since the war was an emotional experience. I was worried lest the bombing should have destroyed much of its beauty. But, in fact, my chagrin was caused by the sight of all the banalities and vulgarity of modern commercial taste: the flickering neon signs, skyscrapers, chromium and harsh-coloured umbrellas and awnings at roadside *bistros*. Fortunately the old part of the town of Nunes is unscathed, and in the becoming hour of twilight the *Maison Carrée*, Roman arena, silver balustrades, terminal figures and fruit-like sculptures of the Fontaine Gardens remained as beautiful as before, although the recent drought had dried up the fountains and the waterways were now a bit rank.

Progress through the dense traffic on the outskirts of Marseilles was slow: we suffered a dusty inferno of fumes, suffocating smells, and cayenne-peppery heat. Negotiations to get ourselves and motorcar onto a ship for Tangier seemed limitless in their delays and irritations. At last David, smilingly triumphant, emerged from an office with the necessary papers, and soon we were enjoying the breezes, regular meals and gentle comforts of a small steamer.

The Tangier quayside scenes were infinitely grotesque. The frenzied desire on the part of the native population to make money by almost any means was hilarious to watch. The porters, guides, touts, beggars, pimps, hotel concierges, were all jostling and shouting like monkeys in a panic. The tourists were perplexed and ridiculous. By a miracle of good luck we were within a short while free to drive away to our new life.

Tangier seen after an interval of ten years: less colour, more sprawling, the light hardened, the natives more scraggy and ungainly. Faced with the *fait accompli* of the present, the past faded rapidly; once familiar streets, squares and people were dead to my memory. The summer heat had dried up everything, and we missed the flowers. David, always appreciative of every Moroccan aspect, pointed out its beauties and ignored the squalor.

The villa residence we had been lent proved to have cool rooms from which one could see the sunshine, but from which the sunshine was barred; a terrace where one could sunbathe; a dining-room with stained-glass window decorations of a modernistic nature; and a huge white kitchen with a huge white refrigerator.

It became apparent that no one was interested in life outside Tangier. There were no English newspapers, and although doubtless much of importance was going on in the great world, soon it was only the local happenings that became important. The vet's wife has come back from her holiday in Switzerland just in time, for it seems her husband ... The already unpopular lessees of Barbara Hutton's house in the *kasbah* have caused a furore by cutting down a hundred-and-fifty-year-old fig tree attached to the house: letters of complaint, feuds. The banker's wife has been bitten by a dog and the police are sent for and told to look for a brown and white mongrel that has become violent; they find and shoot. Later that afternoon the violent dog returns and again mauls his mistress; the police have shot the wrong dog.

So the first days passed.

I wrote a long letter to Greta, but since I did not know where to send it, kept it in my attaché case. Here it is:

> *Mektoub,*
> *9 Rue Alexandrine,*
> *Tangier,*
> *Morocco.*
> *Monday, August 23rd — 10 past 11 morning.*

To Mademoiselle
Address unknown.

A great many things have happened since my last letter: you have done a cure, you have written me a letter which I have not yet received, and I have left England.

It was such a relief to get away from London at last. The final days were spent working against time with my unfortunate Maud — who has had to have a cancerous breast cut off, but, after a long recuperation, seems

45

totally recovered and in good spirits. On the very last weekend I spent with my mother at Broadchalke a most devastating 'flare-up' happened, quite suddenly, about a detail; but, in fact, that was only an excuse for the explosion which I had hoped to avoid since my departure was so imminent. But the rocket went off, ignited by the fact that my mother has been much too close, on top of me, and has come to feel my country house is hers. I hate to make my mother unhappy, and these unpleasantnesses are so degrading to the soul; but I must be allowed my own life. I am now middle-aged and temperamental, and cannot be treated as a naughty child. *Assez!*

On arrival in Tangier I was a bit disappointed that the city didn't seem as beautiful as it used to. I remember such wonderful coloured walls — very pale blue and pink and white, like marshmallow. Suddenly it all looked a bit drab and colourless; but then it is the dried-up-time-of-the-year, and when I was here before there were everywhere wonderful spring flowers. But it was exciting to be again on African soil: brilliant sun, a wind blowing. We were brought to the house which has been lent to us, and very surprising it is. Large, white with blue shutters, Moorish style modernistic: an old Fatima, with fringed head-dress, running around after us, plucking at our sleeves and making incomprehensible noises in Arabic.

To begin with, it was extraordinary to find oneself in a world that is totally unlike, and apart from, the other one has known. Suddenly one felt suspended in time: nothing to hurry about, Allah wills everything, and everything is ordained. It was refreshing to give up one's former rhythm of life and do nothing but 'take it easy'. The Arabs are beautiful to watch in their idleness, and they have a marvellous dignity no matter what task they are employed in.

Then, apart from the exotic and strange Moorish life, there is the fantastic coterie of Europeans: black-market gangsters, Spanish crooks, French expatriates, the different Legations, and the eccentric English — the old ladies, dressed by Liberty's, who have lived here all their lives, and the decadent young ones who come here merely for louche reasons.

Well, now a week has elapsed and we are installed. The cook is good and we tried him out by giving a dinner on Saturday night. The Arabs love a party, and the servants dash delightedly down to the market for last-minute petrol for the stove, or wine or butter or something they've forgotten. Thanks to David, who is a well-known Tangerine, we have quickly found our own place in the life of this strange, remote and fascinating town.

The pattern of the day is something like this: Nine o'clock the houseboy brings in the tea. He says there is no bread — or no electricity — or no water; he needs money for marmalade. The morning is spent amending my play, or writing reminiscences of my camera career called 'Photobiography', David, on his return, telling entertaining anecdotes of what has happened in the market. Then we rush off in the car to bathe at Cap Spartel, surely the most wonderful stretch of sand to be found anywhere. It is the Atlantic we are in, and the water is rough and very cold. The sun on the sands is so hot it is painful to run back to our niche behind a rock where we have picnic lunch. An exhilarating afternoon exploring the enormous grottoes. Back home to sleep for one hour. By now the heat of the day is subsiding. A bath, then drinks with some of the strange characters who are already our intimates here. David and I are always late for everything, but everyone else is also; dinner isn't until the Spanish hour of ten o'clock. Again the electricity has been cut — on account of the drought — so the frigidaire isn't working and we have to have candles about the house, and they make the place hot. After a long evening of talk at home, we go down to the petit socco and sit at a cafe and watch the extraordinary pageant of people pass by: all types, all forms of vice personified, and yet everyone behaves extremely well and the evening is quite an innocent one. After 'the à l'Arabe' (mint tea) and some coffee and Perrier, we decide it is long, long past bedtime. We have forgotten to buy the mosquito net — so once more are irritated by these small airplanes buzzing into one's face just as one has started to doze. We have also forgotten to get the bread for breakfast, or to call at the British Post Office for a registered parcel. We will make the effort if there's time before Jay Heslewood's picnic tomorrow. But the days go by without one's making any effort. Bianca Mosca, a dynamic London dressmaker of Italian descent, after three weeks boasted triumphantly: 'Today I bought the packet of hairpins I've been meaning to buy ever since I came here!' Being robbed of all initiative is surely good for the nerves, and the life is extremely healthy and the sun breaks down all one's secret reserves of rheumatism or lumbago. The complete change is quite a shock to the system — and one is apt to get ill. It seems that in such heat one must drink an enormous amount of liquid.

I am now settled down to let one day slide effortlessly into another — and I trust, during the time here, I may get much of my play finished, for it is an excellent place in which to work. I have told my poor amputated secretary, Maud Nelson, at home, not to worry me with interruptions, and I trust it may be a long spell here; but I can never make plans in advance and the unexpected may so easily make all hell break loose.

We have plans for a midnight picnic tonight in the Hercules Grotto — with flares, and music, champagne cooled in the sea, and toasted marshmallows. It is a birthday celebration. Other dates this week: an Arab dinner; a Russian lady is opening a flower shop here — I have painted the sign for hanging over the door. David and I clock-in at our Consulate to keep the Union Jack flying. Otherwise, like the Arabs we have no plans. Until I hear from you — which I am expecting to do any moment now — I will not seal this letter.

Have just got your letter from Aix, and am grieved to think you have suffered so much. The indecision about the work must be agonizing. I expect, like most film companies, they are being exasperating, but I only trust things turn out so that you will make a beautiful, dignified picture.

Now I am sending you a wire to come here. I doubt if you will be able to, and I don't know how it would turn out if you were to bring your 'partner'; but as it seems the only way for us to meet, I shall trust to luck. You would adore the life of the Moors here, their repose and philosophy; but maybe the climate is too violently different for you after the cure?

I shall wait to hear from you before sending you this letter, so scratch
away. In the meantime am writing you another ...

With fond devotion and deep respect,
I remain
Your obedient but noble servant,
Cecil.

Of the local personalities one is gradually assimilating through
one's pores the idiosyncrasies of the three wonderful Greens:
Ada, Feridah and Jessie. The matriarch is Feridah Green: she is
ageless at eighty-three. Tangier's oldest English inhabitant, she
is adored by the natives for her lifetime's work on their behalf.
Her father was Ambassador (for such in the Victorian period
was the Queen's representative), and for many decades Feridah
has been the uncrowned 'Queen of Tangier'.

Feridah's appearance reminds me of an enormous old toad.
Her pince-nez fall from her upturned nose: her skin is dark,
blotchy and wrinkled: her hands flutter like butterflies or
sometimes tremble agitatedly. She has a deep nasal voice, a
slight French accent, and uses unaccustomed words. Only
elderly and remarkable people develop such rare and original
personality. Feridah has complete assurance and mastery over
her feelings, and says, only and exactly, what is on her mind.

In early days Feridah enjoyed a life of comparative affluence
but the years have brought poverty with them. She now lives in
two rooms of a part of her former house which she calls 'The
Wart'. The other rooms in 'The Wart' are occupied by
meagrely-paying guests. Her 'living' room, which she describes
as 'a mixity-maxity affair', is a maze of W. Heath Robinson
gadgets: the furniture, curtains, bric-a-brac of china kittens,
picture calendars, and a good piece of porcelain, were given by
friends.

Around Feridah's neck, hanging on a string, is a police whistle with which she summons her servants; before each blast she instructs anyone standing nearby to 'Clap your ears!' She has managed to circumvent most of the difficulties of living in this climate, but she has not invented a technique for preventing the flies from crawling over her face. She flicks her brown, mottled hands, but her tormentors come back to settle by the dark mole on her cheek. Each time a guest comes to the house, Feridah shouts to a servant: 'Flit!' The guest is made to put hands over eyes, and is forthwith sprayed. She is surrounded by many scruffy domestics who look after her more for love than the small pittance she is able to pay them. She had, for a man-of-all-work, the faithful Hummel. When he died recently, Feridah was distraught. However, she soon took the loss stoically, and only her nearest relatives realized how much his death meant; it was discovered that for forty years Hummel had not only been her willing slave but also her lover.

For much of the day Feridah sits in her so-called garden, where a lot of rusty old tin cans are filled with cuttings of half-dead geraniums and zinnias, overlooking a scenic view of Tangier of which she has become fond.

'You see how nicely that tree has grown? The girth is enormous: the tree must be sixty years old to give such shade. I know I planted it ... I had cows down there in the byre from 1906 to 1911.

'This place is full of history: Ulysses in the *Iliad* — or was it the *Odyssey*? — came to all these parts: this is the garden of Hesperides. He describes the caves as being lined with parsley and violets; there's still a small purple flower that grows low on the ground which is supposed to be the flower he mistook for violets. And Hercules had to do his twelve — was it? — difficult tasks here. He lifted the load from poor old Atlas, who was later turned to stone and became the Atlas mountains; and it was here that Jason cut the gorgon's head. The Carthaginians, the Visigoths, the Romans and Portuguese all came here. Nelson always wanted to exchange Gibraltar for Ceuta; the local people are proud of the fact that Pepys was a visitor and have made a Pepys Club.'

Feridah is mobile only to a certain extent with the aid of two sticks. But she manages, twice a week, to be driven by a doctor to the Children's Welfare Centre, which she instigated numberless years ago, where she gives medicines and files the cases of the eighty various mothers and children who come for aid. The air is filled with shrieks of babies about which their tortured-looking mothers are able to do nothing. When her morning's work here is over, Feridah sits enjoying a cup of tea and gorging herself on horrible, stale cakes.

Back at home Feridah has more work to do settling family squabbles, checking up on abuses (stallholders who sell rotten melons and old fruit at reduced prices to the children, who then get 'Tangier tummy') before writing to the local paper, or bringing the abuse to the authorities.

'Oh, I'm not a missionary; I don't fight for the betterment of the Arab. I just try to set a good example: that's the most important thing the English can do here. I don't agree with the way Arab women are treated; they should be more emancipated, and taught how to read and write. But I can't alter the men's attitude, and I certainly don't want to alter their religion — it's a very good one. If I had come out here as a missionary I should have said: "Here's this Bible. In it you will find everything that Mohammed has said; read it, it may teach you a little more about Mohammed."'

Feridah invited David and me to breakfast with her before the ritual, which has continued for twenty-five years, when she gives her Friday morning rations of flour to fifty of the most needy Arab women. She was sitting on her veranda with her brass tray and pots in front of her, wearing a washed-out pink dress, that might once have been a dressing-gown, with a wristwatch hung on by a safety-pin. Her hair was parted in the centre and fell in two tight, small plaits. Feridah was as amused as we were by her appearance; at one moment she took the pigtails, tied them on the top of her head, then, bored with them, pushed them backwards. She was in extremely good spirits at this early hour, and her eyes, which brim with amusement on all occasions, were like twinkling dawn stars. She threw small pieces of bread for the tits to come down from the trees.

Once a week old women leave the pathetic caves where they live, and come to the bottom of Feridah's garden where they are given just enough flour to ward off starvation. The Greens provide this with money they scrounge from their friends. Bundles of depressing rags sit around waiting for Feridah to check their identity. They are apt to become emotional when going up to Feridah, and clutch at her hand and kiss her, but Feridah will allow no sentimental nonsense. 'Here — stop crying! Have a sweet!', and she pops a peppermint into a crone's hand. Under Feridah's auspices, these ancient women brim into individuality and develop human characteristics: one old hag, in trousers and a large straw hat, becomes quite a comedian.

A pair of scales: the flour is weighed: each gets an equal share. Feridah plucks at the arms of the women to feel how plump or thin they are, and ticks their names off on her files, which also contain descriptions of the women whom Feridah helps:

Bad-tempered, but not bad.

Rather idiotic.

Gave on face value — looks so miserable.

Terrible legs.

Husband died — five beastly children (and she appends their names).

Seemed pathetic — caught stealing — turned away — given another chance — stole again — died '48.

Via the radio programmes and news bulletins Feridah is in touch with the England she has hardly ever known, for Feridah, so typically British in all her ways, has only been back to England once since she first arrived in Morocco as a small child. 'Don't you miss it very much?' I asked.

'Oh, no — I think it's a horrible place! I haven't been back there in this century. When I went last time I had had a lot of malaria and other tropical diseases, and the doctor told me I was a bit run down and suggested that a change of air would do me good. That was in '99, in July, and I stayed till October. I always say if I went back now, I'd take a Moor with me to look after me and to help me with the money. The other time I didn't know what to pay for anything, and the shop people looked at me in blank amazement. And I wasn't accustomed to being answered back — no one answers me back here — and I hated it. But some of it was nice. I remember I was so excited when I first saw hops growing. I was in a railway train, and I shouted to all the other people in the carriage: "Those are hops!" but they didn't care a bit.'

Talking of the changes that have taken place in Tangier Feridah, trying to swat a fly, said: 'You're quite right — it used to be much prettier. It's lost a lot of its colour, and so many of the Arabs wear hideous European clothes and that ruins the picture. It spoils it if they put on even one thing that doesn't belong to them — like a pair of braces, or suspenders, or shoes — especially boots which do something wrong to their walk. They used to look so attractive in the *souk*, all moving about in yellow shoes. Then, of course, motorcars shouldn't he allowed in the *souk*.'

Re Lacratelle's remark about the lack of soul in Tangier, Feridah agreed. 'I think he's a little bit right there. Tangier was never a great town; it's a port and a fortress, but the people who are filling the place today haven't lived here long. There's no tradition, and I think it's rather those sort of things that give a place a soul. The country folk who come from the twelve neighbouring villages to sell their wares create the best element; they have a communal life and their own integrity.

'But Tangier itself is just a boiling pot of visitors and of people coming here for no good reason. And these behave so *badly*! I try to stop my ears to the things people come and tell me, because I don't like hearing about such goings-on. But the English who have come lately have been perfectly awful! The Moors know that, and little wonder they feel no respect for them; the Moors have a very high moral code.'

Feridah's cousin, Jessie Green, is said to be about sixty-nine years old, but she seems to be perpetually youthful with her mouse's eyes twinkling, her cheeks flushing like briar roses, and the slim hips and limbs of a preparatory schoolchild. With her bossy, cherry-lipped mouth that curls in disdain or amusement, her large nose with expressive, rocking-horse nostrils, she could be described as a *jolie hide*. Her most apparent quality is one of leisure. She is never fazed or hurried, yet always on top of every situation: often brusque, but honest to a fault. On her allowance of 200 a year she creates an impression of style and affluence. She is neat, pin clean, with pretty hats, shoes polished like mahogany, and freshly ironed dresses. She appears cool even in the intense heat of a Moroccan summer. Ten years ago she broke her hip and it has never mended; her sticks give her added distinction for she wields them with infinite effect.

Jessie, as a girl aged seven, came to Tangier from England to stay with Feridah, who at once adored Jessie, as did Feridah's father. In fact, everyone adored Jessie so much that she was prevailed upon to remain here permanently, her parents saying: 'Although we love Jessie best, there are eight other sisters, so perhaps we must spare her.'

Jessie, in turn, soon learnt to love the Arab world, and she, like her cousin, has devoted her life to its cause. She is staunch and remorseless in her fight against the colonization by the French, and considers that Tangier should be for the Moors.

The recent British Minister here was a figure of general unpopularity. Jessie hated him hard and strong. He infuriated her, and often she had to dig her nails deep into the palms of her hands to prevent herself from being rude to him. She once told him that the French do not know how to treat the Moors, and that their methods of punishment by incarceration were all wrong.

'You don't mean, Miss Green, that you'd rather a boy had his arm cut off for stealing an apple?'

'Yes, I do, sir.'

'Can I be hearing you aright? You can't seriously wish so barbaric an atrocity?'

'Yes, I do, sir.'

'Well, I've been on a tour of inspection. I've seen the prisons and reform houses, and consider the French have tackled the problem pretty thoroughly and done a rattling good job.'

'How long was your tour?'

'Oh, I suppose it took nearly two weeks.'

'Well, I've been here forty-five years, and I know a bit about Arab mentality, and I don't think they should be behind bars where they are cooped up with a lot of wicked and degenerate people. The boy with the arm cut off did wrong; he understands that quick form of retribution, and it is a terrible example to others not to do likewise. But the ones that come out of prison start straightaway to corrupt the others. Oh, the French don't begin to know how to administer here! They just suck everything they can get out of the Moors, then squeeze them dry, and leave the land parched and useless.'

Jessie is without any of the inhibitions or prudery of most spinsters; she has, in fact, had a number of love affairs. One great romance was of such importance in her life that she has never been able to recover from it entirely, and to this day it must never be mentioned. It seems Jessie became enamoured of a married Portuguese (who was Minister here) and, in spite of their passion for each other, the wife would not give him a divorce. Eventually Jessie had a complete nervous breakdown and lost the power of speech. Finally she had to be sent to a school to learn all over again how to talk. Even to this day you can notice in her speech a slight hesitation — a stutter, a splutter.

We were drinking on Jessie's terrace: dusk. I remember noticing a splendid young woman passing by with a pot on her head as Jessie said: 'There goes Sandia, the gardener's wife; she's such a charming creature.' Later we heard cries, yet we couldn't quite believe our ears so went on talking. Then the cries continued, and suddenly Jessie shouted: 'I believe I can hear someone calling my maid, Ayisha.' We stopped still. We could hear 'Ayisha! Ayisha!' but the sound seemed far away. Then we all ran out and discovered that Sandia had fallen down a well. The well was so dark and deep that we couldn't see her but imagined that she must be in the water drowning. Then we realized she was wedged on a ledge, and as we kept leaning down and calling to her, she repeatedly thanked us for coming to save her — how good it was of us! To keep up our spirits she started to sing. But imagine the horror and the psychological effect of falling down a well! The symbolism of being at the bottom of a well! Imagine it!

Well, Jessie hobbled off on her sticks to telephone the police and the fire brigade. In moments like this you don't know who to telephone: you can't look up in the telephone book 'Department of Wells'. But Jessie got on to some Spaniards who sent out an emergency contingent; all the time the gardener's wife was singing on her dark ledge. Then from over the hedges came some neighbouring gardeners and workers, and very expertly and without any trouble — and, unlike Arabs, very quickly — they organized that one man should go down the well with a bucket on a rope. Three men lowered him until he managed to reach the wretched Sandia, and then both were pulled to the surface. Sandia was laid out on a rug. Her legs were in a terrible condition — cut to the bone and broken badly — but she kept saying how very kind everyone was, and how wonderful that they should worry about her.

Later Jessie observed that if the woman had just slipped and fallen down the well, she would surely have gone down head first. Jessie believed Sandia had jumped; how else could she land with both feet on this ledge? She believed the woman had done it on purpose because lately she had been very depressed since she had lost one of her earrings.

During the recent war, Jessie was asked officially if she could find out why a German airplane landed each week in a certain distant village and, after a short while, took off again. Jessie discovered that in this village lived the parents of Abdul, one of her servants; so, with her two sticks for support and two servants for protection, she set off with three mules. She visited Abdul's parents, then circulated among the other villagers to ask if they had seen the airplane. Yes — it came every week to find out the amount of corn the neighbourhood could produce so that, in the event of the Germans taking over, they would know what provisions they could rely upon from the locality. With this information Jessie set about the return journey to report her discovery. But, in the mountains, Jessie and her servants were chased by Spanish police. The two servants shouted to Jessie to kick her mule in order that it should rush ahead as fast as possible, while the servants would disperse in other directions. Jessie, kicking like mad, tore ahead and eventually reached safety; but the servants were caught and put in prison, and when they would not give the reasons for their expedition, were tortured. 'We came to see Abdul's relations,' they cried in misery. Jessie, back in Tangier, spent her time making protests, and trying every conceivable way of bringing pressure on the Spanish Consul until, eventually, the battered and bruised servants were freed.

Jessie is full of stories about great personalities she has known since her arrival in Tangier. The social history goes back to days when Reggie Lister, the Consul, was shot by a jealous Arab whose friend he had purloined. But perhaps more entertaining are her stories of two remarkable Englishwomen.

In the eighties a young Englishwoman with red hair and a bulbous nose, named Emily Keane, whose father was the

Governor of Wandsworth jail, acted as companion to a Mrs Perdicaris and her children. One day they went for an outing on a boat, and only after it had left England was Emily notified that they were *en route* to Morocco. Mrs Perdicaris then explained she was escaping from her husband, and that her lover was on board. Thus Emily became the children's governess and settled with the family in Tangier.

Here, from time to time, Mrs Perdicaris was visited by the Sherif, the head of the Church of Wazin, who was dark, ugly, ungainly and without attraction, but was an enthusiastic, ardent lover. One day the Sherif noticed Emily washing her long, auburn hair. Immediately he fell in love with her; he proposed marriage. He promised that if this woman would accept him he would not try and influence her to change her religion; he would promise to divorce his former wives and never take upon himself any others. The governess insisted that the marriage should take place in the British Consulate; to this the Sherif consented.

Emily's parents came out from their modest home in England to be present at this extraordinary marriage. The Arab world was thrilled by the turn of events and all were delighted — all but a few fanatics who said that this holy man must convert his wife from Christianity. The Sherif told a parable of the cone of sugar. 'Fetch me a loaf of sugar.' The blue cone was placed on the floor; several ants were placed on different sides at the foot of the cone, and they started to climb to the pinnacle. 'It is like this with all of us. My wife in her Christian way is endeavouring to make her way to Paradise, just as the Hindu, Mohammedan or Jew. We are all trying to get to the peak of the cone by different paths; that is the only difference.'

Emily, now the Sherifa, discovered she had a gift for medicine. She became particularly keen on vaccination; she vaccinated and vaccinated: she made countless cures. The natives believed the holiness of the Sherif had been invested in her: when she went out they touched the hem of her skirt. The auburn-haired Englishwoman became a power in the land. Her voice always appeared as if she were suffering from a bad cold, and as she acquired the habit of taking snuff her nose appeared more swollen and enormous than ever. She gave birth to two sons, Mulley Ali and Mulley Hammet; but, because of the clogged nose, she was only able to call them 'Bulley' Ali and 'Bulley' Hammet.

Later, the Sherif took to drugs, left his wife, and married many more times. Eventually he married as often as once a week because he liked receiving wedding presents. He became ill: he became blind. The Sherifa came to tend him. 'You are my eyes,' he said to her; and she nursed him until he died.

Emily's success with the Moors was due to her logic and sound common-sense (of which the Moors are sadly in need). When they came to her with their family troubles, or land troubles, she took an original, unexpected point of view. 'You're going to have to tighten your belts. The harvest has been very bad, but you've got to buy grain for next year's harvest — otherwise you'll find yourself with nothing next year. Buy now! Look ahead!' (The Moors never look ahead.)

Another of Jessie's old cronies is Miss Denniston, who arrived in 1895 from Ireland to start a convent in Fez with a Mother Superior and nineteen nuns. Since no road existed to Fez, they had to trek by mule for many weeks. Miss Denniston soon saw that the Mother Superior's efforts were making no progress at all; the natives were quite happy to sing hymns to a harmonium and derived much benefit from the medicines that were doled out to them, but nothing would make them change their religion. By the time the Mother Superior and all the nineteen nuns died, Miss Denniston had become a legend in the land. In respect to the memory of the Mother Superior she continued to play the harmonium and say a few perfunctory prayers, but she knew her real work consisted of administering medicines to the diseased who came in their hundreds each dawn to lie outside her house awaiting the moment of admission.

One year Jessie Green was paying her annual visit to Miss Denniston, and lay in bed listening to the murmurs of the crowds below, then to Miss Denniston hurrying through an appointed service, and to hymns sung to the harmonium. Then the real morning's work began. Jessie shot out of her bed in high alarm when she heard Miss Denniston, in Arabic, demanding: 'All those with smallpox hold up their hands!'

On my first visit to Morocco before the war, David and I had made a pilgrimage to Miss Denniston. She was at that time a diminutive, white-haired woman of fantastic vitality and energy living in a Miss Havisham state of disorder while a crowd of locals remained outside her house day and night in the hope of merely setting eyes upon her. Miss Denniston had that classless distinction of all great eccentrics, and with the years had acquired tremendous authority, or what in the theatre we call 'star quality'; but there was nothing theatrical about this down-to-earth character.

Now Miss Denniston has gone blind, and after all these fifty years as 'Queen of Fez' she has been transported back to the bosom of her family in Ireland. But it is a cold, comfortless return. Miss Denniston is not understood by her compatriots; they think her a crazed old soul and do not pay attention to her idiosyncrasies. She writes to Jessie for comfort — long, impassioned letters — but they are indecipherable for the lines are written one on top of another.

Ada Kirby Green, now an elderly widow, was married to Feridah's brother who was in the Colonial Service and served as Commissioner in Nyasaland. One of his posts was in the tsetse-fly zone, and he was largely responsible for enforcing the use of deterrents. Here the family slept under nets on the veranda with flares burning all night to keep the lions from eating the children. Ada's people were tea-planters in Ceylon, and she and her children were dark-skinned and dark-haired. But today Ada is very spectacular with her head swathed, wimple-fashion, in a pale champagne-coloured chiffon to match her flowing dresses. Throughout the day and most of the night she sits with a parrot on her shoulder, and peacocks strolling around her bric-a-brac — crowded drawing-room, inhaling a cigarette through an ivory holder, at least eighteen inches long, which she holds in her trembling hand. An old soldier from Gallipoli once came up to Ada and, referring to the cigarette-holder, asked: 'I suppose that's swank?' Ada replied: 'When it's gone on for forty years, doesn't swank become a habit?' Sometimes Ada confesses: 'It's never a mistake to say what you mean, but sometimes I shouldn't mean what I say.'

In her deep, dry voice, with intermittent interruptions for bouts of smoker's cough, Ada converses and proves herself quite as big a character as the other Greens. In fact she meets her family in public but little, for they are apt to steal the others' effects; but in private they are devoted and intimate.

Ada, cigarette-holder held high, held forth: 'I think that redheaded man did quite right last night to throw that bottle when the band played "Deutschland Uber Alles". Some people said he was a guest and shouldn't have behaved like that, but I applaud him. It's too early to forget what Germany has done to us; murdering our sons, exterminating people in prison camps, and creating horror on such a stupendous scale. It makes no sense of all the sacrifice if we forgive so soon.

'I hate people who are always on the crest of the wave. In the war that "telephone man" was "in" with everybody. He was "in" with the Germans and Spanish, and he knew he need not bother about us because our stock was low and our propaganda bad. But now he's "in" with us too. We make it too easy for those people. How forgiving we are to our enemies, and how sharp to our friends!

'Ah, you talk about the charm of Tangier in 1938! But what about '04? In those days everything was so easy. You went everywhere on your mule or your pony; you went out to dinner in those long dresses, and your servant wrapped the huge rug from the saddle over your dress like a parcel; and when you went to the *souk* a boy looked after your pony. All the Arabs had respect for the English in those days; to serve in an Englishman's house was considered an honour. It was before all these delinquents and degenerates came here to escape the law and behave outrageously. Now there's so much riffraff, and no charm left.

'It was a great shock for me to come back from Basutoland and find people calling me "Ada"; you see, I'd been "Mrs K.G.". Then I met Somerset Maugham, and he said: "Your trouble is you haven't been contradicted enough." And he was right: I hadn't been contradicted for twenty-seven years!'

In Ada's household drama is seldom absent. She had given instructions that a cat 'with its eye out like a beam' must be shot. The Arabs preferred to stone it. 'That's terrible: first a leg broken, then its back.' But, worse, the house boy had just met with a terrible death. It was all his own fault. He was bored by anti-tetanus injections, so when he was bitten in the mouth by a dog, he refused to be helped and at once got hydrophobia.

There are quite a number of Russian expatriates living in Tangier. The most beautiful is Ira Belline, a niece of Stravinsky, who 'walked on' as a goddess in the Diaghilev ballet *Ode*, later became one of the best theatrical costumiers in Paris, then after the war migrated here with her aged and difficult father and her epileptic brother. Ira, with her head swathed in a turban and wearing dirndl skirts and sandals, is a true and talented artist and raises the standards of taste merely by being a part of the local scene. But she has tried, without success, to eke out a living by selling to the unappreciative population her neo-romantic paintings of native life; her attempts at running a pretty junk and flower shop have both failed. Yet she has lost her nerve about returning to Paris, and will continue to remain as an adornment to Moroccan life which, although she seems filled with Russian gloom, gives her such acute aesthetic satisfaction.

Truman Capote has also added to the variety of this holiday. He has been lured here by the delights I promised him, but he is disappointed. He and a friend, Jack Dunphy, are living on a mountain top under a corrugated-iron roof. It is hellishly hot and altogether unattractive, but he cannot afford to move and he is good at making the best of a bad job. Also staying in the same compound are Jane and Paul Bowles so it has become an interesting writers' community.

When first I became friends with Truman two years ago, he was fluttery and wraith-like, enjoying many affectations and frivolities. Now he has developed considerably; he doesn't think of himself as a pretty little kitten any more, and pays only a minimum of attention to his appearance which has become comparatively rugged. For days he will go without shaving, for months he lets his toenails grow; his rooms become untidier, the dogs make messes on the floor; he will never write that telegram at the right moment, or send his suit to the cleaner. He takes little notice of the less important exigencies of life, for he reserves all his energies for his creative work.

Truman manages, in a unique manner, to keep a happy mean, between his writing, and doing things for others. His consideration for Jack Dunphy and for his dogs prevents him from being selfish. In fact, surprisingly enough, he is in many ways quite a selfless person, willing to run errands for friends, never appalled at the idea of having to motor to fetch someone from a train, or take them out in a boat for a day. He seems to have a mastery over time, and is seldom hurried or conscious of its advance.

At twenty-six years old, Truman still looks so young that bartenders are likely to consider him under age and refuse to grant his request for 'a martini — very dry and very cold'; here the Arab urchins treat him as a child and are apt to taunt him. Yet he can also appear like an authoritative sage, and it is possible to envisage him, if not like a contemporary Socrates, then a higher-class Alexander Woollcott. He speaks with total conviction, and manages to convince many of an extraordinary wisdom.

During his short span Truman has known many aspects of life, during which various vicissitudes he has spent his time learning, absorbing, and remembering. His knowledge and interests are extraordinarily varied: his horizons stretch wide. In whatever part of the world he may happen to be, he knows exactly what is going on in other parts of the world. (I've seldom seen him read anything but newspapers and magazines — *Time* magazine from cover to cover — yet at some time he has read all the classics.) The training to read, given him when he was working on *The New Yorker* where he had to scrutinize thirty newspapers a day in order to pick out stories that might be worth developing in 'The Talk of the Town', has enabled him to get the gist of every article at a glance. People of all kinds become the keen objects of his study, and their secrets are laid bare under the microscope of his eye. He has the warmth to draw them out, and little do they realize that whereas he may be sympathetic to them, he is also vastly indiscreet. But it is surprising to discover that much of contemporary life, and many of the interests of civilized people, pass him by. Whereas it is unexpected that he knows much about finance, and has admiration for those in big business, he is totally uninterested in painting, works of art, classical music or architecture; wild horses won't drag him to a museum.

But not only does Truman expound on subjects ranging from medicine to the whaling industry, he manages to carve beneath the surface. He analyses reasons for certain phenomena, and can often prescribe a cure. It is fascinating to see him, beetle-browed, chewing sideways his lower lip as he tries to solve a problem of human behaviour, to come up a few moments later with a sensational discovery. He has a basic schooling in the theories of Freud, but brings his own very personal idiom to bear on everything he thinks and says. I often go to Truman for advice on a great number of personal problems. He understands me perhaps better than I do myself, and is remarkably lenient to my faults; conscious of them, he glosses over them for he knows enough to leave well alone.

Even during the last year I notice that Truman has added stature to his character. Many times I have admired his reticence during our times together. Sometimes he would be utterly outraged — as when Jack Dunphy was gratuitously rude to some girl who came to say goodbye to them; but he knew that, at that particular juncture, there was no use in making a further scene. Neither did he argue with Jack who, when dining with David and me, started to inveigh against Gertrude Stein and Alice Toklas, knowing what great friends they were of mine. Truman quaked to see my fury; but it was only on the following day that Truman explained that no one had more admiration for the two literary ladies than Jack, but that occasionally he could not resist throwing explosives into fires just for the devilish fun of it.

Neither does Truman bear malice or take umbrage or remember scores. Except in a few instances — when his bile can overflow — his hatreds are rare. In general he is magnanimous and does not seem to resent people taking advantage of him.

Jane Bowles, who is perhaps one of the rarest talents on the American literary scene (and, alas, she has published but little), is as wise and witty in life as she is in prose. Her appearance is likewise unique for, although nearing middle age, she seems still to be a child with her shorn-off hair, gangling, spindly legs, and wide-eyed wonder. She was sitting on our veranda discussing the mentality of Arab women: 'I don't think they ever love, but they have no horror of marriage to an unknown man because it is something they have been brought up to expect. It is never a question of romance, of waiting for the prince of their dreams, but of a satisfactory arrangement. The family chooses a certain man because they consider he will look after this woman, and will give her, rather than love, children. Marriage is foremost a question of progeny. In Morocco religion and law are as one, for it is against religion — therefore against the law — that a native woman should marry a European who doubtless would wish his children to be brought up as Christians. It would be less difficult for an Arab man to marry a European woman for the children would undoubtedly be brought up in the Muslim faith. The nearest that Arab women come to love is allegiance. They are loyal to the man who looks after them, and they trust the men they live with, but they hate other women.'

Returning from Tetuan, David and I were exasperated by the insolence of the Spanish Customs officers at the border. After their lunch they decided that nothing should disturb their siesta, so we must wait until, grudgingly, they decided to wake up and search everything in our luggage. It was no good getting angry, but quite effective to laugh superciliously at them. (They're very childish, and a child hates being laughed at.) When David and I started sniggering at them, then finally burst into derisive laughter, rather than continue to suffer such humiliation they decided to let us go without further investigation. When we'd crossed the frontier about a mile, the chauffeur, a Roman Catholic, asked if he might get out of the car and pray to the Virgin Mary for helping us through the Customs.

'Certainly, if you wish it; but do you consider we should thank her for being kept waiting three-and-a-half hours?'

'Oh,' said the chauffeur, 'we must thank her for not letting the Spaniards discover the three hundred thousand francs I had hidden for my family in the brake linings.'

Thereupon we all got out of the car and prayed like billy-ho to thank the Virgin Mary for our escape.

The other servants told us of the dishonesty of our thieving cook. He was discharged from the Minzah Hotel for leaving with thirty-six eggs in the sagging bag between the legs of his Arab trousers. The gardener tells us the cook has stolen six roses, and shows us the tired, dead flowers, hidden but waiting to be taken home; it was a sad sight. It was not pleasant to tell him we did not need his services any more but, after his departure, we found many of our so-called 'valuables' hidden, prior to being taken away.

I am impressed by the dignity of the Moor and his casual behaviour about money. I love the twilight on the opal-coloured walls of the old city, and the light in the *kasbah* at night. I enjoy the bathing, with the choice of the Atlantic or the Mediterranean. I am mesmerized by a twilit garden in Shauen where they are hanging cotton curtains among the trees and flowering bushes as they prepare the stage for an evening of music. The flowers which grow in this mountain air are of all seasons: roses, anemones, and Michaelmas daisies. The air is heavily scented with a combination scent of 'death lily', *dame di nocce* and kif. The night silence is disturbed only by calls to prayer, crowing cocks, and distant music.

We remarked upon the curious fact that so often Arab wives who do not love their husbands rather surprisingly become widows. It seems that the husband has just died gradually, naturally. But, recently, Jessie Green learnt of one way, known to the Moors since centuries, whereby the wife gets rid of her husband: she goes to the cemetery, cuts off the hand from a corpse, and each time she makes a soup for her husband she seasons the brew with a morsel from the hand. The process is a slow one: nobody suspects; yet, after six months, the poisons from the rotting, putrid flesh have done their deadly work. The wife is free.

The fleet's in! Three American destroyers are here on a goodwill mission. That means hundreds of sailors will go to the brothels and return home with clap. The tarts are all out, the pimps are running round, the market place is overrun, the souvenir sellers have put balloons, belts, tarbushes and coloured sweets on long poles. The usual drunken rows. The special police knock the sots on the head with their truncheons, and down they go like ninepins; then the 'corpses' are carried back to the ships.

David remains as much as ever a Tangier enthusiast, but for me a certain disenchantment has set in. The bourgeois house has become unsympathetic, and the nearby villas seem to encroach with a hostile ugliness. It is midsummer and we are parched in the oven heat. For sightseeing there is little except the public gardens planted with cannas and decorated with cannon, and the exterior of the Sultan's Palace — for no visitor is allowed inside the thick white walls, or permitted to see the tiles of mosaics of the mosques. The police are corrupt, and every other evening we are plunged into darkness through a cut in electricity caused by some local blackmailing business tycoon. Likewise a sudden stoppage of running water.

Tangier life is a strange mixture of Arabs who are not pure Arab, of Jews, Spaniards and French, and of English people who, uprooted, live here either because they are too poor to live elsewhere, have been involved in financial 'monkey-business' at home, or know it does not matter how badly they behave.

September, 1949: return from holiday

Relief at leaving Tangier. The visit had lasted too long, and its beastly gossip had begun to asphyxiate. (Last night's 'Black Magic' party with its witch-doctors, snakecharmers and drunkenness turned out to be rather more sinister than intended, ending in a vicious brawl in which I found myself in the extremes of rage accusing a local tycoon of having supplied German submarines with oil during the war.) Yes, I was glad to leave that echoing, hollow villa of ours. David did not resent my leaving him. I was grateful to him for his being such a spunky, high-spirited guide. And I was sad to say *au revoir* to Feridah, Ada and Jessie Green.

But I now had Truman Capote to accompany me on my return, and it was a joy to converse with him, undisturbed except by the hum of the engines of the ship that took us towards Marseilles. When we arrived Truman remarked: 'Well, at any rate, Marseilles is a real town, and the shops are real shops.' And we ate a real lunch — even though the hour was early, eleven o'clock — before I had to dash to the railway station for Paris.

In the train I found myself alone for the first time in two months. I sat thinking about my holiday: it had been productive. My drawing and painting amounted to very little, but I'd finished writing my 'Photobiography' and made notes for a play on Tangier with a background of Moroccan skulduggery with Feridah Green as the leading character (of course to be played by Margaret Rutherford!). But my Gainsborough play was now uppermost in my mind, and I knew I must somehow contrive to take several months off in order to concentrate, undisturbed, at Broadchalke. Nothing must prevent that ... not even love — though there was precious little prospect of that at the moment.

RETURN TO PARIS: GRETA

September, 1949

As the train wound through France, the places David and I had earlier motored through came back in reverse order: Montélimar, Lyons, Vézelay (would I ever again see that *tulipiere*?).[2] I bought a batch of newspapers and discovered Richard Strauss is dead, Harewood married, and — most stirring item of all — *La Divina*, as they call Greta in French and Italian newspapers, is in Paris.

September 28th, 1949

After eleven hours the train arrives in Paris and, immediately, I leave a note for Greta at her hotel. I await results: they are unexpected. When I am unpacking, the telephone rings. I pick up the receiver, expecting to hear the sullen porter who has mislaid one of my bags. I am surprised by a very bright and chirpy voice: 'Is that you, Beattie? Well, I never ...' Greta is in a good mood. The 'Duchesse de Langeais' film, which she had been planning to make in Italy this summer, has been shelved and the relief is great. It had been a bad day when she signed a contract to do an English version of the picture in which she had admired Edwige Feuillière. Anyhow, everything is in abeyance; she seems to be full of vitality.

I am so pleased at the prospect of seeing her in half an hour. We are to walk in the park. I dress myself with particular care, then rush along the streets, getting very hot in the late summer sun, to collect my hat from a hotel where I left it. Greta does

---

[2] Due to the kindliness and executiveness of Diana Cooper, the *tulipiere* — that thing of great beauty which I had spotted in the sad lady's antique shop — soon arrived at my house in the country to become one of my favourite possessions.

not like to see me without a hat ('One of the boys, eh? — no hat!'), and I must not be late.

As I am awaiting Greta's descent from her room I am waylaid by, of all things, an alarming Hollywood gossip-writer — the worst luck! Out of the corner of my eye I spy Greta in a big, dark-blue, Puckish hat, and I motion her to rush past her sworn enemy. This she proceeds to do, then returns too soon, so we three must talk together. From Greta's manner one would have imagined that she and the columnist were indissoluble friends; with apparent regret the two part from each other.

I had expected that Greta's recent and most abominable harassment by the Italian Press, and her sufferings from the chicanery of film crooks, must have left her a nervous wreck. Yes, her body appears thinner, her chest now quite flat, and her waist incredibly small; but I am again staggered by her wonderful beauty, and tell her so. She shakes her head. 'I still have eyes to see, and I know how I look,' she says sadly.

We hurry into a blue car that has been put at her disposal — a natty-looking vehicle with a built-in natty-looking chauffeur — and off we whizz to the Bois. 'The same place,' she instructs the driver, and it is to the same place that she had walked alone yesterday that we go; but yesterday a man had followed her, and she was frightened and had turned back. We walk arm-in-arm in the highest spirits. I am more thrilled to be with her than with any other person. All worries and doubts and speculation about the future go by the board. I am caught in the mesh again, and happy merely to be her slave.

So life is to continue as before — or would it be the same? At any rate, this was no moment to be serious, to make any longterm plan. Better just to let things slide along naturally, and take one's happiness where and when it happens to be.

'The little man' and she are leaving Paris on Monday for New York. By degrees, she tells me the story of her European trip. For two months she has been over here, and for two months the film people have assured her, from one day to another, that they were ready to begin the picture; then, by degrees, it became apparent there was no money in the bank. So the company induced her to go to Rome. Here she discovered they wished her to smile at rich Italians so that they would put up the necessary cash. But no — she would not do that.

'These picture people are a tough lot, and they lie — they lie — they lie all the time. And by their lying they've wasted a year of my life; they've prevented my doing other work, but they've got me under contract. Eventually I've got to go through with the picture; but it isn't very pleasant knowing that, sometime in the future, you have to work for people you don't like.'

Then she described how the Italian Press had made her life a misery — a dog's life: night and day a car had been parked outside her hotel, and if ever she went anywhere the car followed with photographers. So she had remained in her hotel with the blinds drawn, for her rooms looked onto a courtyard and those living opposite stared in at her windows.

'In Rome the Press photographers are bandits — bandits — and if I'd had a gun I swear I'd shoot them. As it is, one day I had a stick, and oh my! — how I did want to break their cameras; but there'd be such a scandal. They're just determined to get you in front of their lenses — or else! I only went out twice: once to a gallery and once to a church. And I got no peace just because, a long time ago, I used to make films. It's awful to think that you have no private life at all — that an individual can't have any freedom — and that if the papers are after you there's nothing to be done!'

I asked: 'Why didn't you agree to be photographed when first you arrived? You have done it before.'

'Yes, four times — but you don't know how much I hated it. It's my character to hate it, and I can't alter myself. You think maybe you can get away without submitting to the humiliation — and then, when they discover you've eluded them, they're after you, and they try to make you give in. Once that happens, war is declared.'

Greta considers that this is a debased period when true values are turned upside down, vulgarity is encouraged, and often the worst people assume power. But, in spite of all her complaints, she does not bear anyone a grudge, and holds no bitterness towards mankind. She still feels her lot is an exceptionally fortunate one.

We have an idyllic walk in the sunlight among the trees, and then in the blue car we career about the streets of Paris. Since we each have separate luncheon engagements (she, of course, tied to 'the little man'), I get out of the de Sota half-way down the Champs Elysées and take a taxi. We pass one another and wave, and when I blow kisses she pouts, with one finger wagging from side to side to say 'stop'; but her face, always so full of expression, is, in spite of itself, now expressing pleasure.

Later in the day, by arrangement, I meet her in the company of 'the little man' who immediately impresses upon me how clever he has been in dealing with those crooks — how, if it had not been for him, they could have found themselves in dire trouble. But, as he tries to justify himself, it is obvious that he is concerned that he is partly responsible for the fiasco. He is an amateur in the movie world, yet seemed to think he could take them all on at their own game, even dispensing with the services of a tough agent. He and Greta do not appear to be stimulated by each other's company, and when seen at meals are silent. But she gives him a feeling of importance, and she is touched by his loyal devotion and his efforts on her part. She has come to think that *he* has become a martyr, and thus they are bound to each other.

'Could we three dine quietly together?' I asked. It was inevitable that the 'friend' should be included. Perhaps because the invitation came through me to her, and not through him and on to her, the reply was that if, at six o'clock, they were less tired, and I had not fixed anything else, then we could all go out. But, at the appointed time of six, Greta telephoned to say they were both too tired to be of any use to me at all. 'Let's skip it tonight.' Luckily, I had made alternative plans.

DAY AT CHANTILLY

Sunday, October 2nd

Sunday! I set off in high spirits as the day was playing up to perfection: a most wonderful sun, the countryside looking so crisp and verdant, although already some of the trees were beginning to turn primrose yellow.

I told Diana Cooper at lunch yesterday, before she left for England for a weekend, that I'd had such a nice walk in the Bois with Greta. Diana then, enchantingly and typically, suggested I could take Greta down to stay at her house in the park at Chantilly, or at any rate for a Sunday lunch. 'Two or three of you, if you like,' she said tactfully; maybe she knew of my cross. When I remonstrated that it would surely be too much of an imposition, she replied: 'But the servants will like it; they love notables.'

As it happened all went well — or, at any rate, so I write the day after — for I feel that 'the friend' was not displeased to notice that Greta and I behaved very casually — in an almost matter-of-fact, offhand manner — towards one another. It was the first time he had seen us together for a long while, and in the interim there have been so many fusses that I must have appeared to him as some ghoulish, unknown quantity, always to be contended with, yet never seen. If he did suffer pangs of anxiety and jealousy he managed to hide them, and I did my best to keep his ego titillated; on the return journey in the car I talked to him most of the time. Occasionally throughout the day I scrutinized him with a steely glare of hatred, but I don't know whether or not he detected it.

Scenically the day was a dazzling success: the sun gave a diamond sparkle to everything, and the dove-white little Château de St Firmin, with its lawns sloping down to the lake and the fountains, was seen at its most romantic. Greta at once became like a child in her appreciation of the countryside. Even in her absence, she loved Diana, for she said she must be a woman who loves rural things. 'This is such a happy house — I feel it. It's got such a nice atmosphere: and sunny — every room is sunny. And oh! I love the smell of the walls. Walls in a European house smell so good!' and she put her face close to the library bookshelves. It was like that scene in *Christina*.

Outside she exclaimed: 'It's such good, clean air here — refreshing — with such a lot of nip in it — and everything's green and smells fresh.' She hurried into the park and marched into the long grass until, suddenly, she halted and, loathing the idea of going back to America, she said: 'If only I could rest and have a spell in the country, I'd feel so well.' This was music in my ears. I tried hard to induce her to stay with me in England, and we talked of the advantages she might enjoy. She replied: 'You see, I'm such a very fair person. I can't leave my partner to go back alone and just say: "Well now, I've got a better invitation and I'm staying."'

Yet perhaps I'd sown the first seed that might take on growth and develop a longing for her to stay in the country in England. I am convinced that once she tastes the life of Wiltshire she will realize why she has been so unhappy all these years on Second and Third Avenue in New York. Full of glory she said: 'But there's no asphalt here: everything growing, and it's so "helty"' ('helty' — not 'healthy'). This was what she had missed for so long, yet had not realized it.

At luncheon Greta ate more than usual, and Jean, the butler, served a most delicious meal. 'The friend' described their recent visit to Italy and the people's reaction to Greta. When they drove towards Rome she had at first imagined the boys in the country lanes were shouting 'Greta'; but, in fact, they were shouting: '*Cigarette*. On their way back, after so much publicity, the blue car became so well known that they did call: '*Viva* Greta!' 'The little man' mentioned that the film tests — the first made of Greta for ten years — were excellent. Greta admitted that they pleased and reassured her, for she felt that her eyes had a depth that had not been conveyed in earlier pictures.

But 'the little man' does not succeed in giving Greta much interest in everyday life, and remarkably few things seem to impinge on her consciousness. When I described how beautiful Vézelay had been on our motor trip to the south, she had not even realized that they, too, had stopped the night in the same place. 'The little man' told me how, the night before in Paris, they had been to see the marvellous collection of a rich Jewish banker. The banker explained that, during the war, his priceless possessions had been taken to Germany; but now, thank God, he had got them all back. Greta asked the banker: 'You sent them to Germany for storage?'

By protecting herself against the worst aspects of Hollywood she has become remote from too many of the activities that ordinary, nice people generally have in order to receive pleasure from each day. The result is increasingly hard on herself. I felt that Greta was about to realize the mistakes she has made, and which have become a habit. She is still more beautiful than anyone I have ever seen, and has an extraordinary aura and magnetism about her; but, unless she soon starts to take on a new life as an actress, or cultivate some interest, she will find herself enduring a living death.

After lunch the three of us set off for a walk through the park to the great chateau of Chantilly. Greta admired the sage-green avenues of formally planted trees, the clear, bubbling water, the thick grass, and the animals. (She gave half a cigarette to a goat.) Mercifully ignored by the populace at the chateau, she appreciated its beauties while criticizing its ugliness (very Germanic and heavy she considered some of it).

We stopped at a little farm, a circular cluster of small buildings of painted brown and white beams with thatched roofs. One of the doors was open, and we went in to see a large room painted in *trompe l'oeil* of trees and flowers with walls and ceiling making a Fragonard-like world. The room is now used as a storehouse for corn, and sheaves were stacked against a wall; other mountains of corn were undulating on the distant painted landscape. The stacked corn, and the intoxicating smell as one entered, created a magical impression. Greta became like a person possessed. She wanted to lie and roll and bask in the golden colour; she knelt down and gathered a bouquet of wheat sheaves.

The day had been one of nefarious adventure with hidden handclasps, Asiatic winks, and surreptitious squints to express the boredom. I was pleased to feel that my hold over Greta had not entirely lost its power in spite of the 'friendly' influence being, perhaps, greater than ever. On the way home Greta whispered: 'Won't you take me to Montmartre tonight?' But I knew she was only saying this because she knew I was going to the theatre with my little Greek friend, Lilia Ralli.

But I must admit that I felt slightly rattled when, driving back from dropping Lilia home, through my taxi window I suddenly spied Greta and her friend in the famous blue car. They seemed very much interested in one another, and Greta was looking at him with a smile of affection and his head was close to hers. This was a revelation. The glimpse also made me realize that Greta is really by no means a delicate, tired invalid and that, though she likes to think that she is easily worn out, she never rests during the daytime and can keep going for an eighteen-hour stretch without a tremor.

AGAIN PARIS: BORIS KOCHNO; DIANA; DUFF; EVELYN WAUGH; BOB BOOTHBY

November, 1949

Came over for the last lap of preparations for a ballet I am to decorate for Boris Kochno's new venture. I am feeling very nervous: that an Englishman is replacing as designer the so much loved and keenly mourned Bébé Bérard is placing an extra emphasis on my contribution.

Today was one long series of frustrations. Four days before opening — two of which are holidays — Boris could be found nowhere: the scene painters have not started on the set: Taras has not even completed the choreography: no one knows anything. An appointment with the costumier, a new young man, was several times delayed; then I discovered, close on closing time, that he was about to embark upon the clothes for the principals in colours wide of my mark.

The French enjoy leaving everything till the last moment when, I suppose, they pull themselves together with a Herculean effort — let's hope! But it is an agonizing procedure for someone like myself who plans in advance, likes to be prepared, and allows time for the last-minute change.

Saturday

Boris has appeared and says that his lighting can make my set and costumes any colour that I like, but I have never worked with colours that are so basically drab when meant to be brilliant. Looking at the stage I feel as if I had an attack of jaundice: instead of scarlet I am given brick-red satin, and cricket pavilion paint is applied to the set instead of viridian. After two days everything is still appallingly casual. It was a relief to get away, and escape from chaos at the Theatre des Champs Elysées to take the train, in torrential rain, to Chantilly to stay the night with Duff and Diana.

Suddenly the atmosphere was of a celebration. 'You've missed such beauty! There was a *panne d'électricité* and we had everyone in here in candlelight — it was too beautiful!' Diana was exultant. 'And you've missed the hunt service this morning. We got to Rambouillet by ten, and the congregation was all in pink coats, and they blessed the hounds. And you've missed such a wonderful row going on upstairs. The Cabrolles missed the Ghislaine Polignac-Chuck Basildon car which had their lunch in it, and have arrived wet through, exhausted, starved, and they're fighting it out now — it's wonderful!'

I sat in Diana's bedroom while she dressed for the evening's festivity — a local hunt ball. While doing her hair in the glass she remarked: 'My face looks terrible.' Half an hour earlier, wearing a scarlet tricorne, she had struck me anew by her beauty. Now, meaning to indicate my recent astonishment at her continued beauty, I lamely replied: 'Well, it didn't,' to which Diana, with a wry laugh, concurred: 'No, I know it *didn't.*'

Duff came in and, apropos the morning hunt service, Diana asked him: 'Why should the Church celebrate the killing of a stag?'

Duff, a dry martini in his hand, said: 'The Church isn't against hunting. There's nothing against hunting in the Bible. A stag has to be destroyed,' he continued; 'the damage it can do is appalling. It can eat a whole field of turnips.'

'But that's no reason for the Church to bless the killing of it.'

'Why not?'

Diana: 'We all know adultery's charming, but we don't have a church service for it!'

'But the Bible is against adultery, and anything the Church is not against can be celebrated by a special service.'

'Well,' I interpolated, thinking of the horror I'd left behind at the theatre, 'I don't see why we shouldn't have a service to pray for a successful ballet season?'

'Certainly not — a very good idea!' said Duff. 'But do be quick, Diana — we're already late.'

'Now do stop worrying me, Duffie — you know the others won't be ready for hours!'

By degrees the guests assembled: the men in knee-breeches, pink coats, yellow and purple and green coats — very pretty. Diana, wishing to appear *à la chasseuse*, decided to wear a red cape — but what to put with it?

'This is just like dressing for an Albert Hall ball. What about this top worn with that bottom?'

The impromptu was made into an art medium. To a swarthy maid Diana confided: 'Oh, Naomi — I do love you! You've altered that button beautifully.' Naomi giggled, and proffered her choice of separate tops and bottoms.

'No, I'm going to wear this skirt. Mr Beaton likes it, and he's the arbiter of taste in England.'

'But this is France,' replied Naomi.

Dinner very noisy. Everyone in good spirits and I think, like me, felt they had come to the end of a long day and an endless week and could now enjoy themselves.

Later, as we were assembled in the hall to leave for the ball, Duff rushed past the guests with eyes popping like an owl and shouted at the cowering Naomi: '*Où est Jean*?' Naomi didn't know or care. His Excellency, with fists clenched, leant so far forward towards Naomi that I thought he would lose his equilibrium.

'*Où est Albert? Où est Bertrand?*'

At last the missing Jean was produced: he appeared greener of visage than ever. Duff had words to say to Jean, though to me they were incomprehensible: yet somehow in the frenzy I gathered that Duff had '*sonné*' so many times, and there were four servants in the house, and why couldn't there be someone to help the guests with their coats? Why could none of the servants ever be relied upon? '*Salauds — salauds!*' spluttered Duff. Jean, by now emerald of face, answered indistinctly: 'Very well, Your Excellency, I'll go.'

'Yes, go tomorrow!'

The guests were appalled. We filed into the cars, and the princes and princesses, dukes and duchesses, barons and baronesses, counts and countesses all said: 'How does he manage to keep the servants? We wouldn't dare lose our tempers like that! He behaves as if it were before the war!'

Duff was soon in the sweetest of moods. The ball at Royaumont was a noble sight with fine French furniture, crystal chandeliers, and yellow chrysanthemums with orange or green centres — and the ladies dressed to kill. All the Fulde-Springer family have instinctive taste and a great knowledge of works of art. Max, tonight's host, is no exception, so it was not surprising that the festivities were outstanding and continued until dawn.

Next morning I slept late. Diana in the adjoining room busy telephoning.

'May I come in?' I asked.

I walked in, wearing pyjamas. Diana, in her pink-flowered sheets, wore her nightcap like a baby's bonnet. Enthusiasm typical of Diana: 'The new bride is coming! Anne and Michael Tree!' It is always a birthday morning with Diana. Jean, still very green in the face, was by the bedside and gesticulating with long, bony fingers to inquire how many for luncheon?

'Eighteen. The Windsors and sixteen other people.'

Jean likes notabilities so he was quite pleased about the impending party but, of course, had to show his displeasure of last night's scene.

'It is not my fault if His Excellency cannot find his shirt studs. There is no order in his methods and he does not let me take control. Why blame me if there was not enough partridge or pheasant for dinner? It was those two extra guests.'

Diana: 'You know, Jean, it wasn't either of those things that irritated His Excellency. It was the fact that not one of you four servants were anywhere to be found when we wanted to leave. He rang and rang, and you had shut the door of your room so you could eat in peace. He was extremely displeased — and with good cause.'

'All the same, it's no use being taken for a *"salaud"*.'

'No, Jean; but we've been into all that. There will be eighteen for lunch.'

'Very good, my lady.'

Door shuts. Diana's eyes up to heaven. 'Lord! I've been dreading it all night — couldn't sleep a wink! I was so afraid he really would go!'

Duff appeared two moments later. Eyes very much askew, he was fully dressed in a smart grey suit, with a protruding stomach and bottom and shining shoes. 'Well, how was it?' he asked.

'All right — I think good will come of it; but you must take a high line.'

Duff and Diana are a loving and extraordinary couple: they understand one another completely. Of course it would have been beside the point for Duff to excuse his outburst to Diana.

'Well then, now, Duffie — about lunch.'

Chantilly again

Cast: Diana, Duff, Peter Rodd, Lady Kitty and Frank Giles

Duff considers there has been a greater revolution in England since 1914, or since 1939, than there was in France in 1789. Admittedly it has been bloodless, but the life of taste, culture and refinement, as we knew it, has gone for good. The Socialists are determined to get rid of private enterprise which, he says, has made England rich. By giving the masses so many free benefits, such short hours and the promise of security, there is little incentive to work. People in England today do not work.

Giles opined that the Socialist theory seemed to be working well — that the figures showed that we were 'getting back onto our feet'.

'Rubbish!' cried Duff suddenly, red in the face and quivering like a turkey-cock. 'The Socialists are ruining the country. If they continue another four years England cannot recover. England has to export — can't live on her own resources. We are fast going downhill. Even the masses are turning against their leaders, striking against the people they put in. Before the war the postmen didn't strike against the Government; now it's not only the postmen, but everyone, who is striking.'

By degrees the two Gileses exhibited more strongly their Socialist tendencies. Duff became more angry. Kitty Giles shouted back. Duff, wild-eyed, said: 'I much prefer Communism to Socialism. In Russia those who work are given rewards.'

Suddenly Peter Rodd, who had been sitting behind a plant, brought out a whopper. 'If you have a baby you would be ashamed not to give your baby milk.'

The astonishment was as if a bomb had dropped in our midst. For a moment complete silence. Then Diana recovered enough to ask: 'What on earth has that got to do with this argument?'

Peter Rodd continued stubbornly: 'If you have a dog then you give it milk; but if you cannot get milk you would be ashamed.' Another embarrassed silence followed. Then Rodd again went on, but was howled down by cries of derision: 'Don't let's be sentimental — don't let's talk about babies and dogs!'

When the opportunity arose Duff continued: 'Sir Stafford Cripps is a maniac — a righteous man like Robespierre — a menace. By his lust for power he will ruin England. His brother once told me: "If my brother Stafford ever gets to power he will wreck the country, and I'm off." And sure enough, when Stafford became Chancellor of the Exchequer his brother migrated with all his possessions to South Africa. All great good men are a menace: they bring nothing but misery to the world. Gandhi has done more harm than any gangster. Gangsters only work in small ways. They murder old women and orphans — but what else are old women and orphans for but to be ill-treated? No — good men do the greatest harm in the world.'

But Duff had obviously lost heart in the argument. Nobody, from Rodd's moment on, really believed anything they said. Disintegration complete.

Arrival of Evelyn Waugh

Evelyn has arrived for a few days. Diana admires him immoderately. She is a true friend of his, though I cannot imagine how she, the most straightforward, unpretentious person, puts up with Evelyn's snobbery. When I criticize Evelyn — whom I find intolerable — Diana defends him, but admits she can't bear his 'showing off', being so boringly pompous, and pretending to be deaf.

Of course I am prejudiced. That wise old marvel, Morgan Forster, wrote somewhere that even in later life one can never forgive the boys who tormented one at school. During my first morning at Heath Mount day school in Hampstead the bullies, led by a tiny, but fierce Evelyn Waugh, at once spotted their quarry in me during the morning 'break' as, terrified, I crept around the outer periphery of the asphalt playground.

It had been a relief that the first two hours of school were not as appalling as I had imagined they would be with cruel masters cracking rulers on one's outstretched fingers, or birching one's naked buttock. But my worst anxieties were realized almost immediately after the 'elevens' bell rang, and with a shriek all the boys, no longer under the supervision of a beak, rushed out to play games of their own devising. Evelyn was already an experienced bully and his expert eyes had seen in me, from a distance of thirty yards, a mother's pretty and excessively timid darling who was an easy victim for ridicule and torture. My arms were turned back to front and my face spattered with spit from the pea-shooters.

Heath Mount's literary master was a young man from Cardiff, Aubrey C. Ensor. He was amused by Evelyn Waugh and by me, and it was in my mother's house that he tasted for the first time fish in aspic. When he visited the Waugh household he expected to find Evelyn's father some sort of human monster, since his son had given such bad accounts of him. When the ten-year-old Evelyn suggested walking Mr Ensor home along the Spaniards, the man who taught us English remarked that he was agreeably surprised to find old Arthur Waugh such a delightful person.

Evelyn, who even in front of Mr Ensor patronizingly called him 'man' contradicted. 'Oh no, man, he's terrible — he likes Kipling!'

Having survived the rigorous bullying that continued at this school, by the time I arrived at St Cyprian's boarding school in Eastbourne I had learnt that bullies are often the most easily deflated when they meet with opposition. In sheer self-protection I learnt to overcome my shyness, and at the first sign of aggressiveness to show fight in return. When, several years later, I came across Evelyn, I took the initiative and taunted him. He respected that. I find it unattractive when schoolboys suddenly assume the manner of very grown-up British men. I was amazed at the rich fruit-cake *basso profundo* in which he now spoke, and the elderly pomposity that he had prematurely acquired. It seemed to me the most ludicrous affectation.

After Evelyn's novels had brought him fame, he lived in a large house in the West country, with his coat of arms carved in the pediment over the front door. The Waugh parents went to stay for a weekend. Evelyn showed them the rooms they were to occupy. 'This is your room, Father,' Evelyn pointed, 'and this is your wife's. And I hope you won't mind sharing the bathroom between the two rooms.' Mr Waugh Senior replied: 'Since the woman to whom you refer as my wife and I have shared the same bathroom since we were married, it will be no hardship to do so again this weekend.'

There was another reason for my dislike — and it was mutual. Both Evelyn and I now moved in more exalted spheres than when we lived in Hampstead and Highgate. In our own way we were both snobs, and no snob welcomes another who has risen with him. My particular snobbery was more in the nature of wanting to become part of the world of the '*cultun*'. I was magnetized towards the Sitwells, Gerald Berners, Lady Ottoline Morrell, Viola and Iris Tree, Raymond Mortimer, and certain of the Bloomsbury set. Evelyn was attracted by the foibles of those who lived in large, aristocratic houses. He cultivated the Lygons at Madresfield, got elected to the 'best' clubs (where he taunted newer members or visitors), and fostered a fascination, though in many ways despising it, for the highest echelons of the Army and military etiquette. He drank port and put on weight, and attempted to behave in the manner of an Edwardian aristocrat. He was very conscious of what a gentleman should or should not do: no gentleman looks out of a window, no gentleman wears a brown suit. In fact, Evelyn's abiding complex and the source of much of his misery was that he was not a six-foot tall, extremely handsome and rich duke.

We seemed to have certain friends in common and, since we met quite often, it was expedient to put the old hatchet away. Its burial was only temporary. However, for a time a truce was enjoyed. Evelyn seemed to find me amusing, laughed full-bellied at my jokes, while I found his observations about people and general perspicacity quite wonderful. His novels were written in a prose of which I was never tired. Ostensibly we were friends, Evelyn sent me inscribed messages of good will on the front pages of his latest works. But I was always aware that I must not let him find a chink in my armour.

As fellow guests of Duff and Diana at Chantilly, we played a subtle game of cat and mouse. I flattered Evelyn by taking him around the precincts and photographing him in every conceivable posture. (The most significant snap was of Evelyn scowling, with outsize cigar, as he leant on a gate marked '*Defense d'entrer*'.) Then, to show how versatile I was, I bade him sit still while I made a crayon sketch of him. I knew that Evelyn, sitting back, pot-belly proffered, was peering with incredibly bright popping eyes and vivisectionist's knowledge, awaiting like a tiger the opportunity to tear me to shreds. But I was never off guard. When he saw the result of the sitting he exclaimed: 'Oh, that's cheating! Anyone can do a passable drawing with a red pencil.'

Evelyn has a talent for making a complimentary word sound suspicious. A mutual friend, Bridget Parsons, gave a cocktail party at which the sudden rush of guests appeared to be overwhelming. Clean glasses ran out. Bridget asked one or two of us if we would take the 'dirties' into the kitchen where they would be washed. As I passed, Evelyn, standing warming his rump in the fireplace, remarked to the man enjoying the pleasure of his company: 'What on earth is he doing with those glasses?' I shouted into his ear trumpet: 'A buttling job.' Evelyn sneered: 'How extraordinarily *kind*.' After Evelyn had been to a small dinner at my house, he referred to me for some time as 'an extremely *hospitable* person'. Somehow he managed to convey that my chief role in life was to entertain people, and most certainly for some sinister, ulterior motive.

I wonder if Evelyn ever really likes anybody? I believe his second marriage to be an exceedingly happy one, but I cannot imagine his ever loving anyone. Diana says she loves him though she is fully conscious of the unkind and cruel things he does to people. Once the two of them were motoring together through Marlborough. At some traffic lights they came to a stop, and an anguished pedestrian put his head through the car window and said: 'I've got a train to catch. Can you tell me the way to the railway station?' Evelyn gave him elaborate instructions. The man ran up the hill in a muck sweat. Diana put her foot on the accelerator.

'How clever of you to know where the station is.'

'I don't,' said Evelyn. 'I always give people the wrong directions.'

I have heard Diana and Evelyn being appallingly rude to one another — really vilely, squalidly rude — and yet Diana is deeply touched by him. Today, however, Evelyn did get Diana's goat. He had the impertinence to criticize the breakfast tray: he said it 'wasn't fully furnished'! Diana, even several hours later, was still exploding with wrath. 'There was I, trying to get the trays ready for everybody — with Marguerite in bed ill having her you-know-whats. I was doing my best in my nightgown, bare feet and bald pate. Well, I let him have it. I said: "Really, Evelyn, it's too much to put on such an act!" and I gave him the full benefit of everything that I'd been bottling up about his pretentiousness. It really rankled with him — but it'll do him good!'

Bob Boothby

Bob Boothby booming in his rich port wine baritone:

'Winston is getting very erratic and strange now. God knows what would happen if he took office again, but he still wants the levers of power. He still continues to exasperate Eden whenever he can. The other day he was dining in the House, and gave a sidelong glance at Eden, and asked how old was Mr Gladstone when he formed his last cabinet? He was eighty-two — Winstone is now seventy-five. Eden is becoming anxious.

If he doesn't lead the party soon, he never will have achieved his ambition. But if Winston does form a Cabinet, it's one in which I'd like to serve. It would be a hell of a joke. Winston will either put everything right by violent and unconventional means, or he will pull the whole country down with him.'

Someone asked: 'But why must he continue to want power? Another term as Prime Minister must surely be an anti-climax.' 'Why? Winston said: "When I first came to the House of Commons it was ambition that spurred me on — just a lust for power. Now I want to continue out of anger."'

Part III: Here and There, 1950-1

GRETA'S ARRIVAL

New York

I begin to realize how weighed down I have felt during the last year in England: I've lost so much of my zest. However, on arriving in New York, in the shining sun and electric ozone, my spirits suddenly soar. I feel I am a changed person.

My new-found enthusiasm is in contrast to the general gloom that very soon I realize is felt everywhere, due partly to the reverses in Korea — which have been sudden and decisive — but also on account of the prospect of a world war against Communism. Many people think we are on the brink of disaster. There is no feeling of stability: the Stock Market is low; everyone is fundamentally disturbed; the elevator men talk of doom. Few people have any faith in their leaders. The President's letter of abuse to a music critic who had written disparagingly of his daughter's concert has not only caused him to be a figure of fun, but has made people realize that their fate is largely in the hands of someone who can so readily lose his sense of proportion — a man without sound judgement.

But, selfishly, everything seems to portend a little more auspiciously for me. My rooms, incredibly high on the thirty-seventh floor — in fact, at the very top of the turret of the Sherry Netherland — overlook half of New York. They command both the East River and the Hudson, and a great length of Fifth Avenue and Central Park below: at dusk the effect is unbelievably dramatic, and quite unreal. I had forgotten how successful are my decorations that I did for these rooms on my last visit; I am happy here.

Before I have unpacked my bags Lincoln Kirstein telephones: 'Balanchine wants you to design a *Swan Lake* for him.' My delight at this news is quickly followed by an even greater surprise: Greta had come unexpectedly to New York. We arrange to spend the first evening together.

Greta flew from Hollywood three days ago to consult Laszlo, the Hungarian skin-virtuoso, about a rash that had broken out on her chin. Laszlo seemed to have everything under control by now; but the tortures of the 'Duchesse de Langeais' film project continue, and Greta feels not only thoroughly humiliated, but unnerved.

'Here I am committed to do another moving picture! Why should I allow myself to be so miserable? I feel dread as I lie awake at night, and my bed goes through such a merry-go-round! I should be going to Kounovsky, the exercise man, and getting limbered up, but I'm in no fit state. How do I know what I'll look like on the screen? It's eight years since that last picture: that's a long time. Before no one had to worry about my camera angles, but now it may be different. When I was young I remember being so distressed when older people had to move only in certain ways, in certain lights, to show only one side of their faces, so as not to appear old. Perhaps it's now happened to me!'

Greta confessed that she had been so run down and unnerved that, one day, she broke down completely in front of her doctor.

She wept. He said: 'Go ahead — it'll do you good; cry away! What is the matter? Tell me a few things about yourself. What is your private life? Have you got a boy friend or a girl friend?' The latter question gave her such a surprise that she immediately stopped weeping. Next time she went to the doctor she asked: 'Did you think I am a lesbian?' 'Good heavens, no! I meant any sort of a friend: you're too much alone.'

Greta mentioned that she had seen the Windsors coming out of a gallery on Fifty-Seventh Street, and she and everyone else had stared. 'How horrible it is not to have any privacy! I felt so sorry for them.'

'Did they stare at you?' I asked.

'Oh no, no one saw me — only I thought such is the price of fame. Fame, fame, where is thy sting?'

Several weeks were spent most contentedly going to see museums, or moving pictures. Although I was sad to leave for England, I was restless to stir up activities over my play which seemed as if, at last, it was about to find its way onto the stage.

On our last evening together before my departure, we dined in a Russian restaurant. We ate *schlashlic* and drank vodka. We joked about the prospects of our marriage; her reply, 'I probably will,' became a tag line. Obliquely referring to 'the little man', she admitted that it had been difficult for her to spend the evening with me, and that although it was hard to break a habit, she could not give up her life to nursing a human being. I felt that perhaps she was thinking a little more about making a life for herself with me in England.

Our parting was highly charged with emotion. G hurried back to her hotel to continue our farewell by telephone. She asked: 'Shall we do our trick of waving to each other?' 'Yes, hold on.' I went to my turret window, and waved to her across at Hampshire House with a bed sheet which I had flung out into the night breezes. Then, in the clear night air, a new star was born as a moving standard-lamp light sparkled outside her window.

Most farewells are sad, but tonight I was happy; I believe that, with the years, our friendship has been cemented. 'With me that generally happens; I have few friends, but they always stick,' Greta said.

TAORMINA

It is twilight: the electric lights begin to go on one by one in the Piazza. Now the shutters that have been closed during the heat of the day are rolled away to reveal shops with walls lined with rolls of stuff for curtains, for upholstery, for suits and shirts — so inexpensive and so beautiful; striped yellow and pink cotton brocade, raw silks and Sicilian stripes of all colours and variations. You can take your choice of fabric to the tailor with the large bow-tie who sits on a dining-room chair sewing out on the main street. The populace watches the progress of your latest garment, and when, two days later, you wear it proudly in the Piazza, you will receive nods of approval. Other brilliantly lit shops reveal pots made of dried orange-skin, beautiful baskets, pralines as big as walnuts, tuberoses. For none of these things need you pay now if you have not the exact money: none of the shopkeepers has any change.

Truman Capote, small and spectacular, sits in the Piazza under the same tree at the cafe with his shopping bag and his dog Kelly. After a long day on the terrace of his pink house among the vineyards on the far side of the mountain — D. H. Lawrence once lived there — working on his novel *The Grass Harp*, Truman has come down to collect his letters from the post office and to buy cold ham, cheese and tomatoes for his evening meal. As he sits eating a sherbet ice he can tell you about the life here — for nearly a whole year has passed since he arrived when the hills were ablaze with pink and white blossom.

Truman describes André Gide hurrying through the Piazza like a bat in flowing black cape, tall stovepipe hat and velvet shoes with silver buckles, followed by a lot of little local boys to whom he gives presents of chocolates and candy as he comes to rest under the statue in the garden by the taxi rank. Truman points out the local celebrities: 'That woman is quite a good painter: she's living with the man who runs the antique shop.' 'That's "the panther".' A beautiful young hustler pauses on the look-out for prey.

A French essayist drags up a chair and informs you that you must uproot yourself and go to Syracuse where Archimedes shouted 'Eureka' in his bath and discovered the displacement of water by weight. 'Nor can you come all this way without seeing the draped skeletons nearby at Servoca; and with the present political situation who knows where we may be this time next year, so you had better hurry off to Palermo.'

The Frenchman had not over-praised the beauties of Palermo. Monreale, in its varied golden richness and strange mixture of Saracenic pointed arches with Norman architecture, is the most splendid palace-chapel. Many have heard of the baroque statues of Sicily, but the works of Serpotta, the sculptor, were a revelation. Serpotta has decorated nearly a dozen churches here, but the best are to be seen in the Oratorio del San Rosario, where the altar piece is by Van Dyck, and his Virtues are represented by Louis XV court ladies posing in their corsets and plumed helmets with the flamboyant gesticulations of Cécile Sorel at the Comédie Française. At the Oratorio de Santa Zita, Serpotta has created an apotheosis of children: hundreds of cupids are depicted in every sort of dilemma and ecstasy.

On the outskirts of the city of Palermo the Villa 'La Favorita', built for Marie Antoinette's sister, and later used by Emma Hamilton, is a small architectural jewel in the Chinese style. It is still in mint condition, and its pastel decorations make the more usual sweetpea colourings seem crude and vulgar; an almond green and cinnamon buff is a recurrent combination. Touches of English taste were introduced at the time of Nelson, and the library is charmingly and inconsequentially hung with Chinese and English sporting prints and coloured engravings by Richardson. The walls of Emma's bedroom of fawn silk covered with sprigged muslin, could be copied today, as also many of their labour-saving devices. (The hot dishes came up from the kitchens below onto the dining-table itself, for the Queen of Naples did not wish to set eyes upon her servants.)

Of the outlying villas, Palagonia, in the district of Bagharia, is a story-book fantasy with its monsters of every shape in the garden. The Prince of Palagonia in the seventeenth century married a woman of such loveliness that he was terrified lest someone, marvelling at her beauty, should abduct her. So the Prince dotted his garden and lined its walls with statues of double and triple-headed monsters, and figures of every mis-shape and outsize, perhaps to frighten the would-be lovers away, or to keep his wife in a continual condition of terror. Inside this Alice-in-Wonderland palace the ancestral portraits in the ballroom, instead of being painted, are carved in coloured stone so that the earlier Princes and Princesses of Palagonia gesticulate blindly in their marble ruffs and frilled cuffs from their oval niches in the polychrome marble walls.

It was night time when we returned to Taormina. As we drove through the hot summer night every scent gave us its particular welcome: eucalyptus, warm hay, chutney, cinnamon; urchins rushed to sell us sticks of jasmine heads splayed on straw sticks like a Catherine wheel with which they further scented Taormina's evenings.

Next morning, so great was my joy at returning to this beloved spot that I woke unexpectedly early, pulled back the shutters, and savoured the mountain freshness to its full. It was too early for the household to be awake, so I took myself off for a walk. Already people from the outlying districts, the farmers, the shepherds, were coming down from the mountain tops with bales of pale gold hay on their heads. Some were bringing baskets full of purple, scarlet and emerald vegetables to the market square, others leading goats. In the distance the sea was combed with a pattern of different blues and greens.

The sun is fiercely hot and bites at your pale, sensitive skin; the beaches are rocky and the flint-like stones at the water's edge cut your feet like knives. The sea, coming as it does from the Straits of Messina, strikes cold at first, but it is exhilarating and you can remain bathing for hours on end. If you borrow a mask with breathing-tube attached, time becomes endless: you have embarked on a Jules Verne world of discovery. Every stroke of your arms brings you to some marvellous new surprise. Longhaired plants wave to and fro in unseen currents: you are in a tropical hothouse of exotic foliage with speckled leaves and fringed edges. This new seascape is Victorian in its colours of browns, chutney, fawns and cream. Shoals of huge dappled fish appear among the inverted skyscrapers of rock that dig down deep beneath the earth. Suddenly the monochrome is shattered by an armada of electric-blue fish. Sensing danger, they disappear abruptly into some cranny which is covered with mauve and orange anemones. Any moment you may expect to find a drowned sailor looking like an engraving by Gustave Doré lying on the sea bed with pearls in his eyes.

So fascinating is this exploration that you forget you have been swimming for two hours, and you return to ordinary existence with sea-stars in your eyes.

PROBLEMS OF A PLAYWRIGHT

June 8th, 1951

At last things seem to be moving. Unless some catastrophe such as a general strike overwhelms us, or war is declared (and the threat never, never seems far distant), I feel that my play is really going to be produced.

God, it's been a long time! I can't even remember now when I first started to write the bloody thing. Perhaps the seeds germinated when I was still at Cambridge and enjoyed looking at that Gainsborough *Conversation Piece* in the Fitzwilliam. Then I read a life of Gainsborough and was intrigued by those poignant little children — his daughters — whom he painted chasing butterflies, and who posed for many of his 'fancy pieces'. Coming with their father, from the countryside which they all loved, to make his way in the grand world of London, the bright lights went to the children's heads. After serious setbacks in love they both ended up as dotty old maids — so snobbish that they ennobled the tradesmen who were their only visitors; thus the milkman, before he could leave the milk, announced himself as the Duke of Churn.

I suppose the urge to write plays came as only a secondary enthusiasm to my original desire to design scenery and costumes. As a 'prep' schoolboy I had a toy theatre with my own watercolour imitations of the scenery at Daly's, the Shaftesbury, and even the elaborately mounted melodramas or pantomimes at Drury Lane. The 'characters' in my productions, shoved to and fro from the wings by means of long metal prongs, were given their lines from the haphazard quotes published in *The Play Pictorial*. My father, quite an accomplished amateur actor himself, did not commend me for my reading of the explanation scene from *The Whip* or *The Hope*. 'Father-Brenda-you're-both-wrong   it's-all-a-terrible-mistake!' 'You mustn't run the words together,' he said. ' "Father" — pause — "Brenda" — pause —. At Harrow School I wrote a particularly revolting piece of whimsy, *à la* Barrie, about someone falling in love with a Bacchante. While at Cambridge I took a train, during a vacation, with Jack Gold, a fellow undergraduate, to a lodging house in Charmouth in order to write a comedy about a farcical American hostess, Mrs Corrigan, who was at that time barging her way into London Society. But my attempted dramatic collaboration fizzled out, as did my attempts to collaborate with my brilliant and witty friend, John Sutro, nephew of the dramatist Alfred Sutro.

Later, I embarked on a series of 'drawing-room' plays inspired by certain country neighbours. One piece was about a particularly exalted lady who fought against 'moving with the times'. Another play was inspired by the friendship of Lady Crewe, when her husband was Ambassador in Paris, with Lord Alington, a most fascinating, unconventional young man who showed her Paris night life. But this play, called *Government House*, was, in facts based mainly on evocative letters from Trinidad where Jame, Pope-Hennessy was serving as ADC to the Governor. My plot, in which Her Excellency fell for a young man on her husband's staff whom she eventually sacrificed for duty's sake, was identical to that of Maugham's

Caesar's Wife. Although Binkie Beaumont of H. M. Tennent was patient enough to read it, he quite correctly pronounced the characters as cardboard. A somewhat too near-the-knuckle comedy came nearer to being considered 'stageworthy', though if it had been produced, my great friendship with Juliet Duff and her young adorer, Simon Fleet, would have ended.

A year passed while I worked on the Gainsborough play. The first time I read my completed script was in America when, one Friday night, I was staying with those two stage-struck enthusiasts, the actress Ruth Gordon and her playwright husband Garson Kanin. Anita Loos was also there, and I could not believe it when, soon, my audience of three started to ripple with laughter, and react in a far more enthusiastic manner than I had ever hoped for. I must have read the play well, for there seemed never to be a dead moment during the entire, and very long evening. In fact, with the final curtain the enthusiasm was so electric that I imagined all my ambitions in the theatre were about to be fulfilled. Of course that night I could not sleep.

Throughout the weekend my play continued to be the topic of conversation, and when Peggy Ashcroft arrived to stay, late on Saturday night after appearing in *Edward, My Son* on Broadway, she was at once given my script to read. Her report next morning was more measured; but she liked the play, and she said: 'It stands a good chance of success.' Indeed encouragement continued when Binkie Beaumont accepted it for the firm of Tennent.

But the next theatre season opened and there was no sign of my play on the list of forthcoming attractions. Binkie reiterated his intention of putting it on; Peter Brook would like to direct it, but said we must wait for the right cast. Since I was quite well known in other fields, they both said so much would be expected of my play ... But never a doubt then that things would not eventually turn out for the best. I remember one day meeting Binkie, quite by chance, off Piccadilly, and we stood at a street corner in a howling gale talking of a possible cast. I could hardly believe my good fortune when he asked: 'Would you like Sybil [Thorndike] as Mrs Gainsborough?'

But the delays continued. Then came a letter from Binkie to say he had decided not to do my play after all. It was difficult to bear such a disappointment; but, in spite of the monopoly of H. M. Tennent, there *were* other managements.

After torturing procrastinations, the American firm of Aldrich & Myers decided that they would present the play in England. If the trial run of the provinces was successful, then the entire package would be shipped immediately to the US. Aldrich & Myers employed Henry Sherek, who had previously turned down the play, to put the show on for the firm.

The most important step was to get the right director. Peter Brook had long since gone to greener pastures; Peter Glenville had shown enthusiasm for a while, then also disappeared to the US. Then Norman Marshall, with a long list of worthy theatre successes behind him, showed willingness to launch the leviathan. He told me: 'I like your play; it has great charm; you've brought in the facts of history so covertly. It's a well-knit, polished piece of work and needs little rewriting; possibly the last scene of the last act could be amplified.'

It proved difficult to keep Sherek talking about the subject on hand. Also, he had his own fish to fry: he decided to put on a revival of *His House in Order*, and asked me if I'd mind if he asked my assistant, Battersby, to do the set. Naturally I could not refuse; but it was not long before I began to notice that on Sherek's and Battersby's schedules the Henry Arthur Jones play took precedence.

Will Sauguet be asked to do the incidental music? Will I get favourites for the cast? Sherek seemed too anxious to get all the other parts filled right away. I must try not to concede to some decision that I do not believe in. I wanted Roger Livesey for Gainsborough, but he was busy. There were no stars out of a job. Then Norman and I went to see Laurence Hardy in a small and unsuitable part in the revival of Flecker's *Hassan*. When, next day, Hardy came to be interviewed, Sherek made agonizing jokes in an attempt to put everyone at their ease. After all our stomach muscles were aching with over-contraction, Hardy was signed.

About twenty people came for auditions, and as each character stood up and recited my sentences they had an unfamiliar ring; many fell clumsily on the ear. All such readings are a cruel business. Agents send these wretched victims to appear on an empty stage, without make-up, in blinding light, to read a part they have never seen before. It is hard to coax the hopelessly inadequate ones off the stage without hurting their feelings — or undermining their confidence for life.

Sitting next to me in the stalls, Sherek held forth about his wife's ancestors, and how he worked for Montgomery in the war. When Norman, he and I adjourned for lunch, he talked of smart foreign travel, the Gilbert Millers, and meeting Queen Mary at the dentist.

Sunday, June 15th

Rehearsals start tomorrow, but I am so unnerved by frustration that I tremble lest there be some unforeseen, last-minute snag such as the money not forthcoming, no theatre available, or the impossibility of getting a cast.

June 24th: end of first week's rehearsing

The growth is slow at first but, like springtime, as soon as the first shoots are seen the burgeoning process follows rapidly. We assembled for rehearsal on Monday. The experienced stage director said that he and the cast always hate a first day — it's like going to a new school.

I was delighted to hear my lines read by such expert actors, though towards the end of the last act I wondered if the whole play didn't vanish into thin air. Only later did I hear that Norman was depressed. He seldom pays compliments or shows what is on his mind, and when we leave the theatre together, we talk of things other than our play.

How fortunate that Michael Shepley, always a good actor, should have agreed to play Christie — for he gives enormous style and individuality to a part that is very sketchily roughed in. Angela Baddeley is most true and real as Mrs G. Laurence Hardy as G has all the vitality and fire I'd hoped for; I am so grateful for his youthfulness and for his enthusiasm, and his deep, strange, coky-crackle voice.

Sometimes an actor asks me a question which pulls me up with a jolt. 'Did Margaret really forget her shopping bag, or is that a ruse to exonerate Mary from theft?' 'Are we to know here that Margaret did steal the ring, or only later?' Gainsborough himself asks many questions about the motivation of certain speeches. 'Why does he rush out of the studio in a bad temper?' 'What are "these things" he has to remove?' I find I have been careless, but Norman is a most helpful buffer and plays along with me in a kind, considerate manner. For the most part I am satisfied with my play. I only trust a few other members of the audience will be as responsive as I am for I try not to laugh at my own jokes, and it's hard not to cry at the emotional scenes.

Actors do not talk about the prospects of success of a play, or whether they like it or not; but every now and again Michael Shepley or Hardy have said: 'That's a nicely written little scene!' I am elated as all the time I am looking for reassurance.

Day by day some sort of hurdle is overcome. For some time Margaret would mispronounce certain names, and other actors would put the wrong inflection on a line. By degrees, there seems to be more understanding of their parts. Time is running by, imperceptibly and relentlessly. The progress seems slow but, I suppose, with professional actors the directions given each day do add up appreciably so that the general effect will soon be seen.

June 30th: a week later

The week started badly. At home all has not been easy. I am on tenterhooks about the state of my aged mother's health; the accident of breaking her wrist has given her delayed shock. My secretary Maud is away with asthma. One of the worst aspects of this nervous disease is that it often strikes at times of anxiety and stress. Poor Maud! I'm afraid she is incapable of looking after my affairs.

At the theatre things are in a rotten state. Our young hero never turned up for his fittings; Hal Stewart, the stage manager, complains to me that my assistant is never to be found — then, when he appears, does not show much tact; he mopes, glowers, and shrugs his shoulders pettishly. Some man brought in by Sherek to do the incidental music (Sauguet, they say, would have been too expensive) has composed some tricked up bastard eighteenth-century country airs that make me puke. Our hero now practises mashie shots while he is on stage. He does not understand the part, and thinks the whole play is a bore; maybe he is right, but this does not give confidence to the rest of the cast. Then, suddenly, the golf-playing *jeune premier* has sacked himself and a substitute (whom I have never seen) is on his way from the theatre. Sherek always acts on the minute: a decision is made there and then. Norman has proved himself so utterly dependable that I have confidence in his decision about the new man who has the contours of my aquiline friend Nicholas Lawford of the Foreign Office, but none of his charm.

However, there are pleasant surprises: the painting of the set is everything I could wish for — it is a beautiful pearly grey. By degrees, an actor comes on without a book and, slowly, they are all learning their parts. Hardy develops a fine temperament; Michael Shepley builds Christie into a definite personality. And Norman works all day long at a remarkable pitch of concentration: his mind like a flash, his manners and kindness to the actors impeccable.

The organization and ramifications of putting on a play seem endless. I see nothing of the financial side, though I know there are weekly salaries being paid, and much business transacted in the office; but I am amazed at the variety of activity connected with the merely physical side of the production. The auditions for the cast are scarcely over when auditions for understudies begin; the bills soar, the 'props' accumulate.

By the end of the week we have achieved half-time in rehearsals and, with only two more weeks more to go, my heart is in my mouth.

One week later

This has been a gnat-biting time: so many unexpected little jabs. Angela Baddley is a great asset to the play; but a bomb sizzled, and nearly exploded at the costumiers. Since Angela has recently become so thin, I suggested we might have to give her bodices a bit of padding. When Angela caught sight of a colossally grotesque, stuffed corset she fumed: 'It's a question of my not having any padding, or else my not playing the part!'

In my highly unnerved state I cannot help imagining the worst. By the end of the week I am really out of sorts, crotchety, and letting off steam onto Maud, my secretary, who has returned to work panting and still short of breath. Now that we have only one short week in which to go, we have to be careful and fight the unexpected in the calmest, cleverest way possible.

July 14th

After three weeks of rehearsal the company are getting fretted and nerves are raw. I arrived at the stage door on Monday: a note from Battersby to say that he has resigned as my assistant. But more distressing to me is the fact that the *jeune premier* seems incapable of getting a swing on the lines. As soon as he dries up, all the other players disintegrate; they, too, dry, and rehearsals become a nightmare of slowness. On the Wednesday evening run-through, every time Angus came on the stage, the pace was let down to a crawl. We could do with an extra week of rehearsal and preparation. All of a sudden, there are no more rehearsals: nothing but a terrible lull.

July 28th: Brighton

I am writing in the hotel bedroom in which I have spent many unhappy hours since I arrived here, so full of expectation, two weeks ago. As the train bringing me to Brighton stopped at outlying stations I craned to see if there were any billboards bearing the name of my play; the sight of the first large poster was a thrill. The welcome at the familiar hotel was warm, as it was, too, at the jewel-box of the little Theatre Royal. The set was already up, Sherek in high spirits, while everyone else was impatient for the lighting to be finished before the dress rehearsal.

By the end of the evening the anti-climax was appalling: the play had never come to life. A few people in the audience made no comment. Joyce Grenfell appeared like a lightning-struck sheep, and added not one word. My agent looked even more like a ruined pudding than usual; he merely cleared his throat. Mrs Myers, the wife of the American producer, when asked if she would like a sandwich, said: 'I would like a taxi.' A strange chemical reaction took place in me; suddenly I was robbed of all hope. But perhaps the dress rehearsal disaster was a good sign: it was said to be. Next day I worked non-stop in the theatre on set, costumes and script changes; but the cast was not sure enough of their lines to be given the cuts I now suggested.

But I didn't realize how much cutting was necessary until the audience was there — a terrifying first-night crowd of London friends and critics. A steel-like curtain of defiance seemed to go up between them and the play. The first act went without laughs. Later things warmed up, but never were the laughs as I had hoped for. At the end of the play there were a number of curtain calls, but no great enthusiasm. At the party afterwards my friends tried to give me the impression that the evening had been a success.

As usual, I was awake very early next morning, too pent-up and overtired to be able to sleep. I called for the papers, and with no exception the reviews were bad. 'Trite dialogue.' 'So much good material in it, and it often almost achieves its purpose.' 'Much charm, some lightness, a certain amateurish Harness in the writing, a trace or two of gaucherie, and a rather agreeable and affecting sentiment.' 'Heavy disappointment. Enchanting to look at.'

For two weeks I had had a feeling of sickness in my stomach, but now I was aghast. I felt as miserable as one only does when one falls unhappily in love. My mother and sister were in the next bedroom. I had to wake them with the news that the reviews were bad: I felt more queasy than ever. It was like telling them of a family death: they did not know how to comfort me. What was there to do? Try and swallow the cold breakfast.

I got out the script again, for the thousandth time, and I started to make cuts so that, by the next evening, the changes would be made. We had a midday conference in the hotel: Sherek, Myers and Norman Marshall. Dick Myers said he still has faith in the play, but a lot of work must be done on it, that Angus was a stick, and should be made the central figure of the play.

Under great duress I worked in my hideous hotel room, and managed to find a typist to take down a new scene. It was rehearsed and put into being: but none of it was fun any more. The critics had written failure over my play, and I couldn't get rid of this horrible feeling; I turned even against my scenery and costumes.

However, the cast worked hard, and Norman was very persevering. That sweet man, Duff Cooper, penned me a note from White's, saying that he thought the critics had been unduly harsh, that often resentment was built up when people had had success in other fields of activity and took to something new.

We continued as if the play were a success and, after the first night, audiences seemed really to enjoy themselves. There was always a lot of laughter and many curtain calls. For two weeks here we have been doing business that Sherek says is 'wonderful'. What will happen in other towns I do not know.

After all this jockeying ourselves up, and making small changes at each performance, a sickening cable arrives from the management in Paris: the tour should be cut short, the physical production stored, and nothing further done until they decide what to do on the return of Aldrich and Myers to New York.

It is difficult not to feel discouraged and, above all, guilty (it's as if I'd given birth to a monster); but perhaps one day I shall realize I was fortunate to have had a play put on at all, especially in such style. Yet somehow or other the experience has been too hard and serious with never any spontaneous gaiety, and it has made me feel very much older.

Later. Business has been so exceptionally good that one fools oneself that only the critics are wrong. The cast help one to kid oneself, and at some performances I have enjoyed myself and been carried away by my own play. But somehow or other I must face the fact that the play lacks essential drama, that an audience's emotions are only partly involved. Perhaps one kind, well-meaning fan inadvertently managed to express the general feeling when she wrote that the tragic ending 'almost made her cry'.

I'm so weak and tired — as if I'd been through a severe operation — that I feel incapable of picking up the threads of ordinary existence again.

VISIT TO LOPOKOVA

One afternoon, in order to escape from the atmosphere of the theatre, I took a bus and went to Firle to call on that most stimulating and entertaining of all human beings — Lydia Lopokova the dancer. When I first discovered Diaghilev's ballet, the miniscule Lopokova was one of its wittiest adornments. Pert, chubby, with an unhealthy wax-doll quality, Diaghilev considered her downright plain. When he put on *The Sleeping Beauty* with various stars alternating in the main role, and it came to Lydia's turn to dance, he altered the posters to *The Sleeping Princess.* Lopokova could dance classical roles with exquisite grace, but in light roles, she had a staccato way of moving that was funny, original, and completely captivating.

The art of the actor and dancer dies with their performances; it is impossible later to judge their effect on the audiences of their time. My father used to try to convey to me the charms of the Victorian actresses, Connie Gilchrist and Nellie Farren, but their photographs, and even the Whistler portrait of the latter, give us little impression of the spell that they cast. All the pictorial documents of Lopokova are worthless: the photographs particularly misleading. Osbert Sitwell has tried in words, and with a certain success, to describe her quality, and he likened her waxen pallor to that of Christmas roses. But it is useless to try to conjure up Lopokova's contribution to that very original production of *The Good Humoured Ladies* with its Venetian night scene — surely Bakst's masterpiece of mysterious romanticism — except to say that, as the mischievous maid Mariucca, she supplied a rorty, yet delicate humour that was an indispensable ingredient to an unforgettable and unique evening. When other ballerinas later danced her role they were too pretty and dainty: the ballet lost much of its strangeness as well as fun. Lopokova's indefinable marionette quality embellished *La Boutique Fantasque* and *Petrouchka*, and these ballets also were never the same without her. But her appearances were somewhat spasmodic. Once the London posters proclaimed 'Russian Dancer Vanishes': Lopokova was nowhere to be found. After an interval she reappeared, with eyes even brighter periwinkles than before, having had a wonderful time with a stalwart high-ranking Army officer.

It was an equal surprise when it was announced that Lopokova had married Maynard Keynes, the economist and pivotal member of the Duncan Grant, Vanessa and Clive Bell, and Virginia and Leonard Woolf Bloomsbury group. The marriage was a success. The Bloomsburys were continually amazed by Lydia's innocent '*enfant terrible*' frankness.

Among her fellow dancers Lydia had a reputation for directness of speech. At one time a certain elderly ballerina in the company was becoming so liberal with her favours that the young men in the *corps de ballet* were apt to arrive exhausted for rehearsals or the performances on stage. Something must be done about the situation. The elderly ballerina's husband must be told to control his wife: she was creating havoc; it was most reprehensible of her to behave like a nymphomaniac. Lydia was shocked at the idea of telling the husband. 'No — no! There is nothing wrong with poor Tania except that she has an irritable womb.'

The Keyneses divided their time between Bloomsbury, Sussex and Cambridge. Legion were the stories about her outspokenness and often embarrassing honesty. A certain well-known lady with a husband and large family was seen orbiting London's 'artistic' circles in the company of Osbert Sitwell. The gossip was that the two were enjoying a twilit romance.

Suddenly the lady produced a baby. The church was crowded for the baptism. The baby lay in an elaborate Napoleonic crib in front of the altar. At the end of the ceremony Lydia tripped up the altar steps, peered into the crib, and in a surprised voice for all to hear, said: 'It doesn't *look* like Osbert!'

When Lydia accompanied Maynard to the White House for a large dinner given by Cordell Hull, she was heard, in a lull of conversation, to say to a neighbour: 'Two men — yes — I can see they've got something to take hold of. But two women — that's impossible. You can't have two insides having an affair!'

One day Lydia was alone in her Gordon Square house when a water-pipe burst. In vain did she telephone for a plumber. She then resorted to calling the Water Board. A crew of six young men, wearing high rubber boots, arrived to dam the flood. At the sight of the young men Lydia shouted: 'Oh, you're so beautiful! If only Diaghilev could see you!'

It was said that she was one of the most remarkably intelligent children that had never grown up. When, at last, I met Lydia she proved no disappointment. In fact, I doubt if anyone has had more the power to give me hiccups of laughter than this incredibly unselfconscious droll.

After suffering from a bad heart for ten years, Maynard died recently leaving Lopokova his remarkable collection of pictures and, if little cash in hand, three places in which to live.

When my bus deposited me near her house on the Downs near Lewes, Lydia rushed out to meet me wearing a mercerized silk skirt of cream leaf pattern, cocoa-coloured stockings, woollen socks, straw boots, an apron, and about three different sweaters over a silk blouse. Her head was tied in a maize-coloured handkerchief: a pale grey, shiny face without make-up, but freckled and sunburnt at back of neck.

Tilton House proved to be typical of the Bloomsbury taste when the Omega workshop ordained that nothing brighter than terracotta could be used among the clay, oatmeal and slate colours of their domineering palettes. But Lydia's own personality was very apparent, for everywhere was a mess of all the things she is interested in: yellowing snapshots, bits cut out of the newspaper — how to stop snoring, a review of Roy Harrod's book on Maynard. The chimneypieces, the occasional tables, sideboards, even the piano, were all stacked with tins of food, cardboard boxes of provisions, matches, serried jars of pickles; everything on view. Surprising it was among all this litter to discover, skied high on the walls, a marvellous collection of Modiglianis, Cézannes, Seurats and Picassos. 'Oh, they don't belong to me,' said Lydia. 'They were Maynard's, and they're only loaned until death.' What other woman would disclaim ownership in this modest way? But such humility is typical of Lydia; the impression she creates on the world means absolutely nothing to her. When Maynard flew to Washington during the war to confer about the economic situation, Lydia accompanied him. On arrival they posed on the gangway for the Press photographers; Lydia, grinning, was almost hidden behind a large paper bag prominently marked 'Macfisheries, Cambridge'.

The widow chuckled, and exclaimed in her thick Russian accent: 'I have to ask the trustees for every half-crown, and for a hand-basin for my bedroom, but I don't really want for anything. I live well. I drink wine with my meals; I have here a garden with peas in it, the rooms in Gordon Square, and a flat at Cambridge. When Maynard died I thought I could never live without him, and I suffered a lot. But now I never think of him.' She is utterly absorbed by her new life. 'I go into the raspberry canes and I imagine I'm in the jungle, and I bend my body and it gives me such a feeling of freedom — and I picked these peas for our lunch.' ('Will you have sausages or cold ham?' She rushed off and shouted to a hidden servant: 'He wants ham!') 'Yes, I'm blissfully happy here. I have a married couple whom I gave this nice home to, and in return they do the cooking for me. I can't cook. Oh, it's too much of a bore — too messy! But sometimes I try to experiment — and the other day I ate a squirrel! It tastes rather like a bird — it lives on nuts and apples — and it's delicious, and next time I'll eat half a dozen! But I always make my own bed; I like that, it gives a rhythm to life. And I go for walks, and I read a bit, and the days aren't long enough; twenty-four hours aren't long enough at this time of the year.'

Lopokova once had the historical experience of sharing a sleeping compartment on a train from Madrid to Paris with a large, fattish lady 'obviously made for men's delight'. Lydia said: 'We were very polite, and I agreed to take the upper berth; it was easier for me to climb up.' But at the frontier the lady was not allowed into France, and Lopokova did not know until later that she had been travelling with the spy Mata Hari.

During my visit today Lydia, looking like the Widow Twankey, danced the 'Valse des Fleurs' of the *Casse-Noisette*. She did imitations of the way that Michael Somes moves, leaning slightly forward as if sand was falling out of his behind, and proved in a thousand different ways that there are no disadvantages to old age when one is as completely lacking in self-consciousness, is as interested in as many aspects of life as she continues to be, and is able to laugh as much as ever.

Lydia has taken to English country life as if born to it, though she has never been able to master the language. Describing how much she enjoys riding, she says: 'Of course it is hard on the two halves, but my feet have never come out of the hooks, and I never lost my horse morale.'

When, after the ham lunch at Tilton, we sat quietly talking about the disappointments that one suffers in one's work, and of my tribulations with the Gainsborough play, Lydia made me realize that troubles were only another part of life — that failure is as necessary to experience as success. She calmed me by saying it always takes three weeks to get over bad Press notices. I have one more week to go.

Part IV: Wiltshire Friends and Gardens, 1951

REDDISH: GARDEN PLANS

July, 1951

David Herbert, good at gardens, when asked for his advice about improving my terrace, suggested first of all that it would be an improvement to rid the lawn rising to the paddock of that heavily wired, rose-covered fence that was the sole means of preventing Herbert Bundy's horses and cows remaining decoratively in the semi-distance. 'The eye should stretch to that distant row of trees, so you could feel you are at one with nature — that your garden is part of the countryside.' Of course, of course — how could that suburban-looking fence have been allowed to exist all these years? When once someone has pointed out an obvious fault one cannot imagine how it has been overlooked for so long. One must set about improving the state of affairs immediately. Not a second to be lost!

But the problem of how to keep out Farmer Bundy's animals was a difficult one. A 'ha-ha' would necessitate building a sunken brick wall, and this would cost much more than I could afford. But, in any case, the hill sloped the wrong way and the cows would fall into the trench, or the horses leap across the dyke to enjoy trespassing on my juicy plots. Farmer Bundy suggested an electric wire, but no one else much cared for that idea.

After much consultation the offending fence has been removed, and we now have a barbed line stretching neatly from posts, camouflaged green, placed at intervals. The effect is not quite as one hoped, but with luck one can now imagine the paddock as being almost a continuation of the garden. The evening sun slants across the grass up to the deep shadows of the trees; the cattle graze, the horses frisk about, and the white mare gallops across the view like a Delacroix. The effect is good.

This late summer evening I sauntered into the paddock, and wondered if we could not have a series of posts with roses trained between each to form a string of garlands. This would be more fitting than the barbed wire, and would serve as protection, too; I must think seriously about this. Meanwhile, on up to the end of the garden.

This is the time of year I most enjoy: I must savour my enjoyment to the full. I walked on past the herbaceous things: the stocks, phlox, daisies and evening primroses, and into the kitchen garden. It was dark green at this quiet time of the evening. The lettuces in rows were looking orderly and appetizing, the radishes rosy... But, to my great chagrin, and as a result of the discarding of the fence, a young rabbit hopped across my path; then, frightened, ran among the French beans, and finally took refuge under the potato leaves.

The rabbit has become enormous — as well it should, living for so many weeks off the best that we can supply. No means has yet been discovered of putting an end to the trespasser's sojourn among our prize produce. Perhaps, in future, when making 'artistic improvements' it is as well to realize the artificiality of a garden — that it can only survive if heavily walled against nature and the destructive elements of the countryside.

CLARISSA CHURCHILL, NOW EDEN

Back after Anthony's long convalescent holiday, and once more involved in high politics, the Edens come down to the doll's cottage in the Corot-like valley behind the watercress beds in Broadchalke. 'Rose Bower', which my mother found for Clarissa, has become important in their lives. At first Eden hit his head on doors and ceilings, and had to come down to my library to use a telephone with a scrambler for secret conversations, but now he has a great affection for the cottage and considers it his home. Here, free from the turbulence of Whitehall, he can get on with the contents of 'the boxes' without interruption.

When Clarissa drove over to lunch with me, leaving the Edens, *père et fils*, to look after each other, I noticed the changes since that morning when she sat on a chair in my bedroom and confided that she was going to marry. At that time Clarissa had seemed so independent and capable of living by herself, that one wondered at her ever deciding to 'settle down'. When first I knew her, with her long, corn-coloured hair hanging like bells, she was a most romantic character; a friend of James Pope-Hennessy and the eccentric Gerald Berners, and of publishers, writers and painters. This news came as a tremendous switch.

At the time of the engagement Anthony Eden was so busy, so many were his commitments, that, ridiculous as they admitted it to be, there was no chance of the marriage taking place for several months. Meanwhile, total secrecy. It was amusing to be with Clarissa in Bond Street one morning when, after choosing some hairbrushes to be initialled 'AE' at Cartier's, she popped the letter announcing her engagement to her Aunt Clemmie who was, at that time, abroad in a clinic. On receiving the sensational surprise, Clemmie Churchill returned home immediately, and Randolph then 'took over'. Clarissa described the news of the engagement, and the Press onslaught, as being in the path of a typhoon. Clarissa, beautiful yet unphotogenic, became a public figure. She was too occupied to see old friends, but when occasionally we met, everything seemed wonderful for her. The vistas were endless: she could help to do so much for the arts, she could wield power in the right direction.

Whenever I met her husband, a wave of what I had hoped was long-forgotten shyness would again overwhelm me. Anthony, by nature, himself is shy, Clarissa too. So we made an agonizing trio: three people, all wanting to be nice to one another, stumbling about in the mire. If only for the reason that Anthony had become my great friend's husband, I wanted to be friends with him. I happen to admire his character: his honesty, courage and fairness. But we shied from one another. Clarissa obviously found it difficult to treat me with the insouciance of old times, for she has changed in many ways. Before, when Clarissa passed by my house on her way to and from 'Rose Bower', she would come in unannounced by the back door. Sometimes I'd get a great shock to find her standing silently, like a ghost, in the library. Today when she came to lunch, she drove her car up to the front door and rang the bell — though, typically, did not wait until it was answered before coming in. She no longer wears leather jerkins, trousers, and does not appear as someone from 'another part of the forest': she dresses in a more conventional style. Yet, after a while, she relaxes into being the marvellously sympathetic person I love.

'I can't tell you what fun it's all being: much more interesting than I'd ever imagined. It's fascinating all the time, and there are new developments every day. I'm loving my tea parties for the Ambassadresses, and I get such wonderful notes, putting me wise, from Marcus Cheke, the Marshal of the Diplomatic Corps. He tells me not to sit Ecuador next to Esthonia as they're not on speaking terms, and I must not mind if the Nepalese never raises her eyes as it's the first time she's been out without a veil.'

Clarissa amused me with a story of Anthony Eden, just returned from the Palace where he had to introduce a new Ambassador who was about to present his credentials to the Queen. It seems that a disregard for on-the-dot punctuality is something our present Queen may have inherited from Queen Alexandra. On this particular morning Her Majesty was a bit late for the audience during which several matters of state had to be attended to before the Ambassador (who arrives in a horse-drawn coach) could be shown in. Suddenly Anthony Eden said: 'I think, ma'am, we must hurry through this as the Ambassador has been here some considerable time.' The Queen said: 'Oh yes, and we can't keep the horses waiting?' She saw the joke and laughed.

I suggested that Clarissa write a diary. She gave a wry smile, said she would, and I believe she has written for an hour each night before going to sleep.

Although we did not talk intimately, my impressions are that she is much in love with Eden, has a great maternal feeling for him, and is perfectly content to devote herself entirely to his welfare. But, in spite of the enthusiasm of the moment, I don't think she is interested in politics and politicians. She says, with pride: 'I haven't opened the papers today' (they are full of yesterday's Tory rally), and it is obvious that she is not going to bother to do so. I'm sure she will do the present job well, for she is exceptionally efficient about anything she undertakes; in order to achieve her ends she could be utterly ruthless. Yet, in some ways, she is an unhappy person — always in search of something denied her. I daresay she will suffer a great deal all her life, and it is certain she will not end her days in the milieu of politics.

After lunch I went back with her to the cottage where the Edens were sunbathing on a patch of lawn that was out of the shade. I was amazed to hear her say to her husband: 'I've brought Mr Beaton back here for a walk.' How *could* she be so formal, and how could she inflict such a burden on all of us? I'm sure a walk in my company was the last thing her husband wished for, and I felt an immediate urge to flee. But Anthony suddenly made a great effort to be friendly. He showed me the latest additions to the garden: he made jokes about the wives of certain Cabinet Ministers. Talking of Governor Stevenson (whom he would like to become President of the United States) he said that, when he had met him in his own State of Illinois, he was surprised how little known the Governor was on the streets. When the arrangements about conveying them both in some motor car had gone wrong and they had to walk a couple of hundred yards, more people recognized Eden than Stevenson. Then, with a most charming, wistful smile and wrinkled forehead, Anthony asked: 'Won't you come with us for a walk?' But Clarissa now did a complete volte-face. 'Oh, no, no! He would much rather be left alone,' she stuttered.

For some time now Clarissa and I have shared Stacey as a part-time gardener. He is a difficult, odd character with a twinkle and much humour. While discussing 'Miss Churchill's' garden, he said: 'I must say I had to laugh at the way she put it to me, but Miss Churchill — I *will* call her that, but I must remember it's Mrs Eden now — well, she says to me: "I've been going without too much sleep lately."'

GRETA IN ENGLAND

October, 1951

Bandy-legged old Mr Gould is, apart from being a local publican, a farmer and a car-hire driver. Ever since I came to live in Broadchalke it has been in his old boneshaker that we arrived at and departed from Salisbury station. So great is Mr Gould's enthusiasm and interest in all aspects of rural life that the road in front of him cannot confine his attention even when at the wheel, and in order to see how Mr Gilling's crops are faring, or whether there is a chance to run over a stray pheasant, his eyes must dart in all directions. Often his head is pivoted almost back to front the better to tell us, in his broad Wiltshire accent, of some neighbourly event: how farmer Bundy's cows were electrocuted, of Mrs Bundy's sow's record litter, or of Captain Dale's accident resulting in his old Rolls being a 'write-off'. Yet, although others in the locality have found themselves head-on to some runaway tractor and propelled over a hedge, Mr Gould boasts that he has never yet had a road accident.

In the darkness, and without so many distractions, Mr Gould's driving is no less fanatical. Tonight he was to take me further afield than usual — as far as Southampton, where I was to take the tender out into the darkness to meet the giant ocean liner, the *Liberté*, on its way from Cherbourg to New York. Among its passengers was Garbo who was disembarking at Southampton in order to stay with me. The future was as bright as this enormous, illuminated structure which suddenly towered into the night — all her funnels spot-lighted, each deck a brilliant glow, every one of her portholes a twinkling star.

Greta, wild-eyed and seemingly somewhat terrified, was waiting, among empty glasses, with her 'little' friend in the restaurant. They did not smile on seeing me: it was as if I were coming to make the final transaction of a business deal. The general atmosphere was so grim and overladen with tension that I wondered if, at any minute, one of them would suddenly inform me of a change of plan. Without allowing time for such an opportunity, and with an impatience that was quite ruthless, I snatched my friend by the arm and, in my best Lochinvar manner, guided her down the gangway into the waiting dinghy. It was with the greatest feeling of relief and happiness — too good yet to be true — that I looked back to see the golden illuminated liner receding into the distance.

For several minutes we sailed in silence on the dark liquid waves towards the cold blue light on the jetty. Here we were on English soil — safe at last! But even now I did not find that Greta seemed fully conscious of my presence: not one look or one word of intimacy. But once in the smelly old local car Greta was intrigued by Mr Gould's broad Wiltshire accent. She asked him to repeat certain phrases, and soon, throwing back his head and roaring with laughter, he was completely conquered by the unseen passenger at the back of his car. Even though he is accustomed, in his role behind the counter, to meeting all sorts of unexpected types, he sensed that this was someone quite out of the ordinary. He was obviously very amused and struck by her, but it was many days before he discovered the identity of the lady in the dark.

Mr Gould was only one of the local personalities who at once became friends with Greta. Soon she was on the best of terms with the vicar, the butcher and the gardener. George and Lily Bundy, the general storekeepers, and farmer Herbert Bundy and his pig-keeping wife Olive, were also trusted with her friendship. Greta was surprised and grateful that everyone in the village treated her as an ordinary private individual and that no one, even in the Salisbury market where we went to buy gum-boots, fish or potted plants, would stare at the stranger in their midst.

It was a revelation to watch her coming to life, and loving nature and simple things, and taking to Wiltshire ways as if this was where she belonged. For me it was marvellous to see that the transformation which I had hoped for, was, in fact, taking place.

The autumn weather held good, the leaves remained on the trees longer than usual, and went through every variety of yellow, gold, flame and rose. Soon existence in Reddish House developed into a set pattern. I was under a 'gentleman's agreement' to rewrite my Gainsborough play, for the kindly management who had lost a considerable investment on its preliminary try-out in the provinces were still interested in a further production and the possibility of recouping their fortunes. So my early mornings were spent with a quiet and erudite friend, Hal Burton, who was helping with the latest version of the play. Hal had much experience in the theatre as director and producer and was able to give excellent advice on points of construction. He is a most gentle and trustworthy soul and Greta took an instant liking to him which made life so much easier for all. At twelve o'clock Hal and I would join Greta who, dew-covered and ecstatic, would return from her favourite walk on the downs where the height of her joy was to scratch the backs of a posse of Bundy pigs in their pen. The rest of the day was given to pleasure. We browsed in nearby antique shops, went to see favoured neighbours. Everywhere Greta went hearts were laid before her by people of both sexes of all ages and all types.

We visited noble houses: Wilton, Longford, Crichel and Cranborne. We ventured further — as far as Bath, Eton, and Oxford where Greta ran her fingers lovingly and lingeringly over the stone walls of ancient colleges. 'I love the smell of the walls. Walls in European houses smell so good,' she said at Magdalen College, and she put her face close to the library walls. But Greta loved to return to Broadchalke. She enjoyed its seclusion, she relished the garden and the fact that the vegetables, fresh from the ground, tasted of their intrinsic selves. The salads were unlike those in California, which have such a spectacular appearance but are disappointing in flavour. When confronted with our Irish stew she admitted: '"The Dragon" [her own cook] never made anything like this!'

Greta became totally relaxed and lost many of her inhibitions; she was seldom cautious about being on view or in other ways exploited. She became her true self: she blossomed.

The only worry to our peaceful coexistence was the Press. On the very first morning of relaxation in the green quiet of Broadchalke, the telephone rang a few inches from Greta's ear. I stretched for the receiver and we both listened to inquiries from the *Evening Standard* as to Miss Garbo's plans, and were congratulations in order for Mr Beaton? Greta did not smile. This was my baptism into the ways the Press can hound its quarry when it considers the pursuit is worth its efforts. The experience was alarming. Within a short space of time, nice, rustic and somewhat *naïf* journalists in old tweeds appeared, on instruction from London, from the offices of the *Salisbury Times* and *Western Gazette*. Two hours later, city-suited professionals arrived from Fleet Street for only a brief interview with Miss Garbo. At first polite smiles and refusals. Then an ominous note was heard. Greta, unseen in the background, would not yield an inch. Therefore the campaign intensified outside. A large, black, urban limousine remained waiting in the village street for days on end. Shopkeepers and rustic folk maintained a canny secrecy, and gave away nothing about the luminary in their midst. Once, however, while climbing a steep woodland arcade, we were taken completely unawares by a flashlight photographer. A whacking great ulcer exploded in my stomach, and I tried to hide the *Sunday Express* from Greta next day. But she is a realist, and demanded to see the picture which she perused with the corners of her mouth turned down in the ultimate expression of dissatisfaction.

Perhaps more than a month after her arrival, when the Press had lost interest, an unexpected reporter called while I was in bed working on my Gainsborough play. The cook, unused to the wiles of reporters and easily flattered, had given away the information that Miss Garbo had gone for a walk by herself over the hills past Mr Bundy's pig-styes. When I heard this, I rushed out in my pyjamas in cold and windy pursuit. In the distance I saw the lone figure approaching. I signalled violently to Greta to return by the woods above the house, and thereby avoid an unwelcome confrontation.

Then when Greta decided to come to London the Press campaign started again. Wherever we went there was the eerie feeling of being watched — even dogged. Who are these ubiquitous spies who are there to give information at every turn? It is understandable that the proprietor of a restaurant might inform some journalist friend of the presence of a celebrity in his establishment so that it might be mentioned in a gossip column, but one would not imagine that anyone on Salisbury platform would bother to telephone so that a flashbulb would be 'at the ready' by the ticket barrier at Waterloo. Greta would always be the first one to spot the hastily summoned photographer. Suddenly her carefree mood would change to fretful or sullen.

Only now did I fully realize what havoc the Press have wrought on Greta's private life.

It was not surprising that my mother should become upset that her son who remained, at middle age, unmarried, and whom she had come to rely upon to look after her for the rest of her life, now appeared as if he might be making plans to make a painful change. She was resentful. My mother has never been one to hide her feelings; when she met Greta for the first time her welcome was far from warm. Greta took no time to notice this. A 'situation' arose that made things extremely difficult. I was exasperated. How was it that one couldn't expect support and help from one's nearest, if not — at this moment — one's dearest? I was told that my mother even sank to the melodramatic level of referring to 'that woman'. However, after a while, my mother decided to relent. One cold winter's evening she came home with a pale translucent, green and white bunch of the first hot-house lilies-of-the-valley, and as Greta said: 'No one can resist lilies-of-the-valley.'

My birthday was celebrated by the arrival of sisters, aunts and cousins for a family dinner party. I personally find 'next of kin' gatherings are apt to be poignant, rather than gay occasions. Perhaps others are better at covering up their embarrassment: perhaps they genuinely enjoy the jollity. Apparently everyone else was at ease, and treating Greta as if she were already one of them; there was much joking and laughter. But on this occasion it was Greta who disappointed; she made no effort to put on at full voltage her powers of fascination. Even in appearance she seemed drab. Perhaps, although it was sad for me, it was more suitable for the occasion, and, by not outshining the female members of the coterie, she showed once more her powers of intuition. But for me, the evening was so charged, so fraught, that I felt like one of those tragi-farcical Chekov characters who suddenly rushes out of the room while the slamming of the door is followed by an abortive pistol shot.

It was not because Greta showed any curiosity, or interest, in my beginnings — rather in spite of the lack, that I took her on a tour of Hampstead and the places in which my infancy was spent. Oh, *les neiges d'Antan*!! Where were those little lanes and dales and Dickensian shopping clusters that I found so full of wonder and thrill when I was at the start of all that builds to the experience of life? What a different picture assaults the eye today! One way traffic on vast roadways, huge impersonal community centres, anonymous skyscrapers of cement and glass; every manifestation of modern community-tastes — chromium, cement, neon.

It was only natural that everything should appear now diminished in scale; but the Victorian Dutch red-brick house in Langland Gardens, in which I was born, seemed so squashed against its neighbours that it would be a tight fit for a family and servants. Little wonder that my father, riding up the hill, steered his horse towards the heath and decided that a large neo-Georgian mansion on Templewood Avenue would be more suitable for his growing family and the fulfilment of his worldly ambitions.

But today 'Temple Court' is not what it was when my mother looked after four children and a retinue of ever-changing domestics. It was here that in her hours of leisure she contributed to the decorative scheme of the house by sewing cottonwool-stuffed grapes or apples on the corners of large cushions, or picked for the dining-table a few prize specimens of the roses that grew so well in the clay soil. Now the house, in acute disrepair, was divided into modernized flats. The departed happiness and charm!

Hampstead Heath, typically Constable-coloured, remains just as mysterious as when, with Latin, Shakespeare and algebra in satchel, I hurried past on the way to Heath Mount School in the Grove. Today as we motored along well-known avenues and byways great wafts of emotion poured into me. They were produced by memories of people loved (sometimes they were seen only from a distance) or people feared: Proustian memories of smells of wet earth, or grass, or oak trees, of remembered textures, wet Macintoshes, pools in the mud, and the shiny, crimson mahogany of chestnuts hanging on a string waiting to be victimized by the other boy's conker.

Greta seemed surprised at my ebullience as I pointed out the 'Arts and Crafts' houses of Voysey, Webb and Shaw in Platts Lane, Ellerdale Road, and Heath Drive. The recollections spilled like a torrent as we sped past the walled garden where Mrs Scholte (the wife of the Savile Row tailor), with high Alexandrine Pompadour and corseted Victorian Cretan torso, led us out into her rose garden, and with her paper-white hands snipped off the carefully chosen offerings. Other memories — of homework and rather exciting developments of learning maths, literature or history — were evoked by the white stone pond, which one passed on the way home on the step of Geoghegan minor's bicycle. Jack Straw's Castle brought back memories of August Bank Holiday fairs and the eerie sounds and smells of the merry-go-rounds.

Then I drove Greta along the Spaniards, past that most ghost — haunted of all places, 'Ivy Lodge', where Pavlova, of the raven's hair, hawk beak, and livid white complexion like the pip of an apple, beckoned to her swans on a lake, and danced a bacchanal on her closely-worn lawns for those privileged, god-like persons, her private guests, at a yearly garden party. Greta, head low through the car window, peered at the black, ivy-covered trellis fences, and dirty, inky brick walls. We drove to Kenwood, and I showed her my favourite fashion plate — the Gainsborough of Lady Howe in the flat straw hat and miraculously painted rose taffeta dress. These glimpses of places that had been part of my childhood elicited no information about her early life.

Perhaps the place that appealed most to Greta of all the peregrinations to which she patiently submitted herself was the Soane Museum, with its quiet sobriety of taste and strange assortment of exhibits. But by far her greatest delight was to watch the changing of the guard at Buckingham Palace or the sentries on duty at St James's Palace. In front of any of these men she would lose all self-consciousness as, incapable of keeping still, she imitated the swing of the arms, the rhythm of their heavy steps, the jumping to attention. Unaware of passers-by watching her in surprise, she would lean forward in utter attention, then quiver with shock and delight each time they presented arms. She was completely rapt. 'Oh, look at the swing of their coats! *Quel chic*!' She would scurry after a retreating sentry marching across the cobblestones of King's Yard, and then be almost frightened out of her wits as he stamped his boots and about-turned to face his childish devotee.

One morning I went into Greta's room. She was serious: she had had a letter from 'the little man'. 'He's very clever,' was all she said; but later she admitted that he wrote: 'There's nothing left now but to announce your good news.' However, the question of marriage did not seem to become any more positive than before. Whenever I brought up the subject, Greta would cast it aside or make a joke of it. Nonetheless, I was not unhappy — in fact, the reverse. The fact that we got along so well together — never a sharp word or a ghost of exasperation — made me feel that all would work out well in the end. I only hoped that we could continue like this without some unexpected SOS call from outside to interrupt this most halcyon phase.

Although she knows little of politics she was excited to be in London for the General Election — even insisting on remaining to hear the results at a huge party given by Pamela and Michael Berry. So great were her spirits as the Conservative victories came through, that she did not seem even to mind the attentions of the photographers.

Christmas approached. What to do? Michael Duff invited us to stay in Wales at Vaynol: it would be a real festivity. Yes, she would enjoy that. Then, for no more reason than that she wished to buy a certain cashmere or a pair of brogue shoes, Greta insisted that we should go to Paris.

We stayed at the Crillon from whence I took her to museums and galleries, dress collections, theatres, antique shops and restaurants. Sometimes the shopping was a trifle embarrassing, for Greta would leave a shop, where everything had been turned upside down for her, with a 'Well, we'll come back later'; she was happily unmindful of the attitude of the rather surly assistant. After a few weeks the routine became somewhat monotonous. 'Where shall we lunch today? Which restaurant do *you* prefer?'

The weather was bad, became worse. Not a taxi on the road. Greta never had confidence enough when crossing a street. ('How do we know they have brakes?') I longed to take her back to Broadchalke, and after a while to motor to Wales. After Christmas we would both sail back to New York.

But suddenly, without explanation, Greta decided that she would fly to New York next week. I knew there was no influencing her. Neither of us felt anything but sadness at parting. For three months I had thought only of protecting her and seeing that life was kind to her. She had responded first with courage and then with complete trust; she lost so many of her qualms and anxieties. The whole experience of being together had been idyllic — certainly for me the happiest emotional adventure of my life. For Greta, too, her experience of England had brought contentment. Accustomed to being uprooted, to merely enduring in a foreign country without even the outlet for her creative abilities, she suddenly found herself close to the things that were essential to her. She felt at home. The result was that she became less frightened, appeared to be more secure, less able to make problems for herself though, as always, she abided by her own rules.

I had to return to London for some unpostponable job. I hated leaving her alone in the Paris hotel. I telephoned as often as possible. We exchanged wires, then affectionate letters. She flew to New York from where she wrote that 'it would be soon now that we meet again'. On sailing to join her a few weeks later, I wired: 'Soon.'

NEW YORK: BACK TO WHERE WE WERE

December 1951

On arrival in New York early on a Tuesday morning I am agonizingly delayed on the docks having to clear through the laborious Customs some tiresome presents sent by friends for friends. Midday is already striking when I reach my hotel. Perhaps I am too late to catch Greta before she goes out for the day? Immediately I telephone her hotel: 'Miss Garbo isn't taking any calls yet.' That seems odd as I know she generally wakes at nine o'clock. I try a little later. 'Miss Garbo don't answer.' Perhaps she's in the bath. I try again: still no answer. I leave a message to say I've called. Next morning I call again. 'Miss Garbo don't answer.' I can hardly believe it possible. This is the old treatment! Later that day — or perhaps the next day — a pink azalea, banked by ferns, arrives in a pot with a note from 'Harriet' saying that she had reasons for not calling me but that as I am a busy person the time would fly by, and meanwhile behave.

I write her a very tender note saying that, naturally, there is no reason for her to see me until she is in the mood to do so. But, meanwhile, too much time goes by without a call from her. A whole week passes. Then on the following Sunday she telephones. She is feeling badly: she has had a cold ever since her return here: she has no vitality. She and her friend are both in a bad way: he is going to hospital: both are depressed. As soon as she feels better perhaps we could meet and have a lunch together?

Another interval: but time is valuable. I send her as a joke a cushion with the embroidered motto written upon it: 'Enjoy yourself. It's later than you think.' By the time I return from delivering the cushion at her hotel she has already telephoned. I ring back. She laughs. There is no tensity. We would meet soon — just as soon as she feels a bit better: the '*nasale*' is still bad!

Michael Duff rings on arrival from Wales. 'Couldn't we have an evening out with Greta?' I say he'd better ring her and arrange it. She rings me. Sir Michael has called her: would I make a date for the three of us? As suggested by Michael the three of us have an evening together: I am somewhat distant, but try to appear bright and gay. Greta looks incredibly beautiful — radiant. The evening is full of fun. We drop Michael at his hotel, and I walk Greta home to hers. When are we going to see each other again? She can't make any definite dates until the last moment.

'Why?'

'Oh, don't let's talk about anything depressing.'

I kiss her rather peremptorily on one cheek and leave. I do not, as is my wont, look back over my shoulder and salute her: I just walk on. I do not telephone to her when I return to my room. I feel too hurt that this should happen after the deep, warm intimacy of our times together in Europe.

Two weeks go by: still no sign of her. Then I ring and say that since Michael would soon be leaving, couldn't we three meet again tonight? 'The little man' is in hospital: he has to be entertained: when she returns from the Medical Centre she is always exhausted. 'Well, there is a lot I think we should discuss,' I say, and hang up somewhat abruptly. This evidently scares her for another meeting. It is after another interval of perhaps ten days that she calls me again: would Michael and I have luncheon with her tomorrow?

I decide to have my own little joke. I will not invite Michael and will arrive for an unexpected lunch *à deux*. Where shall we meet? 'At a quiet restaurant, please,' I say. 'I don't like noisy places where we are buffeted and can't talk in peace.' 'Colony' decided. I telephone Michael just to find out what he is doing. 'I don't happen to be lunching anywhere today,' he says; but still I don't extend the invitation due to him.

From a busy morning of costume fittings for Truman Capote's *Grass Harp* I arrive at the Colony restaurant. Greta looks quite tamed and civilized in a grey beret with a diamond pin in it. Her face, as always when she comes straight from Laszlo, is slightly *maquillé*. She has deeper wrinkles under the eyes than I have seen before, but she looks very sensitive and beautiful — though I must steel myself against her beauty. I tell her I have not asked Michael to lunch. She flusters a little, and says so long as I explain to him that just out of 'deviltry' I have not ...

'"Devilry" is the word we use in England — "deviltry" is Irish-American — don't you remember?' A moment later she uses an ungrammatical sentence and when I remonstrate she replies: 'I meant to say it that way: it sounds tough.' Very soon the effects of the two whisky-sours that I gulp, and the aqua-vitae that she has ordered, are making themselves felt, and I find myself bluntly asking for the reasons why she has not seen me since my arrival here.

'Oh, I couldn't tell you those now — I'm tipsy.'

'Well, I wouldn't be very happy to go home, as I shall be doing at any moment, without knowing what I have done to offend you. It seemed to me that there was no cloud on our horizon in Europe: when we left each other it was with great tenderness. I've never pretended to be anything I am not: I have given you my complete confidence, and can only think that for you to instruct the operator to tell me: "She don't answer", is rather shoddy behaviour.'

'I daresay I am a very bad-tempered wretch.'

'Doesn't it make you feel badly to do this to me?'

'Yes.'

'You must be a very unhappy person.'

'I am.'

'You have the power to hurt me deeply.'

'Yet I feel you wouldn't mind very much.'

'You think I won't threaten to jump out of a window?'

'If you did, I wouldn't believe it.'

'You're right. Perhaps, however miserable, I am not the sort to commit "suers" — not just yet at any rate. Of course I have my work and other things to keep me going. Do you like making people suffer?'

'No, but I didn't think you would suffer so very much.'

'Why?'

'I don't think you loved me very much by the time we left one another in Paris.'

'I wasn't as happy with you in Paris as in the country in England, but that is because I loathe the cafe society way of life; it seemed so pointless — particularly for you. But you really think I didn't love you?'

'I don't think you've ever really loved me!'

'Then what have I been doing for the past five years?'

'Oh, I daresay you have enjoyed fooling around. It's been quite a change.'

This is horrible! I hate myself for precipitating a squalid lovers' quarrel — for nagging on when I already sense that nothing can be resolved. Yet I will not give up the battle. I order myself another whisky-sour. I become quite drunk.

'Don't imagine "the little man" has influenced me against you. I had made up my mind before you came. You see, you have such vitality: you can't keep quiet or relaxed: one has to be on the run with you all the time. And I'm going through a bad period in my life; everything is erratic: I'm feeling anxious and uneasy and low, and I can't face up to the pace you set. I don't feel up to seeing you.'

'You can't relax completely when you're with me?'

'You don't know me. You pronounce such strict verdicts. Someone sent me on Valentine's Day a book you once published, and in it you wrote that I have no heart — that I am not capable of friendship.'

'That was written before I knew you. It was foolish, but then as a young man I had a habit of blowing my top. But is it fair suddenly to hold something against me that I wrote twenty years ago, before I knew you?'

I realize how wounded Greta must have been to read these words which I had long since forgotten.

'So then what? We are at the end?'

'Well,' — a long pause while she looks at me askance — 'you're looking very pretty,' she says — 'and you're thinner.'

I do not return her a compliment. Instead I smooth away a lock of her hair and say: 'I know exactly how your hair should be.'

'Oh, do help! I know I look a fright and you could help me.'

'What's the use?'

She likes it when I take hold of her hair, and I imitate her saying: '*Nicht machen.*'

She asks: 'Do you remember how violently you took hold of my hair in that Paris restaurant?'

'And you were furious.' (Now I realize she had loved it.)

Suddenly the strain has gone: no bitterness is left. I still feel a bit bruised, but we are back — more or less — where we used to be. I tenderly escort her to her hotel. Saint Subber and the technicians are waiting to take me off in their motor to see the building of the giant tree for *The Grass Harp*. In the lobby I ask: 'Shall I kiss you goodbye here?' I am putting her to a test for she knows people are standing by and watching her. I kiss her, and she is pleased. We go out into the street and there is the waiting car. Suddenly I am enveloped by theatrical jargon and stage technicalities. But, in spite of the sudden onslaught, out of the corner of an eye I watch Greta walk up Park Avenue; she looks like any other young woman as she disappears into the distance. Who would have imagined such intensity of feeling is going through our minds? I do not know when I shall see her again.

It takes me some time before I return to the other world of the theatre.

Part V: Both Sides of the Atlantic, 1952

CRITICISM

July 1952

I have the acutest antennae for criticism. The unfavourable review of my work is always the one I remember. When I was on my recent lecture-tour in America, my eagle eye would always spot the one man dozing in the audience. At the first night in Brighton of *Aren't We All*, for which I have done the period designs, I sat next to Binkie Beaumont, the impresario. He was amused, but thought it sad, when I told him that when the curtain in Act One went up to great applause for my *vieux-rose* set, I should hear a man behind me saying: 'Awful! Crikey, fancy applauding that!'

When the curtain went up on Act Two, a sunny Henley Regatta décor with which I was very pleased, for it re-created my boyhood's impression of summer and the theatre combined — white garden chairs indoors, blue and white chintz, white trellis-work, hydrangeas — the woman on my left murmured: 'It's all blue this time!'

'AREN'T WE ALL' GALA

The Queen, it was said, wished to give her encouragement to the London theatre by paying one of her rare visits to a play. She didn't particularly wish to see anything of Brechtian gloom, or adapted from the French, or even an American importation, so this 'old-fashioned rubbish', as the critics recently called *Aren't We All*, received the honour.

Such is the effect of Royalty that, although the play has been running for a hundred performances, the entire cast was nervous. Even the old professionals, like Ronnie Squire and Marie Löhr, were saying: 'Oh, we'll be too keyed up to give good performances,' and everyone was a bit too intent on putting their best foot forward. The women insisted that the wigmaker should re-dress their hair, their dresses were sent to the cleaners, and Marie Löhr told me she had walked for four hours to try, in vain, to get a champagne-coloured bow that I had suggested she should put at her stomach. Everyone behind the scenes was giving an extra spit and polish to their job. Paul Anstee hurried off with all the hydrangeas to have them given a certain dye-spraying as the blue had faded in the strong lights of the arcs.

The streets around the Haymarket were lined with people held back by a concourse of policemen. The audience had to be seated half an hour before 'the Royals' arrived. It sat cheerfully talking. There was the usual air of expectation. The Royal Box was decorated with hideous, small, bronze and yellow chrysanthemums. The first thing to be seen was the approach of a bouquet. 'God Save The Queen'. Everyone stood to attention; the Queen quizzed the house out of the corner of her eye, not looking at all self-conscious at being stared at. The Queen Mother appeared, preceded by another bouquet and a bosom draped in white tulle. Then, without a tiara — perhaps with the wish to appear different — Princess Margaret. With precision the two Queens, having been politely cheered, sat down, the house lights were lowered, and the curtain went up.

Throughout the performance the Regal Box was being surreptitiously watched by half the audience, so that the play received scant attention; but the general atmosphere was uncritical and good-natured, the display of manners and loyalty impressive. It was very interesting to note how the Royal Family seem to have acquired a communal manner of behaviour. They have developed an instinctive self-protection so that they should not bump into each other or stumble down a step. They move in slow motion with care and a fluid grace: their technique is so perfected that it appears entirely natural. No doubt but that much of this charm and grace is very special to the Queen Mother. The reigning Queen has developed independently but her charm and interested wonder is inherited from her mother's genius.

The Queen sat relaxed and hunched, with head cocked backwards to listen concentratedly to the play. Princess Margaret had straight neck and back, and perhaps a more artificial interest in the stage performance. But the Queen Mother is an exceptionally bright woman, and tonight was in her most jovial mood, enjoying every nuance of the play's humour with a hearty relish, and alert to all the complicated twists of the mechanical plot. She was having a 'night out', and in such good spirits that she chuckled at many things that the audience would take for granted, and roared at the things that amused her most. In the first interval, when Freddie Lonsdale and I were presented, she said: 'We're having such a good time.' When talking to Royalty I am apt, perhaps out of nervousness, to do an imitation of them to their faces, talking to the Queen Mother in the same wistful tones with wrinkled forehead. 'It's delicious, enchanting,' are her favourite words, and I find myself repeating them. I was being wistful, hesitant, and much too sycophantic when I heard, with admiration, Freddie Lonsdale just being himself. In his somewhat offhand manner, he was saying just the things that he would say to

Gilbert Miller or Henry Luce. 'Oh, we are enjoying it so much — it's delicious!' one of the Royal ladies would say.

'It gets better,' said Lonsdale.

'Oh, but that's surprising! It isn't generally like that! The last act's always the trouble, isn't it?'

'My last acts are the best.'

Roars of laughter.

I thought perhaps the Queen Mother would be bored talking politely about the evening's entertainment, and suddenly I found myself asking: 'Did you have a good holiday?'

'Oh, I've bought a villa,[3] in the most remote part of the world!'

'How brave of you to have nothing between you and the Atlantic.'

'I've taken this villa to get away from everything; but I don't expect I shall ever be able to get there.'

Hearty laughter. If the Queen Mother were anyone other than she is (ridiculous supposition) would one come so readily under her spell? Would one admire quite so much those old-fashioned, dainty movements? The sweetly pretty smile, with tongue continually moistening the lower lip? Yes — whoever she were, she could not be faulted. As it is, everything about her adds to her fascination. Even her professed enjoyment of good Scottish oatcakes only adds to her comeliness. What matters it if her tip-tilted nose is not specially delicate in its modelling, nor the teeth as pearly as they used to be? It is important that she has such style, subtlety and humour, but it is her empathy and her understanding of human nature that endears her to everyone she talks to.

I wish that I could make a better impression on the Queen — not because she is the reigning monarch, but because I

---

[3] The Castle of Mey.

admire her character — her fairness and her judgement — so much that I reproach myself for something inadequate within myself if she does not respond favourably. Yet I find her difficult to talk to. The timing always seems jerky and inopportune. I know I am at fault. As for her appearance, one would wish her to wear her hair less stiffly, or to choose dresses that would 'do' more for her; but one must admit that all these little alterations would make no real difference. The purity of her expression, the unspoilt childishness of the smile, the pristine quality of her pink and white complexion, are all part of an appearance that is individual and gives the effect of a total entity.

Princess Margaret has more than a certain kindness and understanding, and she can be extremely amusing with a good turn of phrase and an appreciation of wit in others.

In the second interval the company was presented. Jolly jokes, graciousness: everyone had his proud moment. The final curtain. The cast bowed and curtsied to the Royal Box. Then the Royal party left. Cheers, hands waving to the gallery. The Queen Mother gets her special round of applause. Exit. Police in control. Sudden release of tension. Shouts, laughter, eyes wild, bouquets, flashlights. For the people responsible, an evening of great achievement. For the Royal Family, no doubt a pleasant enough excursion: one to be discussed very little on their return, and forgotten completely in the busy events of tomorrow.

OPENING OF PARLIAMENT

November 4th, 1952

I've sometimes thought that I would like, one summer, to devote myself entirely to the enjoyment of 'The Season's' attractions. Wouldn't it be a bit of a lark to go to the Boat Race, Trooping the Colour, the Military Tattoo, the Derby and Ascot Races, and polo at Cowdray Park? And how about Cruft's Dog Show? And surely the Poultry Show is an essential? I have never done any of these things: always so tied up I seldom get out of my rut. Can't I regulate my life to have an afternoon off?

The foregoing outburst is a result of the extraordinary exception to my general rule — the fact that, at the kind invitation of Rock[4] and Sybil Cholmondeley, I went to the Opening of Parliament. It was the first time that this ceremony was to be performed by the young Queen.

Rock, being the Lord Chamberlain, has a strategically situated box in the Royal Gallery (which is raised only a few inches from floor level) from which its occupants can have an intimate view of almost everything — from the moment the leading personalities make their entrance up the main staircase before processing into the House of Lords.

I had to get up at sparrow-fart since ingenious arrangements had been made for me to take photographs connected with the forthcoming Coronation. It seems, and in any case robes (or tunics) are not allowed out of the building, that dignitaries are loath to dress up for a special sitting, so my camera was hidden in the robing rooms the night before, and I would be allowed to take some shots before this morning's proceedings. After I had photographed Black Rod in his small room, which smelt strongly of the apples labelled with their different names — Blenheim orange, Cox's orange pippins, Beauty of Bath, Charles Ross, Codling, Bramleys and Anne Elizabeth — in cardboard boxes hidden behind a screen, the Chief Herald,

[4] The Marquess of Cholmondeley.

Bellew, put on the same costume that his ancestor had worn three hundred years ago.

Later, I was escorted from the ground floor to another part of the building where a second camera was secreted in the Lord Chancellor's room.

The preparations for the morning's activity were as unaccountable and entertaining as anything I have witnessed in my extensive behind-the-stage scenes: the same preening and patting before looking-glasses as in theatre dressing-rooms, the same distant murmurs from the already assembled audience; but this time the crowds were gathering outside in the streets and squares as well as indoors. The offstage noises comprised a mixture of horses' hooves in a quadrangle, the click of steel, the purring of limousines, the quiet instructions from the police to the favoured arrivals, and in nearby corridors the chatter of the peers and peeresses. The black-coated servants of the House were substitutes for the stage 'dressers'. Lord Alexander, with eyebrows raised to create an expression I mistook for arrogance, and which is, no doubt, a subterfuge to hide his innate shyness, came into the Ward Room to make sure that his cloak was properly adjusted. Although there was a certain tension in the air this show had been running for the last five hundred years or more, so it had been well rehearsed.

The Lord Chancellor,[5] in his chambers, presented a not-to-be-laughed-at spectacle before my camera, in black and gold with red and gold purse and full-bottomed wig. His face was benign and benevolent with eyebrows that were so bushy that a few thick hairs hung over his eyes. His ears and nose were likewise thickly sprouting. He referred to the peers as 'a lot of old men'.

---

[5] The Right Honourable Viscount Simonds.

I also photographed Black Rod and Black Rod's assistants, whatever they are called, all in black page-boy uniforms with frothing lace jabots. Some were surprisingly aged with spindly legs and gaunt cheekbones. One, with a beautiful sensitive face, somewhat like an old frog, was the son of a man who had fought at Waterloo.

'Big Ben is exactly 10.24. You had better go now, Beaton, for they lock the door to the Royal Gallery.' I was one of the last of the populace to arrive, and felt abashed at having to walk the length of the Gallery between the serried rows of spectators. The Beefeaters lined the blue carpeted route, and I had never felt a carpet more silken and soft beneath my feet. The Gallery, with huge picture-book murals, and Gothic wallpaper of gold and dark green, is a mess of golden Victoriana and, although not in itself beautiful, gives the effect of grand ugliness or ugly quaintness.

Suddenly I found myself surprisingly and happily placed next to the cosy, adorable Lynn Fontanne, so all terror and anxiety immediately vanished. I always enjoy watching my fellow human beings; but now, in their traditional fancy dress — a fancy dress that has been tried, developed and improved until found to be flawless — the show could have gone on for ever. Ancient men with tired eyes, wrinkles, thinning hair, and all the sad outward aspects of age, appeared perfectly cast as unique and remarkable characters, in these marvellous scarlet, black and white clothes. Grand soldiers or officers of state were stiffly encumbered with gold thread embroideries as if they were in their natural everyday habit.

The arrival of parakeetish Princess Alice and the yeasty Duchess of Beaufort was somewhat of a shock, for they bustled through the Gallery on their way to the Robing Room wearing half-length fur coats that savoured too much of the pedestrian life outside this strange and glorious world. No — the women altogether were not ceremonial enough: jewellery, however important, on badly made, creased old evening gowns, was not good enough. They lacked '*hauteur*'. It was the masculine gender who won today's prizes.

I am completely ignorant of the various offices of those near to the Crown, but realized that most of these people had been brought up to do these particular duties, so it was only natural for them to carry the Crown or Sword of State with such consummate ease. It made me realize the futility of trying to be someone one isn't: a lesson to go about one's life-work immune from any false note of pretension and snobbery. In what other country could people dress themselves up at this early hour, with such ease and naturalness, and never be in danger of making fools of themselves? The only impostors here were among the women: those who by some devious means had trapped a man into a marriage which technically gave them a foothold here. That tiresome, pushing little Lady was still wriggling her way up the ladder; with her innate vulgarity of yellow, frizzy, musical comedy curls and sycophantic flattery she stuck out a mile.

Exactly on the appointed minute the various bodies walked slowly through the Gallery to await the Queen's arrival. There was something quite casual about the whole thing. No one appeared nervous — for no one was. The procession of the Heralds, in complete silence, brought vivid touches of scarlet, blue and gold. There was something quite haunting about one, a young man whose name I discovered to be Frere. His hair was sand-coloured, his complexion colourless, his eyes tired. There was something haunting about his composure; with his pale, lovelorn face he seemed to be burnt out by some romantic passion. Now nothing was left to him but to materialize — as he did — a perfect work of art, in his quartered tunic and sombre stockings, as he held the two Sceptres in pale ivory hands.

The Black Rods, in their lamp-black stockings and pumps with silver buckles, seemed to come from the insect world of Grandeville. Brian Horrocks, with his long parchment face and thickly covered head of carefully combed grey hair, was a subject for Tintoretto — and yet, perhaps, something an English master could better interpret.

With a tinkle of swords against spurs, the Queen's Bodyguard followed with more military precision. An aged warrior, in cock-feathered helmet and dashing uniform, was made more poignant by the contrast of his having to walk with a stick — no doubt the result of some injury in long-forgotten wars; was it possible that he had survived the Charge of the Light Brigade? It was he who now gave the word of command as his company — all tall, in splendid feathers — clanked forward.

Up the carpeted stairs came a playing card from 'Happy Families', the 'Pig King' as personified by the Duke of Norfolk, with sadly surprised eyebrows and bags under small, tadpole eyes, impertinent, aggressive snout and sulking pout. His scarlet-vermilion cloth cape was in need of pressing; but I was told that these garments must be thrown into a linen bag to be brought out only for each occasion, and that there is great feeling that they should never be ironed.

The Duke of Beaufort appeared — superb in his tightly-filled kid trousers, enormous shining black boots, and scarlet jacket. His red face winter-weather-beaten, his chin blue with continual shaving; by wearing a pair of steel-rimmed spectacles, the sort that one only sees on elderly countryfolk or in medieval portraits, a note of reality was added to this fairy-tale grandeur. By his side, even taller, and wearing the same awe-inspiring uniform, was Queen Mary's brother, Lord Athlone. With his clear-sky eyes, fresh rosy complexion, crisp, thick white hair, and overbearing physique, he presented an awe-inspiring elderly figure.

Bobbety Salisbury, whose large cranium, pale eyes and aquiline features made of vellum, gave the onlooker an immediate impression of his general intelligence, worldly wisdom, and profound experience of life, moved in staccato jerks and dashes that caused the white satin ribbons to flutter at the shoulders of his long crimson-lake cloak. Rock Cholmondeley, as svelte as a fishing-rod and a-glitter with medals upon gold and silver embroidery, a Pelion-on-Ossa effect, appeared holding the Crown. This precious symbol was placed on a cushion so close to where Lynn and I were sitting that, without leaning forward, it would have been possible to touch the Koh-i-noor and the acorns made of pear-shaped pearls in their husks of diamond. Lord Alexander, with his eyebrows and long cloak properly adjusted, came in with a perhaps too dramatic, dedicated expression on his face, holding the Sword of State.

Princess Margaret appeared with her aunt, the Princess Royal, with the white-skinned Duchess of Gloucester in black velvet at her side. The Princess, her eyes bright and inquisitive, looked from side to side as she walked forward with rolling gait and head slightly thrust forward, and her kid-gloved arms held with prominent elbows. The Princess Royal, without make-up of any kind, her face and lips equally white, with her crown of diamonds lodged in a hard, wiry coiffeur of curls like a lawyer's wig, was of the right scale: her dignity innate.

Indoors all quiet until suddenly, outside the high windows, various rumbling noises told one that the Queen was arriving.

The cheers of the people sent a tremor through the bloodstream. One expected, but did not hear, an organ to roll out a volume of noise. It was the continued insistent silence that made all the more impressive the moment when the tall double doors were thrown open to reveal the young Queen standing with her gloved hand held high on that of her Consort. A moment's pause, then in a slow, ambling march the procession passed towards the Throne where the young lady would make her first speech to Parliament.

The Queen wore gold and stolid white. The long red velvet train, miniver-edged, splendid against the gold and scarlet setting, her stance, with the rigid little head and the well-curled hair around Queen Victoria's Crown, was marvellously erect. She has inherited many of her mother's graces, but, most important of all, she has acquired her frank serenity: her eyes are not those of a busy, harassed person. She regards people with a recognition of compassion — and a slight suggestion of a smile lightens the otherwise cumbrous mouth.

There was nothing formidable about the general mood, which encouraged an ease and sense of relaxation in the spectators, and the procession moved so slowly that one felt tempted to talk to those passing by. The Duke of Edinburgh appeared somewhat hollow-eyed, his complexion pale, and hair beginning to thin.

The Mistress of the Robes, the Duchess of Northumberland, gigantically tall with wonderful jewels, wore a Knightsbridge horror of a dress, a crinoline of coarse, Parma violet nylon-tulle with self-same sausages, that was so daring in its bad taste that the effect was wonderful. The two Women of the Bedchamber in oyster satin were not looking their best in this cold, unbecoming light of winter.

When the procession moved out of sight, one could only imagine the ritual when Black Rod, with the ebony hand at the end of his wand, shouts: 'Open, open!' to allow the doors of the Chamber to give entrance to the Queen.

From where will Clarissa be watching her husband, the Prime Minister? And Mrs Churchill?

Then we hear the relayed voice of the Queen, in high, childlike tones, thanking the Lords and the Members of the House of Commons for their sympathy expressed on her Sovereign father's death. She hopes to follow her father's example, being sure that Her People would accord her the same loyalty and understanding. In the year to come she hopes to visit some of Her Colonial Empire, prays for an early armistice in Korea, promises that Her Government would take full share in the work of NATO, aims to strengthen the unity of Europe, and considers the scheme for Federation in Central Africa. The task of placing the national economy on a sound foundation, curbing inflation and reducing expenditure, must also be undertaken, while every encouragement shall be given to the fishing industry. She prays that the blessing of the Almighty may rest upon Her Government's Councils.

Then, no doubt greatly relieved that her vocal ordeal is at an end, she smiles with added sweetness as the procession returns. Smiles to left and right, and the sea of spectators billows down in curtsies and bows. The Queen and her Duke are through the double doors from whence they came; the doors are shut. A moment's pause. Two tall officers of venerable age appraise the Crown, once more reposing on its cushion within a few inches of my grasp. They speak to one another with an offhand perfection of manners. There is a bond, or link or understanding, that goes much deeper than mere *politesse*. None of these people are looking for slights, for grudges, neither are they surprised or impressed. They live on terms with each other, and do not need the framework of formality that is part of social exchange in other echelons. These people do not need to meet each other at given times at lunch or dinner in answer to an invitation. They come across one another casually in the course of duty or pleasure — in their study, corridor, palace or club. They go about their jobs with ease, knowing their like are not jockeying for position or trying a little knifing in backs. This is the reason for the prevailing mood of generosity. One of the officers of venerable age says casually to the other: 'I'll look after it now, and when the Queen leaves, you can come back and fetch it.' 'It' is the jewelled Crown of State.

The Queen is now bidding goodbye to the Lord Chancellor, to Lord Alexander of the super-arched eyebrows, to vellumy Bobbety Salisbury, to ramrod Rock. Broad smiles; it is now all very gay. The Duke of Edinburgh makes some jolly jokes. The Queen departs. A clash of steel, horses' hooves, and again the distant thundering of cheers from the people lining the streets.

The old fur coats are helped onto shoulders of skinny peeresses. Some wrap their trains round their goosefleshed arms, and the party breaks up. The wives of Labour peers are now dressed to go rat-catching. Lynn Fontanne says: 'Isn't it lovely to be in a crowd that doesn't push!' Rock Cholmondeley, already changed into stovepipe trousers, black overcoat and white scarf (no doubt to hide the fact that he had no collar on); has a broad grin on his face. He is delightedly congratulating the police and the Boy Scouts on the smooth running order, and receiving from his guests the compliments that are deserved.

London was in its usual blue haze, the bare plane trees dripping with tassels like Victorian bobble fringe. Big Ben struck twelve, military orders were shouted in rasping, retching voices, guards sloped arms, a brass band brayed, the crowds jumped on their toes, nannies ran with their charges to follow the bobbing sea of bearskins, and the ordinary flow of traffic, so severely inconvenienced, again began to move. Already the newspaper men were selling the earliest editions with their posters, 'The Queen's Speech', and the photograph of the Monarch in her coach, laughing and jerking her hand at the crowds. The flashlight had caught the brilliance of the Queen's laugh, the glitter and the movement of the coach exemplified by the pear-shaped pearl swinging at her ear. This radiant photograph, much admired by Winston Churchill, had the greatest and most deserved fame; a bulls-eye of journalistic photography.

NEW YORK: THE LUNTS

1952

My first taxi drive from the hotel after my arrival took me to the Lunts[6] for tea. The Lunts, at the height of their stage glory, were among my first professional photograph 'sitters' when first I came to New York in the early thirties. Lynn later said that they wanted to like me, but they had such difficulty in getting through my shyness. However, they succeeded, and when each winter I arrived in New York, no matter how busy they were, they always managed to give me ham and eggs while we sat through the night exchanging confidences. I did some drawings of Lynn, and she always urged me to discontinue my photography in order to devote my time entirely to painting. But it was as a stage designer that I really wanted to work, and although we talked of one day 'doing a play together', the

---

[6] Alfred Lunt and Lynn Fontanne.

opportunity did not arise.

I had unexpectedly received a cable to the boat saying: 'Terribly excited your arrival,' and the moment I came into my hotel room the baggage boy answered the telephone and Lynn was piping a request for me to go round immediately.

At their East Riverside house, Alfred and Lynn both appeared in bubbling spirits. 'What are your plans? Are you very busy?' they asked. 'What do you think would be a pretty period to design a play for? Do you like bustles?' I said I liked all periods of costume. 'But why do you ask? Have you any play in mind?' I inquired. 'No,' said Lynn, 'but I feel that something might drop out of the blue.' She just had the right feeling — something was in the air — she felt it in her bones. I left a bit baffled, but we had made a date to see one another again in a few days' time.

Meanwhile, on the next boat from England Noël Coward arrived. Word soon got around that, straight from the docks, he went to read his new play, *Quadrille*, to the Lunts and that they were enchanted with it. I was most impatient to hear the next move. Would I be asked to design for it?

At last the offer came. The play, set in the year 1866, was sent to me, I loved it, and from that moment on there was nothing but smiles all round. I have never known a production go forward so smoothly, with so few setbacks. Polaire Weissman, Head of the Costume Department of the Metropolitan Museum, showed me all her authentic clothes of the period, and lent Lynn corsets and bodices. Alfred was enthusiastic about the men's beards, tall bowler hats and travelling cloaks. On the boat back to England, Lynn, Alfred and I had long talks in their cabin about the forthcoming production.

'QUADRILLE'

London 1952

At a meeting at Noël's house in Ebury Street I showed the finished designs for sets: the scene builders held no objections. Binkie Beaumont, the manager, seemed quietly satisfied. Noël was delighted. Lynn, without any reservations, was thrilled by her clothes. Alfred was also happy.

In spite of an early start, once more, as with every theatrical production, we were 'up against time'. Rehearsals started. I had hoped to have Lynn's dresses ready before then, but due to the aftermath of war difficulties we had trouble in getting certain stuffs. A particular candy stripe was needed, but it was 'out of stock'. Binkie would not have it painted: not practical — it would not clean. At last some firm was willing to weave the material. Two weeks later the loom broke down, so the dress had to be hand-painted at the eleventh hour. When the costume was at last finished, Noël came to me in trepidation: 'I'm afraid we don't like it.' 'Neither do I,' was my — to him — surprising reply. 'Let's give it to Marian Spencer.' We did, and it suited. In other ways the production went forward ominously smoothly.

I would have liked to spend more time watching the way the Lunts create their stage characters, but there was too much else to do. At the end of one long day's rehearsal Lynn and I went home in a taxi. She put her feet up and laughed: 'Why do we do this — all in the name of fun? It's never fun. It's damned hard work, and we'll fight a lot; but it's interesting and exciting, and if we win through, it will all have been worth while.'

When, at last, we arrived in Manchester for the trial run, the atmosphere was so electric that one felt there must be an explosion any minute. Alfred wanted me in his dressing-room.

He felt lonely, he said: he was strung up. But I was too busy to sit and talk. There were calls from every direction. Bessie, Lynn's dresser, tapped on Alfred's door: 'Miss Fontanne would like to see Mr Beaton a moment.'

'Darling, what about my wedding ring? Will you choose one because I can't wear this: it's so thin and modern. And what about Alfred's ring?'

Then: 'Could Mr Beaton see Mr Lunt a moment?'

'Cecil, this tie — it's a bit puny, isn't it? And how about this watch-chain?'

Again Bessie: 'Mr Beaton, Miss Fontanne.'

'Darling, I wondered what you meant about my eyebrows being thicker?'

Back to Alfred.

Watching the play unfold for the first time before an audience was a revelation. Noël is nothing if not a craftsman, and he knew just how to make his play come alive. Many of the laughs came as a pleasant surprise. Whereas, in the dressing-room, Lynn had looked adorable in her Empress Eugenie bonnet and bustles, now on stage she had assumed consummate beauty. She has the dignity of the true artist. Alfred is that rare thing — a genius of the theatre.

Throughout the provincial tour the Lunts continued to develop aspects of their roles as well as perfecting the production as a whole. After three weeks on the road it was quite extraordinary to note the difference in the playing. The performances acquired tremendous pace; Lynn and Alfred managed to discover many more varieties of mood. Before, the effect of the play had been brittle and crisp; now a deeper emotion had crept in to certain scenes that made them extra poignant and touching. If the play were to run for two years, I knew that Alfred and Lynn would continue making inventions and miniscule improvements right up till the last performance.

Before catching a train to go back to London, I went in to pay my respects to the Lunts. They were making towards the stage, preparatory to their entrances. Alfred turned back and said: 'What a risk you took with the sets, and wouldn't it have been awful if they hadn't worked! Aren't you glad this all turned out so marvellously well?' And Lynn, kissing me, said: 'Thank you for your dear patience.'

ARRIVAL IN NEW YORK: MY MOTHER'S EIGHTIETH BIRTHDAY

November 11th, 1952

Bright sunlit day, a nip in the air. The taxi passed through dirty West Side streets of dark chocolate-coloured walls with peeling posters — relics of a bitter election — and the marks, like drawings by Miro or Klee, of children's games, of houses with dust-clouded windows and dirty, strong-yellow curtains. On the sidewalks the people appeared almost unbearably ugly, and the children playing in the dirt of the gutters with bright puppy dogs generated an inhuman vitality and toughness that dispersed any need for sympathy.

At my hotel (the Sherry Netherland), instead of enjoying the rooms I'd decorated on the very top of the tower, I was told they were unable to dislodge the present occupants and, meanwhile, they would give me 'the honeymoon suite'. It was disgusting.

Friday, November 14th, 1952

Allowed back into my own rooms, I awoke in my black and white four-poster. Chinks of sunlight filtered through the drawn curtains at the window. I looked at my watch. I had slept late — a quarter to nine. Time to telephone back to England and congratulate my mother on her eightieth birthday. By my reckoning they would be finishing lunch at home. I put through the call, went to the bathroom to wash my teeth, and no sooner had I wetted the toothbrush than the telephone bell rang. It had taken only one minute for my mother to be on the line.

She was in a state of elation and joy, obviously very moved emotionally, and soon became unable to talk for a lump in the throat. My sister Nancy then took charge and described the gold link bracelet she had bought as a communal present, and the violets, roses and carnations in the drawing-room, and how the doorbell kept ringing all the time with messages and presents. Somewhat recovered, my mother came back on the wire and said that the whole family were present, that they were all going to a play tonight, then tomorrow to the country.

'What sort of a day is it in New York?'

'Oh, fine — a lovely, sunny winter's day — and I've got a well-paid photographic advertising job.'

Then we hung up, and I went back to the bathroom. As I started to brush my teeth a wave of uncontrollable sadness drowned me. Tears ran like rivulets down my contorted cheeks.

Already looking so old and bald and ugly, my disfigured face had become swollen and red. I was fascinated by this monster in the glass. But my momentary curiosity in this awful effigy in front of me did not prevent my continuing to sob and splutter.

I suddenly realized how near the surface my nerves were, and that although I could not analyse this surging, overwhelming misery, it had to do with death and life, and love and hate.

I have very little in common with my mother; we are temperamentally far apart, and our tastes are dissimilar. She, being a strong character, is tenacious and unwilling to compromise; sometimes the tension is appalling. I become nervous and unstable when I see too much of her, and it is often with a great feeling of relief that I am able to get away and come to America. But, inevitably, my life has become centred around her and she is a great prop to me; apart from my deep love and affection for her, we are closely knit in many ways. Also, I have deep pity for her. I feel these later years have become sadly empty. Apart from her immediate family she has no interest in people: she makes no effort to acquire new friends, or keep up with the ones who remain. She is really very lonely — lonely because the children have grown up and left their nests, and her life, once so bubbling and full, is suddenly empty.

It need not be a 'special occasion' that triggers off these sudden revelations of the utter pathos of life. It can be a glimpse of someone loved crossing a road, or washing themselves at a basin, that causes a stab straight into one's heart. The utter futility of my telephone call, and the no less empty calls that I would make to friends and business associates all morning long, gave me now one of those mercifully rare bouts of wondering whether the great misery is worth while. When the waiter came in with a tray of tea, I was still weeping bitterly and had to look from him, sightlessly, out of the window.

GRETA

November, 1952

First agonizing suspense of would she answer the telephone? For three days I had held back from calling Greta in order that she might hear of my arrival from other sources. Thus she could adjust and prepare herself for my overtures. Last time I arrived here and she did not accept my call, I was horrified and suffered much. Now, as I waited, my heart pounded.

The seconds passed. 'Am calling Miss Garbo,' the hotel operator informed me... 'Still calling Miss Garbo' ... And then release! She answered. Rather dull and depressed, she seemed, with a cold in the nose. The usual complaints about not getting around to anything, not having gone out, not having seen people, not having had time to do anything.

'Why do you want me to lunch anyway? What's the point? What's the use? Where do we go? I'm so sick and tired of all restaurants. Haven't got time for anything. Yesterday was Mrs Bates, the neck woman, and then I had my hair washed. So I just had time for two bananas — no lunch.'

I was reminded of Truman's last letter to me in which he said that Greta was not a satisfactory friend for me as she was so conscious of her own limitations that she had no time for thinking of anything else.

No doubt apropos my mother's birthday, we talked of old age, loneliness, and the human frame getting worn out. 'Oh, I know all about it — you can't teach me anything on that score.' When we discussed the pictures at Rosenberg's, and I said how amazed I was at the use of paint in Renoir's *Dead Pheasant In The Snow*, she said: 'That's been hanging around for a long while — and I don't like anything dead.' Then when we talked of the election, and I said: 'Were you pleased that

Stevenson was knocked out?' she said, most typically: 'I'm never pleased about anyone being knocked out.'

Later, the meeting at lunch made me realize how much less satisfactory most telephone talks are in comparison to being able to watch the facial changes of expression of one's friends as they sit at close range. Greta's elusiveness, her secrecy, and a lot that can appear complicated, are more easily understood when we meet. For some while I looked at her as if she were someone I had never met before. Somehow she appeared conventionalized: her hair was shorter and permanently waved, her eyes less made-up; but her imaginative flights of fancy were as unexpected as ever. I allowed her to pay for the lunch (at Maud Chez Elle) in order to have an excuse for asking for a return lunch next week.

After coffee we ambled along to Lily Daché's hatshop where Greta tried on every sort of headgear. It was like a private pageant for me, and I was entranced anew by her beauty. Few women manage to look at themselves in a new hat without arranging their features to appear the way they wish. For her no readjusting was necessary and she turned towards me, displaying a different hat, with a completely bland, pristine, 'open' regard. Her own taste is for things outside fashion, but each time she put on something absurd or fantastic she roared with laughter. The spectacle of her foolishness pleased her, and in a subtle, oblique way she was able to make fun of the women whose taste would allow them to wear these confections of sequins, flowers and feathers. On Greta they became utterly inconsequential. Yet Greta's physical line and proportion of beauty are such that she can carry off most fashionable frivolities and even make them seem beautiful —

as she did when, working in moving pictures, she had to wear some pretty tasteless vulgarities. Sometimes, as she looked at herself with a pained expression, she would mutter: 'Poor little Miss Garbo,' and when I handed her a little diamante crown and said: 'You'll look beautiful in this,' she said: 'Yes — this should be good.' As she placed it on top of her head, she added: 'Or it would have been a long time ago' — and then the pained, peaked little face looked in the mirror and said: 'I used to be so pretty!'

Two nights ago, Monroe Wheeler arranged for me to go with him to a lecture on Shaw by John Mason Brown. When I telephoned him to apologize that I would be a bit late, he answered: 'Don't worry. And I've got a treat for you. Who d'you think it is? Marie Doro.'

Marie Doro, the actress, was little more than a name to me, and I had never been fortunate enough to see her on the stage. But I remember that when my father returned from business visits to the States, and brought me back theatre programmes and magazines, the one person who struck me as being quite unlike Hazel Dawn, Maxine Elliott, and other buxom beauties, was an elfin creature with highly-arched brows over huge, birdlike eyes, spider's-web hair of what must have been a soft nut-brown colour, and a style of her own — outside the contemporary, yet one that has not lost its validity for us today forty years later.

On arrival at Monroe's hospitable and agreeably homely apartment I met Marie Doro. She no longer bore resemblance to the exquisite little creature that she once was. Now the cobweb strands of silken hair had become white loops and strands — rather coarse, but thick — which gave the effect of making her complexion appear somewhat sallow; but the huge brown eyes still twinkled with curiosity and amusement. The elderly Marie Doro wore black with an old-fashioned brimmed hat, and soon it was evident that she had become an interesting little old lady who has turned her back on her past career, and has now a degree in theology and philosophy. Today she is so interested in the adventures of the mind that almost every contemporary phenomenon is of fascination to her — the developments of science and their bearing on our lives. When she can't sleep at night she listens with great curiosity to the disc jockeys on the radio; she watches Monsignor Fulton Sheen on television, and says of all the lecturers he is the most expert. She is interested in the directions in which theatre is going, and is a real participant in the life of today. Yet her present serenity did not come easily; when her beauty first started to fade, she hid herself away from people and only wished to be forgotten. Then she forgot about herself and thought of others. She took up hobbies, then started to study seriously. Recently she has emerged as an entirely different character from the youthful one, and she has become someone who is fascinating to listen to, has something to say on a wide variety of subjects, and has become a happy and fulfilled person.

But the evening was sad for me because it made me so acutely conscious that Greta will not be able to follow such an example. Unless a miracle happens and she is saved from herself, she cannot have anything but a very empty, lonely and unhappy old age. Does the fact that Greta is Scandinavian make circumstances more difficult for her? Already she must be feeling the effects of her wish for self-destruction by leading a life that is a complete negation of all that it should be. 'No' is always her answer. Couldn't she develop some interest? Couldn't we find someone who would give her French lessons? Her old friend, Gayelord Hauser, had telephoned to her. 'You're not still just wandering the streets?' he asked. 'Haven't you taken a house — haven't you done anything about anything?' 'No,' and she laughed at her inability. But it is no laughing matter.

Part VI: Coronation Year, 1953

LUCIAN FREUD'S WEDDING

Party at Wheeler's

Lucian Freud married Caroline Blackwood. Wedding luncheon given by Lucian a perfect expression of his taste. Unlike most wedding festivities there were no strangers, no unpopular relations, and all the real friends, from far and wide, had managed to climb to the top floor of Wheeler's in Soho. Here the curtains were drawn, candles lit, dark-red carnations splayed out, and at a horseshoe the guests drank too much champagne and ate too much caviar and lobster. By four o'clock in the afternoon one had the impression that it was four o'clock in the morning.

My beloved Peter Watson was as teasing as ever: a goodwill-to-all-men festivity brings out the spikiest aspects in him. Kathy Sutherland, perhaps a little tactless, was telling Lucian's father the rumour had gone round that his new daughter-in-law had eloped with Picasso. The Freud father asked: 'Surely that would be a little over-indulgent of Picasso since he has just recently been married to a seventeen-year-old girl?'

Others present: Francis Bacon, whose body becomes like butter when he is drunk, but his mind more electric and alert; John Minton, very drunk, warm and over-confiding, such a nice, but poignant, tragic personality; James P. H., white and romantic; Clarissa, the naiad, looking oddly conventional in a suburban hat; Anne Fleming, over-excited, her blackbird eyes blazing; the new Baths, Harry Hambleden, the widow Orwell, Cyril Connolly; Perdita Guinness, glowing, brusquely intelligent; and mother Maureen, disarmingly benevolent, because it cannot be the sort of marriage she would plan for her daughter.

The young marrieds, after much wine, lost their passports; but somehow they got to Paris where they will remain in one hotel bedroom for months on end. It seems an ideal match.

PHOTOGRAPHING THE QUEEN MOTHER

Spring, 1953

I realize I am exaggerating when I write the following, but there is more than an element of truth when I say that I did not realize how life can be ruthless, even to queens. We all know what happened to Henry's six wives, and certainly today we have become a bit more civilized; but still human nature can be pretty base. Through a sad break of fortune Queen Elizabeth loses her husband at an early age, and from that very moment her position in life is changed completely. Although she is undoubtedly treated with great love, consideration and sympathy by her daughter who is now reigning monarch and living at Windsor Castle, nevertheless, no doubt unknown to the present Queen, her mother is suddenly given quite casual treatment by many at Buckingham Palace.

The Queen Mother is being taken care of by a 'skeleton staff', and when I went to take the first photographs since her widowhood, the lady-in-waiting confided that they were 'picnicking' here, and that a palace was a very uncomfortable place in which to picnic. Some of the rather higher-up Palace servants let it be known to my assistants that they 'couldn't think why the Queen Mother stayed on here so long — not that she will relish the move to Clarence House for there won't be the number of servants there that she's accustomed to.'

When I passed by the Queen Mother's old rooms there was a strong whiff of decorator's paint, and I saw that the walls were bare and the furniture taken away. Electricians whistled as they walked down the Picture Gallery. The rooms in which we were to photograph were so cold that, even though it is said that the Queen Mother, after her healthy Scottish upbringing, is impervious to the elements, I felt that this below-freezing temperature was beyond a joke. I asked for a vase of flowers to use in my photographs. The lady-in-waiting returned later saying that there was not one in the whole palace.

The 'sitting' augured badly. Nothing went right. A camera shutter was jammed, my feet were leaden. The dark-red curtains I had brought for my background would not, when draped, assume any grace or vitality of form, and what there was of daylight came through the windows with an ugly winter-rawness.

Our preparations were not finished before the Queen Mother's arrival was announced. Her smile and warmth of sympathy made it seem as if the sun had come out. She manages to disperse anxiety and care, even makes it seem impossible that people should ever behave badly, or that things could go wrong.

Of course there is something of the great actress about her, and in public she has to put on a show which never fails, but it is her heart and imagination which guide her. She will always say just the one thing that puts people at ease and make them feel a glow of happiness, because she understands and appreciates the reality of any situation — whether it be tragic or gay.

The photograph session lasted just the right amount of time. When it was over the Queen Mother remarked on the speed at which I operated, and how all her family always enjoyed being photographed by me. This gave me the pat opportunity to ask if I might be allowed to take some pictures of the new Queen.

'Oh yes, I must speak to her. I would like that so much. She's looking particularly well just now. She has such a lovely quality of youthfulness. Yes, she has youth on her side, and an extraordinary calmness and serenity which will come in very useful in the years ahead.'

On my way home I stopped at my favourite florist. For once I would be as extravagant as I wished. I took enormous care to choose a bouquet of all the first spring flowers to be sent to that adorable human being living in that cold, bleak Palace.

Our dear old Scots maid, Agnes, on seeing the proofs of the photograph sitting of the Queen in her black velvet crinoline, sighed in rapt admiration: 'Oh, doesn't she look motherly!' And indeed she does, for she has put on a little weight. This is perhaps another example of her brilliance — that she could now not only play a different role, but should also look the part.

ROYAL PHOTOGRAPHER

May, 1953

Have been wondering if my day as photographer at the Palace is over. Baron, a most unexpected friend of Prince Philip's, has been taking all the recent pictures, so the call saying the Queen wanted me to do her personal Coronation photographs comes as an enormous relief. Another lease of life extended to me in my photographic career. 'Would you please not tell anyone about it yet as, when the news gets out, so many people will ring up to know why they aren't being asked, and the Queen wants you.'

The same night that this message was relayed to me, at a ball at the American Embassy, I saw the Queen for a brief moment and thanked her. 'No, I'm very glad you're going to take them,' she said, 'but, by the time we get through to the photographs, we'll have circles down to here' (she pointed halfway down her cheeks), 'then the Crown comes down to here' (to the eye), 'then the court train comes bundling up here, and I'm out to here' (sticks stomach out). 'There are layers upon layers: skirt and mantles and trains.' She spoke like a young, high-spirited girl.

I also had a short opportunity to thank the Queen Mother for what I am sure must have been her help in bringing about this 'coup' for me. She laughed knowingly with one finger high in the air.

May 31st: Coronation rehearsal

I have not yet learnt to ignore worry — to say 'it may never happen'. An almost continual feeling is with me that things may go wrong. The knowledge that much of my suffering is of my own self-making does not mitigate the pain. Others have the knack of only doing the things they want to — and evade unpleasant responsibilities. Why do I take on jobs that are often fearfully alarming to me?

Why must I so often have to wake soon after dawn to take an aeroplane to foreign parts when, as a result of the Dakota crash in which I miraculously escaped during the war, I am still terrified of the air? These thoughts, strangely enough, come to the surface at my being bidden to the Press Gallery for the dress rehearsal of the Coronation ceremony. This is a coveted invitation, and I should feel grateful that the intention is to make my job of sending in drawings and articles subsequently, as well as taking photographs, easier, by having a previous

171

glimpse of the scene in the Abbey. Instead I am suffering from another attack of anxiety. No doubt my imbalance of mind is due to too much stress and activity at home. I have to cope without any help as Maud Nelson, my secretary, is always away ill. No doubt Maud worries that she is not capable of coping with all my affairs and this nervous stress brings on another bout of asthma. Yet she will not allow anyone in to help her. It is being a difficult time for me.

My taxi drove up at the wrong entrance of the Abbey. Instead of, as I expected, hurling abuse at me for my stupidity, the policeman opening my cab door smiled tolerantly and said: 'All right — you can get out here. It's only a short walk along to "J".' At 'J' I was directed to pass through an awninged passage of new canvas, pungent and peculiar-smelling, at the end of which a figure in a cocked hat and black velvet knee-breeches gave a superior look at the sketchpads and inks I was carrying, then with a grave and silent nod allowed me to pass. I went on down a passage, up one or two steps, then turned sharply into a pitch black cavern. It was a Kafkaesque experience. I stumbled and groped: in the darkness I felt dreadfully alone. There was an inevitability, a finality, about what I must do: no turning back now. Soon all the things I feared would start happening to me. Probably even the scaffold?

I must admit that my dogged determination to continue is often rewarded — as it was at this time. I lurched on without anything appalling happening to me, until suddenly I was in lightness and two goldsticks were kind to me. I'd never, in fact, encountered such beautiful manners before. It was as if I'd attained the Heavenly Kingdom when after an old colonel had taken my ticket, brought it to within an inch of his left eye, smelt it, then barked 'Wheel right,' I found myself in the triforium. Soon the rehearsal for the Coronation started...

After two days' quiet respite in the country cosseting my nervous system, I drove back to London on Sunday night. In the boot of the car were several baskets containing the roses and clematis that I had picked for the Queen's photographs. I had the idea of making some pictures in the Winterhalter manner, with real country flowers on a side-table instead of the usual Palace display of hydrangeas and gladioli. As we neared London the same unflattering photographs of the Queen decorated every shop and public building. I felt I must do better than these, and remembered reading how Carlyle had become so sick of the face of Queen Victoria plastered all over the city at the time of her Coronation that he left London. Soon I began to feel again highly strung and tense at the thought of the intense effort soon to be made. For not only must I write two articles on the ceremony — one to be telephoned in cable-ese for Australia — and do illustrations, but the photographic side not only comprised taking pictures of the Queen in her Crown and robes, surrounded by her entourage, but the Press representative of the Palace, Richard Colville, had compiled a list of each group of the Royal Family with their attendants to be taken together and individually.

I have found that when any Royal sitting is involved there are more arrangements involving telephone calls than one could have believed possible, and so many contingencies to cope with, that one might be organizing a vast crowd scene for an early Cecil B. de Mille moving picture. But in the movies there are trained technical crews of electricians and technicians, wardrobe assistants, and numberless people to call upon. Never having, by preference, had a studio with full-time assistants on my own, I found myself at this particular time in a predicament. However, Pat Matthews, a good friend from *Vogue*, volunteered to come along and organize a technical staff.

The day before the Coronation we started to set up special backgrounds at the Palace, the electricians having spent the morning preparing the light cables. When I arrived early in the afternoon to make final arrangements, and went unescorted down a long labyrinth of unfamiliar corridors, to the Green Drawing Room, I could hear that I was getting nearer to a hubbub of voices. I saw some fur stoles and ladies' handbags lying on gilt chairs. Knowing how many visiting Royalties were in the Palace I guessed that some sort of lunch party must be in progress.

Not until I came face to face with myself carrying a huge blanket bundle of garden roses and clematis in front of a pair of mirror-doors at the end of the Picture Gallery, and peered through a small crack, did I realize that I was about to intrude into an enormous luncheon for the Commonwealth Prime Ministers. Luckily I did stop for, if I had proceeded further, it would have been to run smack in front of the Queen with a dozen distinguished old men lined up in military formation each side of her, to be fired at by *The Times* photographer. I pried at the proceedings. Jolly jokes were made. The photographer asked: 'Another one, please?' as he let off a flash. 'Another one,' repeated the Queen in her high, fluting voice. Giggles, laughter: the Queen quite obviously elated at being the delightful, gay and attractive cynosure of all. She wore a pale, dove-fawn coloured dress, with handbag to match, and her hair curled like a child's for a Christmas party. The excitement, nourished by the newspapers, mounting every day, has obviously affected her spirits, and she seemed to be in an exultant mood with a blush of triumph in her cheeks. She has, about her, a certain humility and slow shyness but, at the same time, innate dignity, and one senses a quality of kindness. The Queen is really the one person of whom we cannot say that she has the fashionable inferiority complex.

The dark-skinned men in the group stood stiffly to attention: a hoarse shout was raised when the flash light went off, and the group then dispersed to the Music Room where a large concourse was smoking cigarettes and cigars: Churchill standing and glowering with his legs apart; the Duchess of Devonshire with head earnestly thrust forward; Princess Margaret, intent with sharp head movements, Hanover-turquoise eyes and cigarette smoke exhaling nostrils.

In the Green Drawing Room step-ladders stretched half-way up to the gilded ceilings, but my backgrounds still lay unrolled in a corner; with much anxiety I noticed that the electricians and other assistants had made little headway. Their jobs were of a highly technical nature, and I found myself useless and unwanted, with nothing to do but continue to take a furtive glimpse of the Commonwealth party scenes from behind a huge set-piece of splayed flowers that Constance Spry must have created for the occasion. The Palace was '*en grande tenue*' and a great mass of hydrangeas, rubber plants and sweet peas gave a 'special occasion' look to the huge, gilded, often dead-looking rooms. Enjoying a 'Bisto Kid's' view of grand life, I was amused to notice how conventional in pattern, and formal in behaviour, all human beings appear when enjoying enforced entertainment. Artificial smiles that are real, heads cocked, jokes that suffice. The Duke of Edinburgh, never far from his uncle Dickie Mountbatten, with his eyes screwed up in intensity, conversed with Indians whose clipped, bird-like pleasantries brought back vividly my days in Government House in Bombay during the war.

I was surprised when Martin Charteris, the Queen's Private Secretary, spied me and came across, saying: 'Oh good, you're here! Now I can give you the information about dinner tomorrow at our house. We're going to be about thirty. Arthur Koestler is our star, and later we're going to roll up the carpet and dance to the gramophone.' He is the most delightfully casual, efficient and unimpressed of courtiers.

The afternoon continued and still the setting-up of lights and cameras seemed to make no progress. The electricians, after they had knocked off for a break, had been forced to wait for two hours before they were allowed upstairs again. (I suppose for fear of running into the Commonwealth Prime Ministers.) Now all hands must work desperately hard to get electric cables running with juice, and backgrounds and curtains and various 'blow-ups' in place.

On the way home, I noticed that the wind and gusts of rain had dispersed the summer crowds who, hoping for some preview glimpse of the Queen, had been sheltering all day in the improvised stands. How cruel if such wintry weather were to continue tomorrow! My stage fright at the thought of my responsibility tomorrow returned with renewed force, and at dinner I drank more than I should. Early to bed, I slept fitfully, and when I was called before five o'clock I was suffering from a hangover and my vitality count was low.

THE CORONATION

The birds had started to sing and the sky was pale grey; already a few electric lights were on in the bedrooms of the houses opposite. An angry wind blew the branches of the cherry tree in the next door garden, and despite the heavy sheets of rain people were already going off cheerfully and hurriedly to take their places in the crowds. I watched a genteel woman, with her husband and small child, scurrying off, complete with umbrellas, Macintoshes and sandwiches; they were utterly respectable and charming, and a complete, happy little unit. I felt a great lump in my throat: I don't know why they were so poignant.

With passes, journalists' Press permits, cards and instructions clutched tightly, and with sticker on the hired car, and my grey topper filled with sandwiches, Indian ink and gadgets for my drawings, I was off on my way.

Remarkably smooth traffic regulations. Already at this early hour motors were bumper to bumper in front: it was fun to peer at the old men, bad-tempered and sleepy at this hour, in cockaded hats with lace jabots, their womenfolk having had, before dawn, a hairdresser to their houses to set their coiffures.

Goldsticks stationed around the cloisters showed us on our way. They were already frozen blue. One of them asked me if I had heard the good news that Hunt had climbed Everest. The iced wind blew in circles round the winding staircase that took me to the rafters, and I felt much sympathy for Hunt. My allotted seat was just near the pipes of the great organ. It was by no means an easy place from which to make drawings: only by peering somewhat precariously over the edge of the balcony could the activities below be seen.

But I discovered that, without disturbing my fellow journalists, it was possible to move about fairly freely, and a vantage point from my rook's nest was discovered from which I could not only see the arrivals coming down the nave, but much of the activity in front of the high altar.

Feeling nervous, cold, and rather sick, I buoyed myself up by eating barley sugar (very sustaining) and chatting to nice Christopher Hussey of *Country Life*.

One has seen many woodcuts, and pictures of all sorts, of the earliest Kings and Queens being crowned; particularly detailed are the prints of the first Queen Elizabeth's procession. In all periods, painters have had a shot at recording the ceremony; with the improvements in the technique of photography the scene has become almost familiar. Yet this spectacle today transcended all preconceived notions. The ceremonial seemed to be as fresh and inspiring as some great play or musical event that was being enacted upon a spontaneous impulse of genius. Perhaps it was the background of lofty vaulted stone — like a silver forest — that made everything seem so particularly surprising.

The words of the service struck one's ears with an impact that had the pure audacity of a poem by Rimbaud. The music sounded pristine and sifted.

The colours red, gold and smoke-blue always beguiled one's eye by the unexpected. The brilliant gold carpet was the perfect floor-covering for the slippered feet of the pages, the train-bearers, and the scarlet, blue and gold-clad heralds, for the bishops and clergy in white and gold. Black Rod made way for a messenger; a mote of light caught a gold sequin fallen on the carpet, on a jewel in a bishop's ring; the sun came out and lit up a posse of scarlet uniformed goldsticks. It was all living and new: it was history, but of today and of the future. It was something that is pulsating and vital to us, and an essential part of the life we believe in.

The guests presented great contrasts in their national and traditional garments. The peeresses *en bloc* the most ravishing sight — like a bed of auricula-eyed sweet william — in their dark red velvet and foam-white, dew-spangled with diamonds. Lady Haddington and the Duchess of Buccleuch in huge diamond 'fenders' were particularly outstanding; but, most beautiful of all, was young Debo Devonshire, sister of Nancy Mitford, with her hair dressed wide to contain the Edwardian cake-like crown, in Georgiana, Duchess of Devonshire's eighteenth-century robes, quite different in cut with the straight line from shoulder to shoulder.

Willie Walton's *Orb And Sceptre* blazes out on the organ as the other Royalties arrive and the procession begins: the minor Royalties, and the foreign Royalties and Representatives of States. Norway, Greece, Nepal, Japan, Ethiopia, Morocco, Thailand, Peru; the Sultans under Her Majesty's protection; Queen Salote of Tonga, a great big, warm personality. Is Russia here? Then the Princes and Princesses of the royal blood: the mother of the Duke of Edinburgh, a contrast to the grandeur, in the ash-grey draperies of a nun. The manipulation of the long velvet trains is in some cases too under-rehearsed: Princess Marie Louise, agonizingly old, but still athletic, is obviously very angry with her fatuous lady-in-waiting for making such a balls-up with her train. The Gloucester boys, too, give their mother a moment or two of anxiety as they tug and mishandle her train. Likewise the attendant of Princess Alexandra is at fault; for that matter, so is the Princess's dressmaker, for he has made her a confection that is far too fluffy and unimportant for the occasion. Her mother, the Duchess of Kent, has the dignity of a carved wooden effigy. The Mistress of the Robes, of towering height, is minimized by the enormous presence and radiance of the petite Queen Mother. Yet in the Queen Widow's expression we read sadness combined with pride.

A posse of church dignitaries portends the Queen's procession followed by the Knights of the Garter and the Standard Bearers. After them the Prime Ministers of the Commonwealth and the Lord High Chancellor. The dour old Scot, Canning, with his lean face, exposed skull and dark crimson cape, does not intend to play second fiddle to anyone; yet, quietly and legitimately, the Archbishop of Canterbury overshadows him with consummate tact. That great old relic, Winston Churchill, lurches forward on unsteady feet, a fluttering mass of white ribbons at his shoulder and white feathers in the hat in his hand; Mrs Churchill, close by, grimaces a recognition as Montgomery and his page, Winston Junior, pass her by.

Then, most dramatic and spectacular, at the head of her retinue of white, lily-like ladies, the Queen. Her cheeks are sugar pink: her hair tightly curled around the Victorian diadem of precious stones perched straight on her brow. Her pink hands are folded meekly on the elaborate grandeur of her encrusted skirt; she is still a young girl with a demeanour of simplicity and humility. Perhaps her mother has taught her never to use a superfluous gesture. As she walks she allows her heavy skirt to swing backwards and forwards in a beautiful rhythmic effect. This girlish figure has enormous dignity; she belongs in this scene of almost Byzantine magnificence.

She moves to the Chair of State. Then the Archbishops and Bishops, having placed the Bible, Chalice and the Regalia on the altar, come to present the young Queen for recognition to the east. '*Vivat! Vivat!*' shout, surprisingly, the boys from Westminster School: trumpets sound to split the roofs and shatter the heart. Then, likewise, the Queen faces her people to the south, west and north. '*Vivat! Vivat! Vivat!*' and each time the trumpets blow the recognition as the solitary figure bows humbly at each shattering volley.

The Queen takes the Coronation Oath, kisses the Bible, and, after the Creed and the Communion Service, the Archbishop says the Prayer of Consecration. The choir begins the marvellous anthem 'Zadok the Priest' during which the Queen is divested of her crimson robes, her Diadem and Collar of the Garter, and, in preparation for the Anointing, puts on a simple white shift. Four Knights of the Garter hold a canopy of cloth of gold under which the Archbishop anoints the Queen with holy oil in the form of a cross. Then the presentation of the Spurs, Sword and the Orb, and, on the Queen's fourth finger of the right hand, the Ring. The Queen's hands are those of an artist, a ballerina, a sculptor or surgeon. When the Sword has been presented, then offered to the altar, Lord Salisbury redeems it for a bag containing one hundred silver shillings, and thenceforth holds it naked and erect.

The crowning is superbly dramatic: the expression on the small face of the Queen is one of intense expectancy until, with magnificent assurance, the Archbishop thrusts down with speed and force the Crown onto the neat head. At this moment the hoarse shouts of 'God Save the Queen' break out. The peers put on their coronets and caps of State, and the peeresses, with long, gloved arms looking like wishbones, hold up their coronets. A fanfare of trumpets, a blaze of violins, an eruption from the big organ, and the guns are shot off from the Tower down the river. This is a great moment, immediately to be followed by the enthroning and glorification of the new monarch. While anthems are sung, homage is paid by a strange concourse of old and young alike. As a simple communicant rather than as Queen of England, she kneels to take the holy wine and bread. Thence she goes to St Edmund's Chapel where, divested of the garments delivered to her during the solemnities, she is arrayed in the robe of purple velvet.

Long delays, pauses and waits, but always something occupies one's attention. A new arrival of uniformed dignitaries. A procession forms, and Mr Winston Churchill comes from his pew to line up for the final exodus. He turns on his heels to admire the peeresses. 'Yes — a very fine bunch of women, a most magnificent sight,' he seems to be saying as he gives them his appraisal. He turns back to see if things are ready. No. Again he turns towards these wonderful women. Also waiting to take their allotted place are the great figures of the war, Lords Alanbrooke, Halifax and Portal.

There is an unfortunate hold-up when the Queen Mother is about to proceed from the Abbey. Someone has mistakenly allowed minor members of the clergy to go before her; a herald is sent to inform her of what has happened. She smiles patiently as she waits.

Rain had fallen solidly throughout most of the ceremony. Uniforms were soaked, horses champing; the Golden Coach was now waiting in Dean's Yard in a downpour. The men in cockaded hats and livery were making little effort to keep out of the rain. I made my getaway before the traffic started.

Back home, I found my mother listening to the radio announcer's banal, genteel, rich-fruit-cake voice: 'On this, this great day...'

I rushed upstairs, took a fistful of aspirins, then off with my clothes and I was able to sleep for nearly an hour before dashing again to the Palace for the photographs.

I awoke minus my headache and much relaxed. Again managing to avoid the crowds, within a comparatively short while I found myself at the tradesmen's entrance of the Palace, to be shown up to our now almost familiar haven in the Green Drawing Room. My sister, Baba, who in the inevitable absence of Maud, my secretary, had kindly offered to help arrange the trains, presented a miserable spectacle, chattering with cold and rain-soaked. Thank God the others — the electricians and assistants — had also contrived to be here. Pat Matthews was calm and reassuring. From the balcony of the inner courtyard we watched the return of the carriages. Baba was proud that David Smiley, our brother-in-law, was the Field Officer commanding the Escort.

Every window framed the faces of Palace servants, and a group of them raised a tremendous cheer as the Queen Mother came back, waving and smiling as fresh as a field flower. Then, to the sound of distant roars, drawn by eight grey horses the bronze gold State Coach, with its Cipriano paintings and dark-strawberry padded silk, bowled through the central arch and back to home. The Queen looked back over her shoulder and appeared somewhat dazed and exhausted.

Not long after, girlish voices were heard at the end of the Picture Gallery. 'Oh hullo! Did you watch it? When did you get home?' From the mirror-doors of the Green Drawing Room I spied the Queen with her ladies, her excited children; the family asking questions, jokes, smiles, laughter, the high-pitched voices of the Queen and Princess Margaret heard above the others. The Duchess of Gloucester was leaning forward from the hips with almost perilous intent. The Duke of Norfolk, his duties successfully carried out, lolled behind one of the mirrored-glass doors. George Bellew, Garter King-at-Arms, leant against the brocade walls. The fair, good-looking Duke of Hamilton beamed.

It was now time for the Queen to be on her way to the Throne Room to be photographed by *The Times* — then she would come to me. I started taking family groups. The Queen Mother, dimpled and chuckling, with eyes as bright as any of her jewels, and her younger daughter, with pink and white make-up and a sex twinkle of understanding in her regard, was now sailing towards me, her purple train being held aloft by her four pages; Prince Charles and Princess Anne, who were running around to try and get a hold on it, eventually had recourse to climbing under the purple velvet. No time to lose! Please turn this way, now that; a certain shape was formed, a picture came to life. Quick, quick! All sorts of Royalties popped their heads in on me: Prince Bernhard; then the Duke of Edinburgh put his face through a door. 'But you must come! You're keeping the whole group waiting!' Exit Princess Margaret and the Queen Mother. Through the mirrored doors I watched the guests in the long Picture Gallery.

Then the return of the Queen Mother in rollicking spirits, and slow voice asking: 'Do you really want to take a few more?' Suddenly I felt as if all my anxieties and fears were dispelled. The Queen Mother, by being so basically human and understanding, gives out to us a feeling of reassurance. The great mother figure and nannie to us all, through the warmth of her sympathy bathes us and wraps us in a counterpane by the fireside. Suddenly I had this wonderful accomplice — someone who would help me through everything. All at once, and because of her, I was enjoying my work. Prince Charles and Princess Anne were buzzing about in the wildest excitement and would not keep still for a moment. The Queen Mother anchored them in her arms, put her head down to kiss Prince Charles's hair, and made a terrific picture. Then, ashen-faced and like the wicked uncle in a pantomime, Richard Colville, who deals so sternly with all of us who are in any way connected with the Press, appeared prematurely and, as if to sound my death-knell, informed me: 'The Queen has already been kept waiting. You must take the Queen now!'

In came the Queen, with her ladies, cool, smiling, sovereign of the situation. I asked her to stand against my 'blow-up' Abbey background. The lighting was not at all as I would have wished, but no time for readjustments: every second of importance. Yes, I was banging away and getting pictures at a great rate; but I had only the foggiest notion of whether I was taking black and white, or colour, or giving the right exposures. The Queen looked extremely minute under her robes and Crown, her nose and hands chilled, and her eyes tired. 'Yes,' in reply to my question, 'the Crown does get rather heavy.' She had been wearing it now for nearly three hours.

The Duke of Edinburgh stood by making wry jokes, his lips pursed in a smile that put fear of God into me. I believe he doesn't like or approve of me. This is a pity because, although I'm not one for 'Navy type' jokes, and obviously have nothing in common with him, I admire him enormously, and think he is absolutely first-rate at his job of making things comparatively lively and putting people at their ease. Perhaps he was disappointed that his friend, Baron, was not doing this job today; whatever the reason he was definitely adopting a rather ragging attitude towards the proceedings. However, I tried in the few seconds at my disposal (like a vaudeville comedian establishing contact with his audience) to keep the situation light and full of movement so that no one could adopt any definite attitude: like a juggler I moved the groups about. Photographs of the Duke alone; he looked extremely handsome. Once I replied in a cursory manner to the Queen's: 'What shall we do now?' 'Will you go into the corner?' 'Go into the corner?' She looked at me with wide eyes and a wide smile. No time for explanation.

Now to the other side of the room: The Queen and her Maids of Honour. Quickly, quickly, because this was just about the end.

'You must be tired, ma'am.'

'Yes, but this is the last thing we have to do.'

While the entire family retired to watch the 'fly past' of the RAF from the balcony (which we watched, too, from the inner balcony), Baba and my assistants toasted the Queen from a glass of champagne from which the monarch had only taken one sip.

A panic-stricken page came in: 'Where are the Orb and Sceptre?' They had been left here on a cushion.

Other groups then appeared. Princess Marina, romantically beautiful and remarkably distinguished but sad, and incapable of keeping her children in a vein of seriousness: they all joked and made staccato noises. It was difficult not to get exasperated with my delightful friends, but they, poor things, were at the end of a long, tiring, possibly unnerving day; they confessed their feet hurt.

It is hard enough to give instructions when taking large groups in circumstances like these, but when one is challenged, and asked for a reason why one's instinct has prodded one to say: 'Move over there,' then chaos ensues. The Gloucesters came in with the two boys pulling their mother's train in every direction. The Duke, in his crown, red and shining of complexion, looked like an Alice in Wonderland character.

'Will you stand on that step, sir?'

'But won't I look too tall?'

'Yes, sir, you're perfectly right. Won't you stand down there on that step?'

'Well, if the others are going to be there, won't I look too short?'

I then suggested that perhaps he might open his cape to let me see more of his uniform.

'I don't think I could do that.'

'No, sir?'

'Well, as a matter of fact, I've got the wrong ribbon [wibbon].'

'Which ribbon, sir?'

'This wibbon wight across here.' His eyes protruded and lips quivered.

But the Gloucesters were chivvied off quickly for the Queen was available again for a few more pictures to be taken, this time, sitting at a table on which were placed my by-now rather sad-looking *'Etoile d'Hollande'* roses and the wilting Jackmanii clematis from Reddish.

Now that's all.

For better or worse I'd had my chance.

I felt somewhat dissatisfied; the sensation of achievement had escaped me all day long. Now I wondered if I had got any worthwhile pictures. Except with the Queen Mother and her grandchildren, I felt I'd never become airborne. The bulk of my pictures had been a smash and grab affair; I couldn't imagine they would be successful. Not only was I depressed, but rather alarmed. If the results weren't sensationally good, the Press would attack me bitterly for having failed with such a fine opportunity. Yes — an unique opportunity had been afforded me. Had I misused the trust?

The rain poured. Still the crowds roared and the Queen reappeared on the balcony. Baba and I went home utterly whacked. But I had now to wire a description of the Abbey proceedings for syndication to Australia and Canada. Luckily I had written a considerable amount of local colour material beforehand; even so, the chore took me longer than expected, and the cables were late relaying through my accounts. No sooner were these sent off than Siriol Hugh Jones arrived with a shorthand-typist from *Vogue*. Siriol suggested an article was not necessary: that 'Notes from the Abbey' would be more spontaneous. I agreed with relief. When the 'Notes' were finished, we drank champagne and talked over the day's events with excitement. After midnight I went to the Massigli party at the French Embassy. I ate enormously: I drank a lot. At three o'clock in the morning I rang up the studio to hear that they were delighted with the colour pictures of the Queen; they thought I, too, would be pleased. I went to sleep relieved.

Early morning visit to the studio to be surprised to find that so many of the pictures were excellent. A heavy morning's work selecting the best and getting them to the Palace; by midday a number of them were passed for publication. The rest of the week was a complicated nightmare trying to supply to the Press the requisite number of pictures. Messengers were waiting in the various rooms of my mother's house for another messenger who never arrived. I talked myself hoarse on the telephone, and only by a fraction of a minute did I catch the Friday evening train to make my getaway to the retreat of the country. I bought an evening paper at Waterloo Station and one of my pictures of the Queen was printed across the front page of the *Evening News*.

WEEKEND AT VAYNOL

July 23rd, 1953

Elizabeth Cavendish was to call by for me at ten minutes past eight, together to take the night train to Wales. At seven o'clock I awoke, strangely anxious, depressed and dazed from 'forty winks' of a most debilitating, even quite sinister kind.

With a cloud of vague apprehension still hanging over me I lay wondering why I should feel so low. Why had I not the strength to attempt to snap out of my introspection by jumping into a taxi and going for half an hour to meet, for the first time, Audrey Hepburn? Anita Loos and several other friends have told me how delightful a creature this young actress is, and how full of talent. Recently she has been given the leading part in a film called *Roman Holiday* which, it is said, will put her at the top of her profession.

A small cocktail party had been arranged by Mel Ferrer who, it seems, is the forthcoming star's boy-friend, and who has shown interest in directing my Gainsborough play if ever it comes on again. I'd thought I might possibly interest A.H. in the part of Margaret. Of course there'd be no chance of that, what with Hollywood clamouring for her; but it might be that by *not* going I'd miss a rare opportunity. But no, why make such a giant effort? Instead, I could relax quietly for an hour. The clock ticked on for fifteen minutes; still I hadn't made up my mind. How silly always to be in such a rush! Even if I *should* go, by the time I got there I'd have to leave. Better remain on the bed. Then, quite suddenly, I decided to go. In the cab I chafed at the traffic congestion that always follows a rainstorm in London on a summer evening.

I was the first to arrive at Miss Hepburn's flat in South Audley Street; I would be the first to leave. I talked to the mother, Baroness Heemstra, a lady with a rather charming rolling accent, who told me that her daughter was dressing, was always late. Wouldn't I have some *hors-d'oeuvres*, a martini? Signs of hospitality abounded. The Baroness said that she had found *My Royal Past*[7] a tonic and relief from the gloom and terror of the starvation years of Occupation during the war in

---

[7] One of my earlier publications — a skit on Royal memoirs.

Belgium. I felt this made me no longer a stranger to this company. The guests, like all film people on social occasions, were unconscionably late. Mel Ferrer arrived: a charming, gangling man resembling a coarser Peter Watson, who, no doubt as a result of his theatrical career, has developed a slightly professional charm of manner. He described A.H. to me as 'the biggest thing to come down the turnpike'.

At last the daughter appeared — a new type of beauty: huge mouth, flat Mongolian features, heavily painted eyes, a coconut coiffeur, long nails without varnish, a wonderfully lithe figure, a long neck, but perhaps too scraggy. Today's stars are brought from a different strata of life. A.H.'s enormous potential cinema success, with attendant salary, seems to have made little impression on this delightful human being. She appears to take wholesale adulation with a pinch of salt: gratitude rather than puffed-up pride. Everything very simple about and around her: no maid to help her dress, or to answer the door to the guests who had now started a slow trickle into the room.

In a flash I discovered A.H. is chock-a-block with spritelike charm, and she has a sort of waifish, poignant sympathy. Without any of the preliminaries I felt that she cut through to a basic understanding that makes people friends. Nothing had to be explained: we liked one another. A chord had been struck and I knew that, next time we met, we would continue straight from here with no recapitulation of formalities. This was a unique occasion.

But the point of this brief précis is to try and explain that, after half an hour, I had become completely immersed in such a very different and new atmosphere that, when I returned home a short while later, I was feeling entirely differently about life. The tempo had heightened again. My morbid mood had passed; I was pleased that I had made this onslaught into another world. How many suicides could be prevented by a change of scene!

A little while later Elizabeth and I were sitting in a sleeper compartment on our way to Bangor to stay for a large weekend party of interesting types. 'Here we are,' I remarked, 'at the outset of an experience. The slate is clear at the moment, but surely the portents are that something will happen, and something very positive, by the time we return home on Monday. Someone will have fallen in love or have had a row.' 'Yes,' said Elizabeth, 'that's what's so lovely.' Few people enjoy life as much as Elizabeth, who all the while is experimenting, and going off to meet it in its many varied forms.

We were going to stay with Michael Duff in his large, rambling, white house, Vaynol, in a large park of rhododendrons overlooking Snowdon. It had been the scene for such a number of greatly enjoyed house parties in the 'old days' before the war. There had always been the most stimulating assortment of people — some of whom would never have tolerated each other if they had not come under the spell of Michael's magic wand. He made everyone appear at their best: sympathetic, cosy, brilliant, or merely physically attractive. So many times I had stayed here for Christmas, and there had always been dressing-up, charades, wild dancing, exciting games taking place all over the house. There was a wonderful old nannie whom I called 'the giggler', who when one was ill made one feel as if one were going back to the womb with her ministrations of bedroom fire, an extra blanket, a softer eiderdown, or a tray of suitable foods.

It was here that poor Gerald Berners, so late in life, had found his greatest love. It was here that Natalie Paley posed for my early photographs covered with the best roses from a sunny wall. It was here that Norah Lindsay arrived one winter's

191

evening in the height of the depth of war, and in the absence of her host lined up the servants in the hall and gave them instructions for her care.

'Now I know Sir Michael wishes me to be comfortable. Well, I would like — very early in the morning, long before I am awake — to have a little housemaid come into my room, quiet as a mouse, and light a huge fire which has become so hot by the time I'm awake that I could cook on it. Then...'

Michael's mother, Juliet, who lives within a few miles of me at Wilton, has with the years become an ever closer friend. But when first Juliet introduced me to her son, we looked at one another with mutual suspicion: in fact, one could say it was a question of hate at first sight. Mother and son talked together as if they were the most formal of strangers; I considered this more unnatural on the part of the son than of the parent. With his ramrod back and nape, his stiff manner and staccato stutter, Michael struck me as being the pompous ass I called him to his face as he spat back some equally unpleasant expletive at me.

But I learnt my mistake. Somehow, somewhere — I have forgotten the circumstances — Michael and I suddenly became real pals, and my friendship with him has brought me much joy, fun, and even a little more understanding of people.

Michael once told me of the first time he ever went abroad. As a boy in his teens, he arrived at Victoria Station, full of expectation for a marvellous excursion to Paris with his mother, whom he considered he saw only too rarely. But, to his dismay, he was greeted with derision. The sight of her twelve-year-old son was too much for Juliet, for Michael was wearing a brand-new tweed suit of ginger plus-fours, topped by a bowler hat. Juliet was unable to make light of the situation; Michael's chagrin lasted long after that weekend. In fact, when he came of age, and his mother suddenly discovered she had given birth to a much sought-after and attractive *parti*, she decided to cultivate him, but it was too late for Michael.

It is sad when parents cannot understand or sympathize with their offspring. It is sadder still that, in cases where the children have most suffered from lack of parental empathy they, in turn, are unable to communicate with their own offspring. Juliet's mother was the distinguished and brilliant Lady de Grey (later Lady Ripon) who, perhaps more than anyone, can be given credit for mixing people from all worlds at her parties. It was she who brought Diaghilev's ballet to London, and then invited Nijinsky to meet Queen Alexandra. Lady de Grey had high hopes for her daughter, but she was disappointed. She told her friends that she would have her gangling daughter so well educated that no one would realize she was a goose. Although Juliet admired her mother, and perhaps even loved her after her death, yet she had no real intimacy with her; and, in turn, Juliet was incapable of understanding her own children, while they in turn...

Michael is handsome, tall of stature with wistful blue eyes. His classical features are those of a very conventional Ouida guardsman, and there is certainly a twinge of the military in his rigid deportment. But Michael is unlike his appearance. He is, in fact, a true eccentric, and this he would consider the greatest compliment. His point of view is always original, his mind full of fantasy, and his intuition uncanny. When in form. I know of no one who can be funnier; he is master of the anecdote, with an instinctive knowledge of the value of the pause, and the stutter adds enormously to the dramatic effect.

Michael has an enviable way of striking a chord of intimacy with all sorts and kinds. His real friends range all over the world, for, in spite of carrying out punctiliously and with enjoyment, his duties and responsibilities, he manages to travel a great deal, and will go to the ends of the earth to stay with someone whom he will admit may be somewhat of a bore, but for whom he has feelings of loyal affection.

Michael remembers people's characteristic movements as if he were a choreographer always on the lookout for inspiration. He does an imitation of how the hostess, Lady Colefax, while talking of 'H.G.' (Wells) or 'B.B.' (Berenson), would be rearranging the salt and pepper pots, the spoons and forks, the toothpick and cigarette boxes, and all the objects in front of her on her dining-table. Lady Granard would send the silver boxes flying the length of her polished table; Lady Crewe was continually dusting her mouth with a sideways pendulum swing of a chiffon handkerchief. Michael also relished the fact that Lady Crewe, out of shyness, would never wait with the other patients in a dentist's waiting-room. Arriving on time in Harley Street, she would send in her chauffeur to inquire if the dentist was 'running a little late', or was he ready for her appointment? If not, the car would drive her ladyship around the squares until, eventually, she could be shown straight up to the dentist's chair.

Michael is a godson of Queen Mary, and there is surely no one who knows more than Michael about the private lives of any reigning family, in no matter what country; in fact, it can be said that he is 'royalty struck'. He collects stories and gossip about any royal personage, and treats his hierarchy with a mixture of complete reverence and a realization of how ridiculous their more exaggerated characteristics can become. He appreciates fully the qualities of his Royal godmother while being conscious of her gaucherie — her never being able to smile in public or look anyone straight in the face. Yet when she is alone and amused by some item of gossip, the old lady will laugh until she has to produce a handkerchief to wipe away her tears. Michael may be summoned to have tea and tell the Queen 'all that is going on', and he watches with fascination while the Queen cuts her cake into small squares, then, one by one, throws them, not to a dog, but into her own mouth. In fact Michael's highest compliment for his adored 'old Dutch' is that she is 'doggy'. Michael's feelings of love, admiration and awe for the old Queen prevent him from ever laughing at her, and though he knows his anecdotes about her are highly amusing, he is too intent and serious himself to smile.

He is amused that 'Old Doggie' refers to 'my woman Shaftesbury' (her lady-in-waiting, Lady Shaftesbury), and that, in fact, all those in waiting are 'women'. Michael relishes their names: Bertha Dawkins, Pussy Milnes-Gaskill, Maggy Wyndham, Lizzie Motion. While relating these incidents, Michael subconsciously punches the air with her inexpressive hands, or prods the ground with the point of an imaginary umbrella. His description is hilarious of how Queen Mary and he were crammed into a small lift on the way up to pay a call on Michael's mother in her Belgravia flat. Michael, nervous at not wishing to touch the Royal bosom, pressed the wrong button. As the Queen and he shot to the roof, Lady Juliet Duff was seen, in a flash on the landing as they went higher, doing a deep curtsey, but with a look of utter astonishment in her eyes.

'Did you know that at Marlborough House her wash basin is surrounded by the most marvellous jewelled toilet set given to her by the Tsarina? Isn't it odd that she should have a sunken bath let into the marble floor, and that her loo is covered with red velvet and is like a throne?'

The old Queen's knowledge of *objets d'art* and furniture was more of a pleasure to her than to the King who once, at dinner, heard the Queen ask Michael if he had bought anything lately? Whereupon King George angrily thumped the table and said: 'There you go again, May — always furniture, furniture, furniture!' In fact the King could become extremely exasperated with his consort, and is said to have sent her out at a Sandringham shoot with the beaters. Once Michael heard the gruff German tones evoking her: 'May, *will* you rattle your brolly!' No one was more amused than Michael when, one day, Queen Mary sent a note through her lady-in-waiting to say she was sorry she hadn't recognized him when, a few days earlier, she had been visiting Batsford's bookshop in North Audley Street. The explanation was that, since Michael was not wearing a hat, the Queen had mistaken him for one of the shop assistants.

Michael finds his most charming topic in Queen Alexandra who adored his grandmother, Gladys de Grey. After the birth of her second son the Queen became deaf, and this affliction made her an even more difficult companion, for she had never been able to master the English language well enough to string sentences together and would gruffly point and say: 'Screen — table — dog — woman,' etc. In spite of her deafness she enjoyed sitting at the opera, and some said she learnt to lipread the singers. When, two years after her marriage, she discovered the infidelities of her husband she packed a bag and, in the middle of the night, started down the main staircase to leave Windsor Castle. But Queen Victoria, though sympathetic, forbade her to go. 'You are Princess of Wales. I know what you are suffering, but you cannot leave.'

One evening at dinner, Queen Alexandra noticed that Lady de Grey was scrutinizing Queen Mary, her daughter-in-law, across the table. The Dowager Queen leant across to Lady de Grey and, in a voice enlarged by her deafness, shouted: 'Ugly old thing, isn't she!' Lady de Grey used to bring back to Queen Alexandra, from her visits to Paris, a great selection of false jewellery which the Queen preferred to the Crown jewels. She was once on her way to the Opening of Parliament when a long row of artificial pearls broke. Although she was, as usual, late for the proceedings, she insisted on remaining in her carriage until every bead had been found.

In widowhood, Queen Alexandra became so irritated with always being in the company of the possessive and tiresome lady-in-waiting, Charlotte Knollys, that once she locked her in the lavatory, ordered the car, and alone motored to Sandringham. The motor, not expected on the route, was continually held up; as a result of several inquiries from Colchester and other places as to whether it was the Queen who had been seen by the local police, Sir Dighton Probyn, her Private Secretary, went to her room to find the royal bird had flown. He was severely reprimanded.

The Queen was particularly fond of sprinting down to Putney to watch the Boat Race and cheer among the enthusiasts on the river bank. Later she developed the habit of getting up from bed in the middle of the night and distributing gold coins in the East End.

Lord Haig, that controversial and now much blamed 1914 war leader, was the Queen's hero. When the slaughter was over, and the Field Marshal was riding in state to Buckingham Palace, she made her ladies-in-waiting accompany her to the gate of Marlborough House. They imagined that once more the Queen was going to enjoy her habit of mingling with the crowds, but when the cortège approached, this small woman, dressed in black, stepped forward into the road brandishing her umbrella. The carriages lurched to a grinding stop just before running her down. Haig recognized the lady, dismounted, and received her homage.

'Wanted be first thank you — give congratulations — even before my son.'

The procession was delayed three minutes.

The Vaynol weekend (a Royal one, for Princess Marina was there to launch a lifeboat at Llandudno) ended with the inevitable practical jokes, and 'ghost figures' found elaborately bedecked in the Royal bedroom. But the wholesale jollity, the wild exuberance of youth, was missing. Neither had there been the element of the haphazard, the great surprise. Sadly Elizabeth and I had to agree, on our return railway journey, that no one had either fought or fallen in love.

TRUMAN CAPOTE

1953

It is rarely that, after middle age, one makes a great new friend, but I really believe I can put the American, Truman Capote, in that category. During the last five or six years that I have known him he has become ever more close, and in many ways he has filled the gap left in my life by the death of Bébé Bérard, some of whose sensibility, natural intelligence and deep-felt friendliness he has shown me.

Our first meeting was not too auspicious. It took place in New York in a crowded, smoky room at a cocktail party given by an over-excited celebrity hunter. God knows why I had bothered to go, for I feared the occasion would be as nightmarish as, indeed, it turned out to be. However, I am grateful to the hostess for she introduced me to a minute, gnomelike creature who had recently had a big *succès d'estime* with his *Other Voices Other Rooms*. This little sprite, who appeared not to be more than fourteen years of age, stood, apparently terrified, smoking in a corner and wearing, most surprisingly, a gold medallion on a chain over his dark-blue sweater.

Amid the noise I shouted in an attempt to make contact. A very quavery Southern drawl replied in whispers: 'I'm feehnishin' a *novella*, end theehn ah haieve a novel on heeand, eeeeendah theehn sum short stureeees.' He closed his eyes while he spoke, but having finished his speech he opened them enough to flicker pale eyelashes, then blinked up at me with wide, haunted eyes, through huge glasses and a bang of canary silk hair. He appeared extremely alarmed by me, and his fingers trembled as he jerked the cigarette to his dry lips. However, he managed to overcome his apparent terror enough to inform me that he thought of coming soon to England. I asked him to call on me. A few weeks later he did so — arriving surprisingly enough in a rainstorm at Broadchalke in red scarf and a hired car. My new house was, as yet, only partially furnished, and we had lunch in the kitchen. We got along. Discussing his *Other Voices* he explained: 'I just wanted to create the feeling that someone was telling this story by the light of a fire in a dark room, and that the story was being told by someone with a gift for expressing himself to someone appreciative of that talent. I write for my equals. I think the reader must work, too — must be allowed to use his imagination. I try to provide the essence — the seed of the matter. When I have provided the reader with the seed he must make it come into flower and watch the petals unfold.' I soon discovered Truman has a way of eliciting confidences, and I found myself telling him about myself as if we had been friends for ever; we seemed to understand one another in spite of the difference in environment and age.

Our friendship developed quickly and, together with his great new friend, the farouche and freckled Jack Dunphy, we spent a summer holiday together at Taormina in a stone shack placed among fruit trees in a beautiful landscape. With anyone else the discomfort would have been unbearable. As it was, the daily trek to buy provisions in town, and lugging the heavy packages back in the heat of the day, was quite an ordeal. My bedroom possessed no furniture except a pallet on which to sleep, and it was best never to use the bathroom. We lived on wine, wonderful heavily-scented tomatoes, sliced ham, bread and cheese. Once, however, Truman decided to vary our diet with a roast chicken. Unable to cut the bird with ordinary household knives, a hatchet had to be taken to it; even so, it remained uneatable. But the simple life and the anything but simple conversation delighted me.

By degrees, Truman's books sold in greater quantity, and the houses he rented in various parts of the world became a little more comfortable. But it was always the contentment of spending our hours of relaxation together that gave me such pleasure. For I found Truman to be intelligent to an extent that is quite a revelation. His mind is like a knife: it cuts through all façades. Sometimes he remains silent for a spell. You can almost hear him thinking out some problem: then he blurts out the conclusion he has come to. It is nearly always original, and most certainly near the truth. Another great asset is his capacity for laughter. He enjoys with raucous relish the company that amuses him. He is an appreciative listener, loves the jokes of others, repeats them aloud — like an echo — then goes into gales of surprised laughter.

Truman does not often display the strange, Southern-mossy, eerie quality that comes out in his writing, and talking to him one feels that his books are only a small part of him, and that, like the iceberg, he shows only a fraction of what's below the surface. To listen to him relating his most recent experience is to realize that much more extraordinary things happen to him than to other human beings. He cannot avoid, at almost every turn, violent clashes with fate. He can never expect some period of quiet and peace to last for long before a typhoon dilemma sweeps everything from him. His poetical side certainly leads him to exaggeration, and the truth is inevitably how he sees anything. The fact that his life is often a torment for him makes it full of 'good copy'. He utilizes these dramas in short stories, or novels. Sometimes he spends a year writing a novel only to discover the subject is not really a suitable one for his talent. By nature he is lazy. He does not enjoy writing and will delay the moment of starting as long as possible. But once he begins to concentrate the outside world is lost to him.

August, 1953: Portofino

The short break in Florida during my American lecture tour last winter should have been a health cure. Instead it was spent suffering from a severe attack of 'flu. The sun gave way to gales and a near hurricane and the palm trees were bent like croquet hoops. Depleted and drained on my return to the Arctic climate of an English spring, I pined for a short holiday in Italian sun, but the activities of the Coronation summer were soon upon me and, before I could get away, I was swamped.

Eventually work was cleared up at home. The corrected galley proofs of my *Glass of Fashion* had been sent to America, and I left England to stay with Truman in Italy in a state of unusual happiness, for a smiling, kindly and totally delightful Eileen Hose had been 'sworn in' as my efficient new secretary. I left her to sort out the appalling mess of my business affairs and knew that for the first time my life was being properly looked after and all important things taken care of.

At Santa Margherita Truman Capote met me with yells of laughter. 'Oh, you're going to have the most marvellous time here! You're going to love every minute of it — the bathing, the people. Yes, everyone's waiting for you.'

We drove down the steep hills through dark, leafy avenues to the fishermen's bay of Portofino. Centred around a gaily-glistening port, the houses are painted saffron and rose. The awnings of the cafes are striped or brightly coloured, and, with high mountains forming an amphitheatre, the setting is reminiscent of a Victorian opera. Here are all the picturesque clichés: fishing boats with tall cat's-cradle masts rocking lazily along the quayside, grey rocks that rise abruptly from the dark-green water to the mountainsides covered with cypresses, umbrella pines, romantic little castles, and weird Japanese *art nouveau* houses built for some eccentric man of means, and now appearing no more habitable than a water-colour decoration on a silk fan.

The steep paths up the hinterland are laid with cobblestones, and only at night, when the port is seen in a warm apricot glow of low-powered lights, is the sound of busy clogged feet muffled.

The first days were as if in a sanatorium. I slept from one o'clock in the morning until ten, and again for several hours in the afternoon. For long periods I lay resting, too drowsy to turn over on my bed, or stretch for a book. At first my dreams were anxious, unpleasant ones, and the moments of half-consciousness were full of vague fears; but, by degrees, the *angst* of my London existence faded, and my mind when both asleep and awake was only filled with happy thoughts.

The day starts early in Portofino. Soon after dawn the fruit and vegetable stalls are pitched, only to be taken down by midday.

The greatest activity is concentrated around the small bay with its hundreds of sailing craft; here is continual work: repainting, scraping, adjustment to mast or outboard motor. The hands of the church clock seem to progress more slowly than elsewhere. It is the women who serve a non-stop public at the cafes. They never rest; they run this most matriarchal of small towns.

Soon I had abandoned myself completely to the pleasure of Truman's company; going out in a boat with him, sunbathing and swimming, for days on end we talked. We discussed our beliefs and doubts, gossiped, argued, talked seriously, frivolously and bawdily. We were vastly entertained by each other's revelations. We would take a small boat out beyond the bay, then leap overboard into the cool, deep water — dark blue, dark green, turquoise, or cobalt it might be. Sometimes the sea was blue streaked with darker blue, the effect like a Japanese print. Further out, towards the horizon, it was pale green with stipples of turquoise flecked with brown — or just amethyst and turquoise. The water is buoyant, effervescing, and with the aid of a mask its subterranean treasures are unending.

I found Truman's authoritativeness very refreshing and salutary. He can clear the air with a word; sometimes he even slaps people down in order to get some sense into an argument. Put him with a group of people who are far removed from him in interest, and he will, after they have recovered from the first shock of his appearance and manner, find themselves utterly beguiled and impressed. But Truman himself does not consider whether or not he is making an impression. He doesn't mind if there should be hostility, is quite willing to make a disturbance if necessary. He is frightened or awed by nobody: he has courage.

Truman appears to have few worries. He enjoys good food, lots to drink, and gets it. He loves his dog, Bunker, and enjoys leisure as much as the bright lights of café society. He is avid for gossip. His obvious enjoyment of a good story, and his hoarse, hearty laughter always make everything seem a little better than you had thought it.

Truman has perfected an American use of the latest slang; there is no catchphrase that cannot be pigeon-holed for effective use in the future. He utilizes current phrases as a brilliant Broadway librettist might. Also he uses with a toughness that is healthy and refreshing all sorts of extremely crude and indecent phrases: 'Oh, he's my dream trade.' 'He's on my shit list.' If, for instance, a typically selfish Italian motorist barricades the road, he will eventually be treated to an astonishing vocabulary from Truman who, as the Goncourts pointed out, like many artists whose thoughts are in the clouds, comes down to earth now and then with a salutary thud.

In some ways I feel anxious lest Truman, like Bébé Bérard, may not survive to make old bones. I am slightly scared that someone who lives so intensely, so warmly, so generously, may be packing into a short span more than many people are capable of enjoying or experiencing in a long lifetime. Truman seems to attract drama: he has violent reactions to everything, and the moment comes when total fatigue takes over. Then he sinks into a death-like, sensual sleep from which you feel he will never recover. When, however, he does eventually surface to a deep, drowsy awakening, he seems reborn to all the wonders and surprises of life.

If Truman, Jack and I should need extra divertissement there are plenty of interesting people in the offing. Rex Harrison and Lili Palmer live on the top of the mountain. A group of theatre people assemble on the terrace of their villa: John Perry, Binkie

Beaumont and John Gielgud. Max Beerbohm is close by at Rapallo. There are sudden yacht arrivals: the *Sister Anne* came bringing Daisy Fellowes and her prisoners; another yacht brought the Windsors. Wallis on meeting John Gielgud at dinner for the first time, said: 'You know England made a great mistake in getting rid of the Dook. He's a very valuable addition to the country, an interesting person. You know, after sixteen years I am still fascinated by all sorts of things he has to tell me — after sixteen years! And yet I suppose you think of me as the devil with horns!'

JOHN GIELGUD

September 16th, 1953: Portofino

In appearance offstage John Gielgud looks, at first glance, anything but an artist. But, by degrees, one senses his poetic quality, his innate pathos. The large bulbous nose is a stage asset: the eyes, though tired, have a watery blue wistfulness that is in the Terry tradition of beauty. He is not altogether happy that he has inherited so many family characteristics, and praise of his mellifluous voice and superb diction embarrasses him.

With the good manners that come from his true spirit, and not only on the stage, he has the grand manner. Unlike his rivals he does not know the sensation of jealousy; he will always plan to do the best for the project as a whole, rather than as a means of shining brightly himself. This has often led him to playing small and ineffective roles, and even obliging someone else by doing the wrong thing for himself; however, in his case the 'wrong thing' only adds to his reputation for his innate devotion to the cause of the theatre.

Once, when I was designing for him a revival of a very poor Edwardian comedy, *The Return of the Prodigal*, he sent me a thirteenth-hour SOS to alter the construction of the scenery because, at one point in the play, he was to lie in a hammock. Although, a month before, he had given the 'go-ahead' for the ground plan, he now considered he would not be in a sufficiently prominent position for an important scene. He was not being so much the 'star' as a 'realist'. He knew that it was he that the public would come to see and therefore it was necessary to rebuild the set.

Something about John appeals very directly to one's sympathy. Often he appears to be deeply unhappy, and seems to make life hard for himself. Then one wonders if he does not take from the parts he plays on the stage the compensatory life he misses in private. One of his most disarming aspects is his knowledge and devilish enjoyment of his own shortcomings. 'I'm spoilt, I'm niggardly, I'm prissy. I come home in the evening and count the books on the shelf to see if one is missing.'

John is the first to admit that actors are often vapid and stupid people, yet he spends most of his time, most happily, in unworthy green room gossip. He relates how, during the war, on some ENSA tour, he was sharing a bedroom with Binkie Beaumont and John Perry, and they talked until dawn about a prospective theatrical venture. Only complete exhaustion silenced them. But the moment John awoke in the morning he carried on the conversation where it had been interrupted, by asking: 'And do you think Dolly[8] can be trusted with the wigs?'

Here at Portofino John has appeared wearing a ridiculous white linen hat, sitting bolt upright in a rowboat as formally as if he were at a board meeting. John is always the first to realize how comic a picture he presents, and in no way resents our

---

[8] The distaff side of Gus and Dolly of 'Gustaves', a well-known theatrical wig-maker.

amusement; in fact, his eyes twinkle with the fun of the absurdity as, unmindful of waves or splash, he continues, in his rich, fog-horn voice, to extol the work of Granville Barker, or where he went wrong with *Hamlet*.

For Truman and myself this was to be a working holiday (Truman was desperately late with the script for his play *The House of Flowers*, and I was still struggling with my Gainsborough play), so when John suggested to us that we should motor with him to Sermione, where he had just been offered a part in a Shakespeare film, we were both loath to interrupt the quiet continuity of our labours. But John badgered us. He hated having to go alone; wouldn't we join him just for a few days? But since Truman and I — unlike the star actor — would not be guests of the film company, and rooms were scarce everywhere at this peak time of the year, would John please be certain to arrange our accommodation in advance?

Once on our way, in the film people's hired motor-car, John confessed he hadn't felt like telegraphing for rooms for us, and in any case it was too late. On arrival at Sermione it was discovered, as we had feared, that there was only one room available for John. Truman and I were crushed. John, ebullient, asked airily: 'Will it cost you very much to go on by car to Verona?' He then disappeared into the arms of the *Romeo and Juliet* company.

When eventually John suggested coming with Truman and me to Venice we now had the upper hand, but we relented and gave him a seat in our car. Each morning at breakfast John would appear fully attired and, in his beautiful *voix d'or*, talk out of the window. 'Really, Venice is excessively ugly in the rain: it looks like King's Cross.' When discussing the theatre he expanded with real feeling: 'I'm sick of doing old plays, and don't have much interest in the younger generation. Perhaps I'm tired.' John has a writer's use of words: talks of the 'mutinously bored cast', and says someone has a talent with pencil-sketches 'as if to touch the bar of heaven'. He is not only appreciative of wit in others, but makes sparkling remarks himself: two actresses in opposition were 'diamond cutting diamond'.

John Gielgud is today undisputedly our most modest, distinguished and noblest theatre ornament. He has many of the virtues and faults connected with the actor; but he is also a remarkable human being — full of the very qualities so lacking in many of his confrères. He has compassion. By any standards he is high-minded.

TEA ABOVE RAPALLO

'Max will be pleased to see you for tea at four o'clock.'

His companion, Elizabeth Jungman, telephoned the welcome news through to us in Portofino, adding the cautionary information that of late the venerable master of *belles lettres* had not been sleeping well and could, without becoming overtired, only receive a few visitors for a rather short time. The previous spring he had had a close shave with influenza. The heat of Rapallo summer was bad for him, so they had removed to the summit of a nearby mountain.

Truman drove me in his little boneshaker around the dusty, circling road to Montellegro. Then we wound our way through sweet-smelling trees and fresh green slopes, and we were excited at the prospect of seeing, at the summit, Sir Max Beerbohm, that rare and wonderful link with the Victorian past. A half-century ago he had already become immortal —

the gentle and unassailable creator of *Zuleika Dobson*, the master of fable, satire and caricature.

He was considered one of the greatest conversationalists of his time, and his gift for describing the physical exterior of his victims was so vivid that one knew exactly what they must have looked like. The youthful Churchill had dry hair like a waxwork, no wrinkles, and the pallor of one who has lived in the limelight. He also had hereditary bad manners, was courteous and brutal alternately. Shaw had a temperance beverage face, and Beerbohm hated the naked look of the back of his neck. Balfour was girlish and seemed dazed. Oscar Wilde he likened to an Assyrian wax statue, effeminate, but with the vitality of twenty men. His heavy shoulders, and his fat, white hands jewelled with huge rings, made him also look like a feather bed, an enormous dowager schoolboy. He had a way of laughing with his hand over his mouth. Of Lord Curzon, Beerbohm said he was 'Britannia's butler'.

More courageous sightseers than Truman and I would take the cable car, whose toy compartment dangled perilously over fir trees as it swung them aloft in order to get to the mountain tip. We, however, preferred to walk up towards the tall-spired cathedral, its bone-white façade blazing in the clean mountain air against the deep blue of the afternoon sky. It was not long before we found our goal, the little *albergo* with a vine-covered *loggia*. Miss Jungman materialized as a pepper-and-salt-haired woman of immense vitality with a strong German accent. She took us into a cool, impersonal dining-room where, hunched at a table set for tea, sat the somewhat crumpled, but dandified little figure to whom we had come to pay homage.

I had first met him some fifteen years ago with his great friend, Sibyl Colefax. (In fact, who did one not meet for the first time at Sibyl Colefax's?) A most suitable dinner party had been arranged in his honour, but it was Sibyl's beloved husband, Sir Arthur, a long-winded bore, and not Sir Max who held forth when the ladies left the room. In fact, the great *raconteur* was not given the chance of more than an opening gambit before Sir Arthur embarked upon a lengthy account of the latest law reports. Max sat back blinking with silent surprise. However, a few days later, he had come, at my request, to my studio to be photographed. He appeared to be enjoying the art of conversation even on such a restless occasion as this. He gave his very definite and, may I say, extremely banal, instructions as to his preferences for poses and backgrounds with such charm that I was obedient. He reminded me very much of my father: he was a pocket edition — with much more style and dash, but their slightly bulbous noses, thin lips and wideawake, blue eyes, with an appealing sadness, were the same. The photograph sitting was not entirely an easy one. Certainly I was willing to respect the wishes of someone whom I had admired for so long, and I wanted to please him. Thus I took a great number of photographs in the fashion at the time when Max first became a well-known figure. But I also wanted to experiment. My assistants were told in an aside to bring out more dramatic backgrounds than the plain black velvet that Max preferred. Reluctantly he posed in mock heroic attitudes. The results of these pictures were those that pleased me most, but they were the ones not passed for publication by the sitter.

Today, on his mountain peak, Sir Max, of whom Oscar Wilde said he had the gift of eternal old age, was still, in spite of his eighty years, the perennial dandy. He was wearing a smart pale-grey suit speckled like a moorhen; a black silk tie; a white shirt buttoned at the old-fashioned, rounded ends of the collar and cuff, with quite a large expanse of white showing above his wrist. On his long, pointed fingers he wore a bunch of heavy rings that drew added attention to his remarkable and almost inhumanly pale hands. They might have been made of old parchment or fine ricepaper — the nails dry and horny, the skin freckled and blotched. Bird-like hands, sensitive and expressive, they added distinction. The hair on his domed head grew in long, white wisps at the temples and above the collar. His complexion was clear and waxen, with a blush of transparent pink on lean, shiny cheekbones; he was immaculately shaved around the white moustache that graced the somewhat simian, thin-upper-lipped mouth (his lower lip more pronounced than that of my father). The eyes were still his most dominant feature. The lids were more hooded than my father's ever became, and the muscles below his left eye had relaxed revealing a red pocket of flesh; he seemed self-conscious about the anomaly. Nevertheless, his eyes communicated a lovely wonder and wistful surprise. They had a bird-like intensity, love-in-the-mist blue, and changed noticeably as he switched his memory from the past to the present.

We sat at a small rickety table. Before us were two plates of fancy biscuits, some very strong Indian tea that our host did not drink, and a bottle of red Chianti wine from which he poured himself a glass. The dining-room was empty. Its ugly cream- and salmon-coloured walls and red-tiled floors resounded to the echoes of children shouting or crying at play; rather a lot of flies were being restless.

When we first settled down at the tea-table, there was an instant's silence. What were we comparative strangers to talk about? How were we to begin? Hesitantly, I broached the subject of Sibyl Colefax. I said that although I had a great feeling of affection, even a little love, for her, I had been much too ready to make fun of her: of her illegible letters of invitation sent from grand houses in which she stayed, and of her use of the initials of celebrities — 'B.B.' (Berenson), or 'H.G.' (Wells), or 'G.B.S.' (Shaw). She had been an early friend to me, and I knew that at my first exhibition I had 'made the grade' when Sibyl had not only appeared at the gallery on the morning of the Private View but had reappeared in the afternoon. Sibyl had a genuine love of friends, an exceptional human understanding, and a taste in all things that was rare and extremely personal. She was too easy a target for jokes, and now I had great remorse.

Sir Max ruminated: 'Yes, Sibyl was a reliable, helpful friend, and she seldom missed a year without making a pilgrimage to visit me here. She will certainly go down to posterity through countless memoirs. No one could have imagined, herself least of all, that she would figure so largely in the history of her time.'

It was evident that Sir Max had an extraordinarily exact and precise memory. Never once, during our afternoon's visit, did he fumble for a name or a date.

We talked of cabbages and coronations, though Truman kept a restful silence: he was busy imbibing every nuance. Sir Max said of himself that although he 'went back to the dark ages', he wasn't quite old enough to remember the crowning of Queen Victoria. He had heard tell, however, that one old peer, Lord Rolle, tumbled over when paying homage, and the Queen had helped him to his feet. 'What a wonderful gesture that would have been for the television screen!'

After a pause, Sir Max observed that the days he had known shared little in common with the present. It was for this reason that he felt shy of making any public appearances, though if anyone were interested he had no objection to talking about his heyday for the benefit of the radio. 'It's so simple and not a bit formidable: they bring a discreet little apparatus to your room.'

His voice was quiet, leisurely and gentle, perhaps a trifle quavery. Yet he articulated every word with precision, giving such emphasis to his syllables that we marvelled at how rich in its effect the English language could be. And through the voice we caught the impression of a still-young spirit, emanating charm, wit and elegance.

I ventured upon the theatre as a safe topic, since here was the man who had been one of our outstanding drama critics. Sir Max complained that, from a certain moment onwards in theatrical history, it was almost impossible to hear what was being said upon the stage. He gave an amusing imitation of the breathless gasps, pantings and half-finished exclamations that certain latter-day actors employed in order to express emotion. But even in the old days of great bravura performances that involved much 'ranting', his brother, Sir Herbert Beerbohm Tree, always had trouble at His Majesty's Theatre with Row H. somehow, those sitting in Row H could never hear the actors, however loudly they bellowed: the acoustics were such that the sound always went straight to Row I. Experts were brought from far and wide. 'Herbert tried everything, but it was all to no avail.' (I asked if he had tried re-lettering the row?)

In any case, Sir Max went on, His Majesty's Theatre was always too large for comedy, even for Shakespeare. The ideal theatre was the Haymarket. 'With only a few people on stage you could always give the effect of a crowd.' But it was in the congenial intimacy of the St James's Theatre that Sir George Alexander did the Wilde comedies so well, 'with conventional scenery but good furniture'. Sir Max recalled that the author, after the first night of *Lady Windermere's Fan*, congratulated the audience on its enthusiastic performance.

What did he think of Harley Granville Barker? Sir Max's bushy eyebrows were raised wistfully. Barker had been an excellent impresario for Shaw, Ibsen and Strindberg, but never appreciated the inner rhythms of Shakespeare's verse. His actors just rambled on, breaking up the metre in a dreadful massacre. 'For that matter,' our host added, 'few actors know what they are doing with Shakespeare.' Gielgud and Olivier are exceptions, and he thought they should have a good influence.

He expatiated on Tree's production of *A Midsummer Night's Dream*. 'Yes,' the old critic concluded, 'it was very pretty with all those little people fluttering about — really *féerique*. But Barker's production had gold fairies! Absolutely wrong! From what little I know about the subject, I am positive fairies were never made of gold. That is an earthy affair entirely.' Certainly very little gold has come the way of Sir Max. Although few writers have acquired his réclame — he has since his first success had a legendary quality — yet his books were sold in very small quantities and today are out of print. It is rather terrible to know that the successful Somerset Maugham criticized Max as being someone whose shirt-cuffs were generally dirty.

We spoke of Constance Collier, the glorious Boadicea of an actress, who, at one time, was said to have been engaged to Sir Max. 'Wonderfully handsome with her Assyrian profile, and a remarkable woman,' he agreed, 'but never really remarkable as an actress until quite late in life. Then she suddenly learned to laugh at herself on stage, and did inimitable caricatures of her former performances.'

About his own work for the theatre, Sir Max said he had once written a short stage version of *The Happy Hypocrite*. It had been put in the shade by Ivor Novello, who concocted his own version and made a full evening's entertainment at His Majesty's Theatre. Alas! Novello, who had always been so successful, suddenly had a failure. The financial reports on his earnings read something like: 1928 — thirty-five thousand pounds profit; 1930 — fifty thousand pounds; 1934 — sixty-five thousand pounds. And then, in the year *The Happy Hypocrite* appeared, he wound up in the black with forty-three pounds, eleven shillings and tuppence! Sir Max chuckled: 'Happily, Novello was able to continue his line of success after that.' As for *Zuleika Dobson*, many people had tried to adapt it for both stage and film, but had never succeeded. He felt, nevertheless, 'complimented by their attempts'.

It was apparent that, with such a store of vivid recollections of Shaw, Wilde, George Moore, Irving, and Ellen Terry, our little host scarcely felt lonely here upon the roof of the world. Rather, he allowed himself the uninterrupted time to digest his memories. Occasionally, he said, he did a little work if he felt like it, though not caricatures any more. 'One becomes too kind with age, and the likenesses no longer have any pepper.' He mulled over the possibility of producing another in that series of radio talks which had done so much to enlarge his public.

Yet, in spite of all, how strange it seemed that this glittering figure from another age of literature and fashion should so early have retired to the remoteness of Rapallo. Since his marriage before the First World War, he had remained in comparative isolation, except for another war, and a few visits to London to arrange an exhibition or to see his tailor. Of all places in the world, it seemed surprising to find Sir Max Beerbohm in an Italian mountain hotel so lacking in individuality and atmosphere that the management had not even been attentive enough to reserve his 'usual' table on the terrace for tea. But such was the force of the personality before us that we felt bathed in a singular calm as Sir Max revived the almost forgotten art of conversation. Perhaps the leisure that impregnated his work, diction and tranquil personality was the very reason for the self-imposed exile of this 'quietist' who had never been known to make a hurried pronouncement or sudden gesture.

Miss Jungman was ever watchful for Sir Max. (At one moment during tea she even got up from the table to flick away a fly that had settled on his domed pate.) No doubt she was a staunch prop to him, as she had been for Gerhart Hauptmann during the last eight years of the German writer's life.

At length Miss Jungman perceived that Sir Max was becoming a little jaded, so she instigated a walk for Truman and me round the mountain top. We looked down on vistas of olive-clad hills, distant gorges and the huge expanse of opal-coloured sea towards Lerici, where Shelley drowned. Miss Jungman explained that she had been friends with Sir Max and Lady Beerbohm for many years. There had been a 'little secret agreement' with him:

'If anything should happen to my wife...' But Miss Jungman had never let him finish the sentence, for it was unnecessary. And when Lady Beerbohm became ill for the last time, Sir Max had summoned her. She came post-haste from Oxford, arriving two hours after his wife's death to take on the duties of companion.[9]

When we came back from our mountain walk, Sir Max was sitting on a parapet sunning himself, his cane held gingerly in

---

[9] Miss Jungman in fact became Lady Beerbohm a few days before Sir Max's death.

one hand and a boater straw hat cocked jauntily to one side. He looked, for a moment, like one of those dapper monkeys that are dressed up to sit on the street musician's hurdy-gurdy. I could not help taking advantage of the situation, and when he turned towards us with lowered head and upward glancing eyes, he saw that in spite of his earlier demurs I was photographing him.

Sir Max seemed amused and even pleased when I said how delightful he looked there. 'Mayn't I take one more?' He beamed, posed for a moment, and turned his head so that his left eye would not be visible. Encouraged, I took several more snapshots. Then I asked him if he would show his hands, as they were such beautiful hands. By way of response he held one arm straight towards the camera, fingers splayed and stiff.

'Now no more, please. It's too late, and I look dreadful.'

I closed my camera.

'But you will let me see them, won't you? And you'll destroy any that are horrors?'

I promised that I would. 'It is almost time for his dinner,' Miss Jungman whispered. 'Max dines at six-thirty.'

We said goodbye, and the lady companion took us into the hotel dining-room to collect some parcels. As we came out on the terrace again, Sir Max could be seen from our vantage point under the tendrils of vines, walking slowly down the steep hill. A dandified little figure, with his cane and straw boater worn at a rakish angle, he looked as if he were sauntering down St James's on a summer morning in 1904. He did not know we were watching him, and as he walked examined one of his hands to see if it were really as beautiful as I had said it was. He turned it around, stiff and fishlike, to admire it from every angle.

ANNE FLEMING

September, 1953

Anne deserves high marks: ten for general intelligence, eight for intuition, seven for sensitivity, and at least five for common-sense. Very good marks, too, for gaiety, humour, and courage. Less than one mark for looking after herself and keeping friends or relations away when she is ill or utterly exhausted. Anne has managed the transference from being the wife of powerful newspaper tycoon, Lord Rothermere, to writer Ian Fleming, with style and apparent ease.

Whereas entertaining at St James's was on an impressive scale, she now corrals the people she finds interesting in her small but congenial house in Victoria Square. This she has made into an oasis for people who are creative in some field. The game of politics is enjoyed by her, and many newspaper headliners come onto her from the House. They bring their camaraderie or badinage with them, and for others used to the more formal social conventions of behaviour, their manners seem a bit farouche and offhand. But Anne does not notice this, and all her friends agree that her parties are more amusing than they were at Warwick House and her cook, Mrs Crickmere, trained by the expert Lady Sysonby, is much better than her former chef. To those who used to bemoan the fact that no young hostesses follow in the tradition of Sibyl Colefax and Emerald Cunard we now advocate Anne.

This week she gave a dinner to celebrate the fiftieth birthday of Cyril Connolly, and the small group she collected had unity and character. A lot of talent, brilliance and erudition was gathered here between 'Empire patterned' walls. They were people, born in all sorts of different strata of life, enjoying the fruits of success in the company of others they respected or had most in common with. The talk was on target: no one wasting time in banalities.

I had been to a ballet, met Lucian Freud and Francis Bacon at Wheeler's, and we had come on together to find Anne's party at its height. Cyril was radiant and feeling very warm-hearted at such a genuine display of affection. His heart and greed were equally overflowing at the tributes given to him. (Caviar from Francis Bacon and Lucian Freud, and brandy from me. He said he would eat the caviar for breakfast.) Clarissa (Churchill) Eden, very white and taut: I asked if such talk was not rather impressive after her summer spent looking after Anthony in the US. She admitted that when Maurice Bowra held forth, she had difficulty in following the flow. Stephen Spender, hair ruffled, white locks on end, tripping over as he went upstairs to pee. Freddy Ayer vociferating, and Peter Quennell benign; when Peter is in a good mood he can be the most polished and delightful conversationalist in the world: lovable too — but woe betide you if he is in a bitter mood.

Anne was enjoying the success of the party so much that she wanted her beloved husband, Ian, to savour every nuance of it. She was disappointed that, at two in the morning, he had disappeared to bed. Anne had stars in her eyes until the last guest stumbled out after dawn.

SLADE SCHOOL

October, 1953

I have gone back to school. Perhaps it should not be considered a return for, apart from the spasmodic sketching classes at my public school, art tuition never came my way. At Harrow our drawing master, an aggressive, white-haired, little lion cub, was W. Egerton Hine, and I was his most promising pupil. In fact, I learnt to paint water-colours of bluebell woods, farmyards and manure heaps, in exactly the same manner as my master. Although this was considered the ultimate achievement at the time, I found that, even a lifetime afterwards, when faced with any landscape I could not stop producing — with ample use of raw sienna and Prussian blue on Whatman hot-pressed paper — imitation Eggie Hines, and this became somewhat of a handicap.

Perhaps it was partly for this reason that I decided to come to the Slade. Also I have always felt the lack of tuition in draughtsmanship and wished to learn the use of oil colours.

Suddenly the rhythm of my life changed. In order to do a full week's work I came to London from the country for five, and not two days a week. Instead of scrambling out of Pelham Place, after a busy morning's work, into a taxi for a luncheon appointment, I now must be in the Underground by nine-thirty (Art Schools do not start early: no complaint there!), so the usual coping with letters, messages and making arrangements has now to be organized with Eileen before that.

At first it hit me head-on when I arrived in a building teeming with fellow-students a third my own age. My old shyness and uncertainty came back with a bang. I was reminded of my first day at St Cyprian's boarding school; but, unlike the Eastbourne preparatory school, this place was well heated, and the students were not hostile. With their beards and long hair, they appeared like the artistic personages in that vast group of the nineties painted by Fantin-Latour. It was a bit comforting later to discover that a certain timidity was also felt by other first-year students. Yet coming as an interloper into a quiet room in which a number of young people are silently working, while live figures are sitting motionless without their clothes on, was a bit uncanny. The brown and buff room with growing green plants, and fish floating in tanks among the plaster heads and torsos, was less alarming. In this room a kind, grey-haired, sepia-eyed man named Townsend gave me a 'position' facing a model of a Greek youth with a sliced-off cranium. He also found an easel for me, and then, tactfully, left me to my own resources. I tried to comprehend my newly-acquired equipment. First, to pour a little liquid into one of the dishes on my spruce palette. But panic seized me: I could not even unscrew the top of the bottle. I was desperate: what kind of a guy was this who couldn't even get at his own turpentine? I knew that I would create an atmosphere of abject hopelessness if I asked one of my neighbours to help me. The veins in my forehead swelled as I made a Herculean effort — and won! Next — the battle with the easel. Of course one leg was far too short: how to lengthen it? It was completely unyielding: nothing would budge it. Could I shorten the other two? One leg moved easily, but not the others; and, in any case, my easel would then be in a position that, if I wished to paint, necessitated my kneeling down or lying on the floor. I tried once more to raise the legs. Appalling noise as canvas and easel, palette and paints collapsed. Oil and turpentine everywhere. Fortunately Mr Townsend reappeared to put chaos to rights.

Slowly I discovered that I had been far too ambitious in selecting such a vast canvas as I had to stretch to put a stroke even half-way up the picture, and it was quite bewildering to see what was appearing on it. After a few days I realized that my still-life, done in warm tones of Devonshire cream and burnt sienna, was definitely Hine-haunted. How could I exorcize Eggie's ghost? I wanted to put my signature to a picture that was undeniably and positively my own. These doubts, when relayed to the kind Mr Townsend, brought a slow, knowing smile to his face. 'Don't bother yet about painting a picture. Just get on with the problem of showing the contrast of the highlights on that thigh with the darkness of the plants in the background, and the half-tones of the figure in shadow.' Although it did not look like a 'Beaton' (and what does?), my large canvas, when completed a week later, was to me quite an achievement.

I was now ambitious to go into the life class room, but Mr Townsend insisted upon my remaining longer doing drawings and oil studies of other plaster casts. Only after several weeks was I allowed to face a real live nude. Mr Townsend gave me a 'front-row' position facing an enormously fat, naked lady, who sat bolt upright on an Indian-patterned sarong. One of her babyfingered, dimpled hands was placed meekly at her side, the other half-covering her sex. On her face this kewpie Eve maintained an expression of the utmost affectation with eyebrows raised superciliously, lids lowered, and a mouth twisted to one side in the most exaggerated pout. She was doing an Oliver Messel imitation of herself.

I discovered what an enormous amount of time and readjustment it took to put this fat, sitting figure within the confines of my canvas. After many rags, soaked in turpentine, had obliterated many persevering attempts, I wondered how on earth, on this now dirty, dark canvas, those brilliant highlights of the flesh-tones could be produced? (Delacroix mixed brilliant colours even to produce the shadows.)

Having, all my life, used water-colours, coloured inks and gouache, it was quite a jolt to realize how comparatively easy a job it was in these media to find the desired colour and tone; it was often only a question of dilution with water. But, quite abruptly, came the discovery that seldom is the desired effect in oil acquired by the mixing of white paint (the equivalent of water in aquarelles). In fact, each brush stroke must often be the result of much deliberation, then on the palette trial and re-mix. 'But it takes so long!' I said in amazement to Townsend. He nodded: he knew well.

I now realized, too, how necessary it is to pay more attention to the planning of the composition. Then having spent several days blocking in my new range of colours, I discovered so many miscalculations in proportion that it was necessary to turn the canvas upside down and start again from scratch.

Sometimes, during the short 'rests', I circulated among my fellow students to see how they were tackling the subject. I discovered some were abstracts: none were classical-traditional. A young man next to me, reminiscent of my friend Philip Dunn, worked with trembling thrust, putting down small, but incredibly sensitive little point strokes. His brushes hovered like butterflies' antennae, then wove the most delicate webs upon the canvas, preparatory to his finding his way about the project. I wondered how I had been able, in the past years, to get away with such slapdash attempts. Although far from happy in my use of oil paint, each day seemed to bring me a little less fear of the new medium.

Although I am diffident at hobnobbing indiscriminately with the students, I feel I am imbibing their muted chatter and realizing a little how different the newest generation is from my own. They are so absorbed in the problems they have set themselves that only occasionally do they surface to the realms of everyday events. Only rarely do they discuss such things as holidays abroad, the pictures they saw in museums, and how they were put up for the night by some monks in a monastery, etc.

Being surrounded by folk so much younger than myself makes me realize, with amazement, that I really am now an elderly person. No matter what I may feel (and I suppose I kid myself for much of the time that I'm still a 'bright young thing'), the fact remains that nearly fifty years have passed since my birth, while many of these students were mere boys at the beginning of the last war. No matter what I imagine about myself, these youngsters know that I am a very different person from them; this is something I have got to face. I realize how much more realistic the younger students are in respect to formal manners and artificial conventions. When needs be, they are ruthlessly critical and unsentimental, yet deep and sincere is their respect for those whose work they admire.

Suddenly a young man of twenty-three (whom I am beginning to think of as a contemporary) said to me: 'You don't know what you mean to our generation. You stand for all the gaiety and exuberance' (these not his words — I forget his) 'of a period that seems so utterly remote to us: the personification of a life that we all admire.' I was surprised. I had thought of myself only in private terms — coping with my own difficulties, never thinking that maybe others were conscious of the results of my previous efforts. I found it easy to talk to this young man, and extremely interesting to hear his views on contemporary painters such as Lucian Freud and Francis Bacon. ('Yes, I can answer that — I've thought a lot about that one,' he said, when I asked why he thought Francis had such an influence on the younger generation. Answer: 'They've had aesthetics, sensitivity, but never before a breaking down of all the rules and associations, a revolution in accepted creeds and standards of painting.') I was somewhat abashed when he said: 'Why, you must have known all the painters.

What sort of a man was Bonnard?' It was as if he had asked 'What was Leonardo really like?'

But most shocks are apt to do one good, and this is being an experience on a big scale. In throwing away much of one's former technique — in, so to speak, emptying the old barrel — there is the danger of not being able to fill up another. There is also, for me, the slight anxiety that, for some extraneous reason, I may be unable to go on with this course and have to quit before these new impressions are allowed to sink in. However, while it lasts it is fascinating to watch at close quarters a young and fresh world.

Yes, definitely I am beginning to feel a little less irritated with the medium of oil paint — even to take it more for granted. I now have learnt that, when I dislike any particular patch of paint, it is nearly always as a result of my having applied it without conscious thought. I discover that other students also become irritated with the passages of their work that remind them of all that they most detest. Although for several days I felt my thumb had gone permanently to sleep through holding the heavy wooden palette for many hours on end, and my arm trembles when, at last, I put it down, I am not tired by standing and my arm can sustain the brush at canvas distance for longer periods. I am again amazed at the strength and resilience of the human body — the most perfect, always-renewing-itself structure ever invented. One of the students, explaining how to get rid of a thickly-coated background, said: 'You rub it very hard with an old brush; but it's very bad for the brush, so it's better to do it with your fingers.'

At none of its various phases did my painting appear to be 'my own thing'. At one of its best moments, my nude looked as if it *might* have been painted by a lesser Bloomsburyite thirty years ago; but when I roughed in some of the drapery the effect was as if de Glehn, or Rockwell Kent or some long forgotten painters from Art Annuals of my youth still exerted their influence.

The teachers insinuate themselves casually through the rooms, glancing slyly at the easels but never seeming surprised at what they encounter. On the whole, they are far from discouraging. It is obvious that there is a long way to go on my journey towards being a painter, but it was thrilling if any little crumb of encouragement was thrown at me.

The models fascinate me: they are a lot of Narcissi, relishing the stares of their audience by the hour, day, month, and by the year for their lifetime. When Mr Townsend told me: 'Look at that nice piece of colour running from the beautiful curve of the thigh,' our corpulent goddess bridled and pursed her lips even further sideways.

They are an arty tribe, dressing or undressing in the Chelsea manner. They do not appear outraged, or even disappointed, when, having remained poised so patiently, they then take a peek at their portraits! If there is one thing the students have in common it is the cruelty of their attitude towards age. I see a rather good-looking woman of forty, rather like the actress Isobel Jeans, sitting on the podium, with slightly veined hands and the beginnings of a scrawny neck; the students portray her as a heap of wrinkles, bloated sinews, sagging paps, or a maelstrom of decaying fat. One Scots youth in particular is an expert perpetrator of terrible witch-like hags, using the models as only the vaguest excuse for inhuman, even diabolic ruthlessness. His portrait of my pouting 'favourite' was outrageous.

The nude men models are more depressing than the women as they move around in the 'breaks', sadly smoking a pipe, and stumping around, hairy-calfed, in their unlaced leather shoes or boots. They would be improved by a coat of sunlight on their livid, liver-coloured skin. They are also in need of a muscle tone-up, their bellies often sagging into that most dowdy of all garments, the half-empty, sagging sack of grey cotton that Victorians insisted on hanging on a string over the offensive male organs.

The two-week pose is at an end, and, for better or worse, my canvas must remain as it is. It is not at all what I should like to paint, but I have learnt that my agitation about the 'look' and the 'manner' in which I should paint is of secondary importance, and that the main interest should be to put down what one sees in as honest and straightforward a way as possible. The integrity of one's intention will be the gauge of whether or not the picture succeeds.

I am being taught that painting is not a question of colouring, but rather of drawing with paint in the round, so that the more expert one is, the more solid one's canvas becomes. I try to learn that all colours are more or less the same, but their effect is created when put into various juxtapositions with one another. Each brush is meant for a particular stroke and should be chosen with as much care as a golfer selects his clubs. Never once during the painting period is one bored. By discarding invention, by looking with as keen an intensity as possible, I see the truth of Delacroix's 'Nothing is more beautiful than the truth'.

A very serious young Cézanne addict remarked: 'The trouble is that with a five weeks' pose there isn't time to get down even a simple statement. It takes me so long to see the relative values, to show that this solid mass here is going in that direction while this part of the face is sloping towards there, and that that background is at a definite distance from the head.' Yes, it does take time. It took Cézanne years. That's why he couldn't paint real flowers. They were always dead too soon and even the paint went bad, so he resorted to wax apples, and when his dealer said: 'Why can't you just fill in that space of empty canvas that you've left? It's so unfinished,' Cézanne replied: 'Well, it's a risk, because if I filled it in with the wrong colour I'd have to reconsider the whole picture, possibly repaint it, and that would mean another one hundred and forty sittings.'

These young people are in no hurry to make their mark in the world. They know everything takes its measured time: that nothing can be rushed without the results suffering. Even I, during my weeks working here, have taken a broader view of time. Certainly the days have not been wasted — all the telephone calls that might-have-been, would have amounted to little. Even if I secretly know that I will never make a serious painter, and that this tuition may not lead to my painting as I would wish, it has nevertheless already taught me much in the way of appreciating other paintings, and seeing the way in which the 'masters' overcame their problems.

The stages I am passing through are painful: suddenly each day has become a question of dogged application. The surprise element is lacking: I have to concentrate even harder. I am willing to agree that painting is really drawing in colour, and mixing colours to create depth, rather than merely filling in spaces with favoured colours; but how does one achieve this?

It was a hard, depressing week, and I began to wonder whether I am not being rather silly in trying to tackle a life's job in a few snatched months — and those probably much too late in my day.

November

The weeks fly by with only the progress of one's canvas to give indication of their passage. I am completely absorbed. So it is everywhere in this building, where a continual growth is burgeoning and students are demonstrating their particular urge to express themselves in front of a dahlia, a crucifixion or an abstract design. Some are involved in the processes of engraving and lithography; while would-be sculptors are covered with plaster and white powder.

One work shown in an exhibition of the students' holiday pictures, was particularly original and strange. It was painted by a woman who had, three years before, been the cook to a Cambridge professor. One day after cutting the professor's lunchtime cabbage, she painted it before boiling it. The professor thought her picture so remarkable that he encouraged her to do more painting, then sent her work to the Slade where she has since been producing pictures of tremendous authority and energy. She now knows that painting rather than cooking is her life's work. Magnanimous of professor.

On Monday mornings I approach my work with a certain freshness and eagerness. I was surprised when told that I was painting with more assurance — that the work was an advance.

Of the various professors who give of their advice Tom Monnington is, to me, the most lively and spirited. He never buoys one up falsely or makes one feel the problems are less than they are, but his rorty humour is exhilarating. Moreover, he did me one particular service. When I complained that

Eggie Hine's ghost still haunted me, Monnington gave me a new range of colours. He suggested that I limit my palette to four colours — excluding blue — and I discovered, with surprise, how refreshing and effective it was to work within these limitations. Incidentally, it was quite a revelation to discover that viridian and crimson, when mixed together, make a luminous grey which Vandyke used for his face shadows.

It is a bit depressing to notice that the other students are nearly all working towards a result that is to be exactly the same as their earlier canvas. Of course it would be ridiculous if one week they were to do an imitation Coldstream, another a homage to Rouault or a fake Miro, but it is rather alarming to come to the conclusion that, whatever one's intentions may have been, the paint and brushes so often carry one along with them to a predestined end. As for my own canvases they are all sadly similar; none of them are anything like my intentions, and far from what I admire. I am told that the progress is a natural one, and that I am allowing myself to see nature and draw from her rather than come with some preconceived idea to the canvas.

Started on a head — an easy job compared to last week's elaborate composition. I tried to see the face in the round so that a fly crawling over it would know it was not flat and would have to hop over its various surfaces. I would not have imagined it possible to spend two weeks on a face. But at the end of the first week there was still a tremendous way to go before the painting would be taken to its ultimate conclusion. One old professor, no doubt in an effort to encourage me, said: 'Yes, yes, you have a distinct talent for getting a likeness. After all, this is a rare enough gift. You should do well in the line of portraiture among your friends.'

At last the hot range of the late Eggie Hines's colours has been jettisoned. Raw sienna is seldom squeezed onto the palette, and the skin-tones seem to be positively opal-like. Perhaps the question of 'taste' and 'point of view' will develop further when technique is more fully and easily mastered.

After these weeks I have perhaps gleaned a bit through my ears, but not enough through my eyes or with my mind. Professor Rogers remarked that I had not simplified a face enough, that I had put in too many shadows and that those that were darkest were unreasonably so. 'That face is a pale mass against a dark background. Now I'm going to do a cad's trick,' and he painted a white layer all over the face. The picture never recovered, but it was an effective way of bringing to my mind the important fact of simplification. (In my drawings, caricatures and other painting media I am quite adept at the knack of omission.)

Claude Rogers spent an hour and a half doing a rough sketch for me of the old Austrian gentleman who is my current model. It amazes me that such a slight sketch can have taken more than ten minutes; but I begin slowly to realize that, unless one paints with a preconceived idea, if one does observe carefully, then necessarily it must take this time. It is being borne in on me, over and over again, that I am trying to work much too quickly. I put down a dab of colour I know is not right, intending to alter it at some future date. (It is extraordinary how one's technique in different media has an affinity: I do just this sort of thing when writing.)

The dark, foggy days haven't helped. My sitter, the fat, old, grey-suited Viennese, is ill and obviously finds sitting with his hands folded over his vast stomach is a strain. I feel an urge to play hookey, and go downstairs to the life class to draw from the nude; but when one is in a mood to concentrate on the exigencies of oil it is difficult to switch to pencil, and my recent drawings have lost much of their former assurance.

Nevertheless, in spite of momentary gloom, these last months have brought lasting benefits.

December 13th

The term is suddenly over. When I took Coldstream out to lunch he asked me if I felt 'it was beginning to work'. I had to admit that I didn't think it was. Perhaps it was not to be wondered that I haven't yet begun to master the medium: it really needs another year or so of hard perseverance. Coldstream said: 'The other students come to us every day for three years!' Nevertheless, the big, rousing shock has been to realize what a serious business it is! There are no alibis, and even if one thinks it possible to avoid a hurdle, one is soon found out trying to by-pass it.

Someone said of Voltaire that he always worked as if he had to begin to make his reputation. Even if one should ever reach the stage when one feels one has learnt about processes and methods, one can still know nothing about art.

LADY BINGHAM

In the Underground, on the way to the Slade, I happened to notice in *The Times* that yesterday the Hon. Lady Bingham had been buried. What a name from the past! Another quickly vanishing link with 'Edwardian Society' broken.

Lady Cecil Bingham, as she used to be known, was an American who married twice, and whose visual parakeet features, and wistful, pale blue eyes, stared out from the pages of weekly magazines under a large Leghorn shepherdess plate loaded with full-budded roses. She had, I believe, a sister named Grace, Lady Newborough, a handsome Boadicea with a blunt, wooden profile who, in her vast Gainsborough hat, her bust so proudly offered to the waves, was the prize-winning bore wherever she sailed. No bore Lady Bingham. At any rate, she always looked as if she was the belle of every gathering, a gamecock, having the time of her long life.

As the years advanced, the earlier prettiness gave way to a 'woman of the world' smartness, and her gown was of draped, twisted gold brocade, and her waved hair dressed high, wide and handsome. When I was old enough to savour the outer periphery of grown-up society, Lady Bingham was past middle age. Her complexion was of the most dazzling pearly whiteness; but the hair, once a golden Edwardian brioche, had become shingled and fluffy, the nose more parroty, the cheeks rouged in an exaggerated lobster-pink that we seldom see, and the scarlet fingernails created an appearance that verged on wit. She wore tubular shifts of jewel-encrusted, pale-gold lamée, with always a wisp of tulle or chiffon to bind her to an earlier period. She managed to combine the flamboyancy of the Edwardian age with the chic of the twenties. There was something wonderfully rich and pampered about her appearance: she seemed to make winter velvet more darkly sumptuous and face powder more feminine and alluring. Her bird-like impression was reinforced by the feathers that she always wore: the paradise plume waving from her head, or the large ostrich-feather fan she carried as she danced. Her small feet and ankles were extraordinarily brittle.

On the ballroom floor she gave the impression that, not only was she having a better time than other women, but that her partner, whoever he may have been, was the hero of the evening — or so it appeared to this onlooker. Nora Phipps used to give a wicked imitation of Lady Bingham at a ball in later years. One saw her smile with the lowered lids, the panache of feathers flying, the jerky movements of the head as she frolicked through the dances; but what one didn't notice was that the game old fighting cock's feet had given way, and that she was dancing on her over-turned ankles.

I was impressed by Lady Bingham's dazzling worldliness and her aura of success. Obviously she seemed to be at every party and race meeting, and surely there was never a shooting weekend at which she and her maid were not present. Yet, although I admired her, and was amused by her, from a distance, I did not wish to know her. She was too good at the worldly game for me — too formidable. Before it was the practice for ladies to become shopkeepers, Lady Bingham started a hat shop in North Audley Street which she named after Marie Antoinette's milliner, Rose Bertin. Perhaps Lady Bingham's hats did not prove a financial success; but they gave her the opportunity to appear in different headgear three or four times a day, and her business did not prevent her making her weekend visits.

It seems that one Monday morning Lady Bingham and her maid were returning by train from Wilton House where they had been staying with the Pembrokes. The maid, with the luggage, sat in a third-class compartment while her mistress travelled first. A few moments after the train left Salisbury station Lady Bingham wished that her maid was also travelling first class, or that it was not too late for her to change carriages. She was sitting in a compartment with a somewhat peculiar-looking man in front of her. He kept staring at her. The train service from Salisbury to London is excellent with only one stop, and this, inexplicably, at Vauxhall — only ten minutes away from its destination, Waterloo.

Lady Bingham prayed that the stranger opposite would take his eyes off her, but he wouldn't. Lady B's nervousness manifested itself by her bringing out her compact and making up her face which, of course, needed no such attention. She powdered liberally the parrot nose, rouged the lobster-malmaison cheeks, applied the brilliant lipstick, dusted the eyelids with blue, adjusted the spotted veil that swathed the turban trimmed with a firework display of cockfeathers. Lady Bingham once more threw a quick glance in the direction of the stranger. To her horror she heard him say: 'Take off that veil.' Lady Bingham, too terrified to pull the communication cord, or remonstrate in any way, obeyed the instruction. 'Now take off that hat.' With painted, trembling fingers Lady Bingham obeyed as the man's eyes continued to devour her. Lady Bingham, white as death under the rouge, did as she was bid. In fact, Lady Bingham permitted herself the humiliation of carrying out to the letter the madman's instructions to take off her overcoat, then her coat and waistcoat (she was wearing a smart *tailleur*), and now the blouse and next the skirt, now the petticoat, now the camiknickers, now the corset, the brassiere, and then the smart patent leather, high, red-heeled, buckled shoes. When the terrified nude was revealed in all her pearly beauty, the madman pointed aloft and commanded her to get up onto the luggage rack. With one arm closely guarding the communication cord, with the other the stranger helped the poor lady up into the required position. 'Now don't move from there,' the stranger commanded.

The train rushed on, past Andover, Basingstoke, on and on, louder and faster to Woking, while Lady Bingham lay on the rack with her admiring audience below. Each time Lady Bingham, during the hour and a half journey, wished to turn her body, her captor barked: 'Don't move!' Lady B, frightened, cold and stiff, could only do as she was bid. At last the train drew into Vauxhall; the stranger had reached his destination. He leapt blithely to the platform, through the window blew a kiss of adieu to Lady Bingham, and vanished from sight. The train started again, and Lady Bingham clambered stiffly down from her perch. Perhaps she would just have time to dress before arrival at Waterloo. Lady Bingham put on the brassiere, the corsets and underclothes, the stockings, the suit, the sable stole, the hat, and the veil. By this time the train was curving into its berth and to Lady B's safety.

On arrival at Waterloo, Lady Bingham's well-trained maid appeared at the window of her ladyship's carriage to greet her with the accustomed inquiry: 'Did you enjoy the journey, my lady?' For once, perhaps in her whole lifetime, the worldly-wise Lady Bingham was baffled. She did not know how to answer. Would her respectable maid believe her story? Would anyone believe it? Yet the proof of her terrible experience was not one that she would too readily exhibit to the public, for it consisted of the fact that, for some days to come, her body was like that of a harlequin, diamond patterned, where the cords of the luggage rack had eaten into her pearly flesh. So Lady Bingham did not reply to her maid, who considered her ladyship's behaviour unaccountably tetchy and offhand.

As I say, I never once met Lady Bingham, although we were photographed together in a small group at some fancy dress ball given by Count Frankenstein at the Austrian Embassy. However, several years later, when I was being baked in an electric bath at Miss McInnes' Health Emporium, I listened to some jolly good sort entertaining the nurses in the cubicle next to me. The voice was deep and rorty: it might have been that of a racy old colonel. But no — I was told it was that of Lady Bingham who was provoking peals of laughter as she lay being massaged. I, too, was fascinated as I tried to listen, for here was someone with a conviction of manner that is only to be found in the tried and true — a quality that is rare today. It was impossible to hear through the walls what the deep voice was saying. Perhaps she was now relating a funny story of her railway journey to Vauxhall.

I wondered how Lady B had managed to survive the war, and these difficult, different years that have come since. The world that she belonged to has almost entirely disappeared. I could not imagine Lady B in the kitchenette-dinette, open-your-own-tinned-food, and watch-the-telly world.

The notice of her funeral gave me a little twinge of regret for the past; but it was short-lived because my Underground train had arrived at Euston Square.

REDDISH: AUNT CADA

1953

After a morning that had been a continuation of the weeks of downpour the afternoon was unexpectedly sunny. I felt so fugged up in my country bedroom, where I'd been pampering a cold for the last few days, that I decided, if well wrapped up in a heavy overcoat, it would be a change to go out into the garden to survey the wintry scene. Only a thin veiling of leaves remained on most of the elms, but a haze of autumn orange coloured the distance. The light was clear and beautiful, but it couldn't last long: the afternoons being so short now, and ominous, inky-blue clouds lowering nearer. While standing on the top of the hill for a few extra moments, the cat came and made a fuss of me; then together we returned indoors and upstairs again to my bedroom. Agnes, the dear old fusspot, cosseted me with hot-water bottles, and I was about to settle down to a self-indulgent, unnecessary sleep when the telephone rang. I didn't sleep after that: Bertie Watson, an acquaintance of mine but a loyal and devoted friend of my cousin Tecia, was telling me of the tragedy that had struck my one remaining aunt.

Since Jessie's death the youngest daughter Cada was the only survivor of my mother's five sisters. Perhaps of all she was the most sweetly sympathetic with her bird-like aquiline features and her love of music; in fact, she was the one interested in the arts. As a boy I loved visiting her when she was living in the Midlands. She had married Dick Chattock, a brilliant electrical engineer who was responsible for lighting and heating the vast metropolis of Birmingham. Their house was on the outskirts of the town, but within motoring distance of Broadway and other beauty spots where we would visit the antique shops with the air of connoisseurs.

My dear Aunt Cada was full of enthusiasm for the beauty of the Warwickshire countryside, and when she rented some small cottage for a springtime holiday, she gave me my first journey on a ferry pulled across the River Severn by a huge chain, glimpses of apple orchards, grey stone walls of the ruined castle and the peacocks at Arley. Here, in her small attic room above the cottage porch, I made a theatre out of a hat-box. My aunt and her daughters, Tecia and Tess, encouraged me to put on a musical comedy with scenery as full of blossom as the neighbouring orchards. But I could not provide an adequate script to go with the elaborate changes of scenes and personages painted and cut from *The Play Pictorial*, so I spent the early evenings at the edge of a neighbouring wood watching the rabbits come out to sniff the air.

All the Chattocks seemed more histrionic than my own family. Cada's father-in-law had been a solicitor, but also a professional draughtsman, and his etchings of winter landscapes, a sort of Atkinson Grimshaw of the etcher's knife, were represented in many museums. Cada's husband was a pianist and accompanied family friends such as Frank Titterton and Olga Haley. The sprawling and ugly Chattock house was alive with strange atmospheric currents that were exhilarating to me.

Tecia and Tess were called upon to perform, to recite, to dance, or play the piano. Dressed in blue satin cloaks they were taken by hansom cab every week to dancing classes and each time they wondered what pretty Marigold Bond would wear. It was nothing for Marigold, at the age of seven, to appear dashingly attired in a black lace dress with emerald sash and black satin shoes and an emerald-green headache band adorning her jet-black hair. My cousins were both solo dancers at the charity galas given at the old Alexandra Theatre, but they were willing attendants on little Eileen Bird, with her mop of golden orange curls, who was the Fairy Queen. Eileen's blue iridescence as a dragonfly was as unforgettable as Pavlova.

The whole Chattock family was always acting charades and enjoyed dressing up. Fancy dress parties were numerous, but each taken seriously. My Aunt Cada scored her greatest success at an annual Electrical Ball dressed as a porcelain shepherdess with crook, panniers garlanded with rosebuds, beauty spots, and a pink powdered wig. The day after each costume-ball the dressing up had to be repeated for Miss Clara Cooper who was the extremely picturesque photographer working in the neighbourhood.

As a final *bonne bouche* to every visit, my aunt took my brother and me to Stratford or Birmingham to see plays, ranging from *The Farmer's Wife* to *Stop Flirting*, which were either going to London or had just finished their West End run. Barry Jackson was the Diaghilev of the Birmingham Repertory, and he was responsible for making interesting experimental productions including the excessively neo-romantic opera, Rutland Boughton's *The Immortal Hour*. My Aunt Cada became great friends with Barry Jackson, and went to rehearsals and 'first nights'. When she took me to see Gwen Frangçon-Davies in medieval silver singing 'How Beautiful They Are The Lordly Ones', Birmingham seemed the Mecca of culture. Barry Jackson, a bachelor, started the Malvern Festival, and soon my aunt became his unofficial hostess — detailed to look after such personages as Edward Elgar, Cyril Scott and Percy Grainger. With quite difficult people she behaved with such extreme tact and charm that she had discovered her 'forte', and Barry relied upon her to soothe ruffled egos and professional jealousies. Of the guests, who included such other disparate personalities as Dean Inge, Harriet Cohen and Wee Georgie Wood, she found Bernard Shaw the most difficult. The guests were housed in a large mansion that, during term-time, was inhabited by a girls' school. Bernard Shaw was invariably awake at dawn and would insist on disturbing the others at six in the morning. My Aunt Cada may have entertained a secret love for Barry, and she became extremely angry when Harriet Cohen, at dinner placed *au bout de table*, sent messages to her host written on the petals of the magnolia grandiflora my aunt had placed on the refectory table. Aunt Cada became a widow and decided to live in London; but she kept up with all her old Birmingham cronies and filled her flat with newly-acquired music lovers.

Being away in the States for such long stretches, I saw but little of my Aunt Cada; but whenever she came to stay with me in the country I loved her appreciation of my garden and her wide bucolic interests. However, I had not seen her for some months, and though I had heard that she had been lately in poor health, it was not anything to worry about for Aunt Cada had, ever since a young girl, been considered the delicate one of the family. At various times almost all of her insides had been cut out, but she had developed into a strong stayer and would, no doubt, live to a very great age.

However, it now appeared that, last Friday, she had been taking a stroll down an avenue of chestnuts admiring the brilliance of their flaming colours, when suddenly she realized she could see with only one eye. She returned quickly to her house and soon after, lying on a sofa, found that the sight had gone from the other eye. The doctors pronounced that she had become totally blind, and there was now little hope of recovery.

As I listened on the telephone to this terrible tale, Agnes, lingering by my bedroom door, made extraordinary recoiling gestures of pure horror as she heard me moan. My mind became over-filled with pictures of Cada's agony. How could she possibly, in her late sixties, be brave enough to start life over again with this appalling disadvantage? Where could she find the resources to fight such stark cruelty?

I telephoned to my cousin Tecia but she was out, so I heard a touching account from the family companion of how brave my Aunt Cada was being; but of how the experience was almost more shattering for Tecia though neither she nor the companion dare show their feelings for fear of further upsetting my aunt. Then Tecia returned from a village shopping expedition to get provisions for the household, and my heart broke to hear her tell in such lucid, unsentimental and medical terms of how the arteries to the eyes had hardened so that the blood had ceased to flow to them: how it was like a curtain coming down first over one eye, then over the other. I do not know how most women find it within themselves to contain sorrow with such restraint; yet, although this disaster had struck the person whom, more than anyone on earth, she loves, respects and admires, Tecia was able to advise me how best to break the news to my mother.

By the evening I had told my sisters the awful story, and then had to face my mother, who was suffering from a weak heart and to whom any shock was dangerous. I was a bit dithery; impossible to relate the full horror: I admitted only that the sight had gone from one eye. Even so, Mummie was indeed distressed and said solemnly: 'This is bad news.' Later, when my mother telephoned for a first-hand report, Tecia was able still to treat her to a fine performance of kindness, tact, consideration and commiseration. She told only what she knew would be advisable: she showed extraordinary fortitude.

Not so me. I wept to myself most of the evening and went to bed early hoping to drown sorrow in sleep. I dozed, but my dreams about Cada's blindness were vivid and ghastly. I woke with a jolt. Those who know about such things say that blindness is preferable to deafness — that those who cannot hear become suspicious and miserable while those that have no sight are often happy people. Blind people are loved, and they provoke others to be kind and helpful to them, while the deaf are not treated with such sympathy. I know that if I had to be faced with such an appalling alternative, I would choose rather to be deaf. I am conscious this would be a proven mistake, but

I cannot imagine a more horrifying fate than to have to founder helplessly in darkness. I dreamt of stumbling in space, and falling for ever — down — down.

It was a relief from continued nightmares when Agnes brought the tray of breakfast and drew the curtains to let in the early morning light. But I knew there would not be that balm for my enchanting Aunt Cada.

Weeks later, when I went to call upon my aunt in a nursing home, I found her appearance small and shrunken. She seemed so utterly pathetic that I felt myself choking with a solid gob in the throat. But if she could wear a sweet smile on her face as she lay among the pillows, surely I could summon up some little vestige of courage and cheerfulness?

By degrees, the inevitable was accepted. The tragedy of blindness was alleviated by the doctors' comfort of hope that perhaps, one day, a fraction of eyesight would be restored. This gave Cada the strength to feel that her long period of darkness was sent as a test and trial, and that, in the meantime, there was still music, and so much to be enjoyed during the remainder of her life.

After five months Cada was well enough to visit me at Broadchalke. For my mother and myself, we could not have had a nicer treat for Easter. We had been looking forward to her arrival, and were excited when Tecia brought her by train, to be met by Mummie and bandy-legged Mr Gould.

I saw the little family group of happy, shining faces sitting on garden chairs in the sunlight. Everyone was cheerful and laughing a lot: I, too, laughed and added a word or two to the general gaiety; but when I saw my poor aunt being directed indoors, I looked, transfixed. She was staggering helplessly, and floundering clumsily, like a child lost in a black world of briars.

She was totally dependent on others ministering to her slightest need. One's sense of pity was stirred to the depths, but one's curiosity is so horrible that one watched with ghoulish interest to see how someone without sight does behave. At meals particularly I could not help looking with an avid interest to see how she could cope with all the simple, elementary things that one learnt as a child, and which now have become an insuperable problem. There is something painful and positively dreadful about an elderly woman with a plate of food in front of her, not knowing how to set about eating it. Fate plays such nasty little tricks when, for example, the blind person lifts a spoon to her lips and finds it is empty, or perhaps little morsels of food escape onto her plate from the spoon, or a thin piece of toast, larger than expected and brittle, falls in half. Cada feels sensitive about eating messily and is ashamed, like a child, when the crumbs drop onto her dress. Yet she eats so delicately, with hands that have become much smaller and more pointed.

When she is being conducted about the house, taken upstairs, brought to the table, or taken up to bed, it is harrowing to see the completely lost expression of her body. A frightened little smile hovers on the mouth, the eyes are wide and wistful. But the whole figure is out of context; it is not someone moving through space — it is someone out of life.

Aunt Cada is an exceptional person. Her gaiety and enjoyment of life have always been her greatest gifts so that, perhaps, she is better equipped than most to master this catastrophe. Although the world is black to her, she is still able to hear the sounds of the birds, news of friends, and human stories. Her spirits do not appear to be low. She tells us that she has never felt so intensely alive to all the enjoyments of the scents of the posies of flowers she is handed, but to which her imagination supplies the form and colour. She fondles a leaf that has just broken out of its bud. She describes how she has developed an extra sense of tread, and how she is acutely aware of the various textures of grass, path, carpet or gravel over which she is walking. She praises the wonders that charity does for the blind with lending libraries in braille, all sorts of special gramophone records, and how everyone should give money for radios for the blind since the programmes bring so much enjoyment. Never a complaint, but continual gratitude for the swiftness with which her doctors acted on her behalf.

After a time in her company one is apt to forget that she is unlike the rest of us. She still uses her eyes as if they could see, she turns her head this way and that, she throws back her head when she laughs, and she makes us laugh with silly stories of her affliction that have amused her. Then one notices a little claw-like hand floundering.

By degrees, we begin to despair at the long-delayed improvement in Cada's eyesight. We secretly wonder if the doctors are merely trying to keep us buoyed up on a fallacy. But not Cada. Her faith is strong enough to convince her that soon she will be well again. If she has her moments of being depressed, she will try to hide them from others. She is a lesson in courage and a solace to us. Terrible, agonizing, diabolical as this is, it is comforting to see that when tragedy happens, the human spirit can remain strong enough to overcome: that if the worst does happen, life is still not only bearable, but also can be sweet.[10]

---

[10] Aunt Cada never recovered her eyesight. She died in 1970.

Part VII: A Trip for a Lecture Tour, 1954

ARRIVAL ON MANHATTAN

1953-4

Instead of some business firm paying my passage over, as is generally arranged, I was this year under my own steam. As the fares on the *United States* are less than on the big 'Queens', a slight economy turned out to be a pleasant experience. The atmosphere of the ship is very easy, and the absence of the usual faces (Lord Bamby, Harriet Cohen, etc.) a relief. The nicest fellow-passengers were museum curators coming over to the Metropolitan. But I talked to few people and was absorbed in my books. I read almost non-stop, and managed to finish Duff Cooper's wonderful *Old Men Forget*, then on to the nostalgic charm of Lesley Hartley's *The Go-Between*, a Colette, a rather poor account of the extraordinary Mizner family, and Paddy Leigh Fermor's *The Violins of Saint Jacques*. I took quick looks at Hobson on the theatre, and Virginia Woolf, disappointingly self-centred, snobbish, disapproving and bitter on herself.

As we passed the Statue of Liberty, and were escorted by tugs to our berth, the usual game of 'grandmother's steps' took place in the lounge as we waited to put a step forward towards the Immigration Officials' desk. During the war so many dramas were played out at the boundaries of various countries that some of the terror remains, and the clip of a steel gadget and the bang of a rubber stamp still haunt one with a little dread. I expected to be asked if I intended to liquidate the President, and had I ever been a Communist or indulged in moral turpitude, when, to my surprise, on handing my passport to the tough-looking man with close-cropped hair and a chest decorated with silver badges, he said: 'Well, first of all, Mr Beaton, I want to tell you how much I've enjoyed your décors for ballets. Whenever your name is on a programme I know it will maintain a high standard. And for your information, Mr Beaton, you must go and see a most interesting experimental play which has just come on: *In the Summer House* by Jane Bowles. It has received controversial notices, but you must see it — and soon — because it may not run too long. It is really one of the most interesting plays we've had — very poetic and strange, and a real addition to the theatre.'

Kind and considerate and faithful as ever, Mr Sirest of the Condé-Nast publications travel department came to meet me on the docks and escorted me through the Customs in record time. Before I knew it, I was back at the hotel telephoning friends and exchanging news. And what news! Little Truman Capote had had to fly from Paris as his mother killed herself by taking an overdose of sleeping pills. Many other friends had died suddenly, but to me the most shocking of all was Duff Cooper's death. While I had been filling my mind with him and his book on board ship — a wonderful document — he had died at sea on a slow boat *en route* to Jamaica. Duff must have known he would die: his life was rounded, fulfilled. A perfectly satisfied, contented man, he had always had good luck, and he died the way he wanted — with no protracted suffering.

Duff had always made me feel inferior: he knew so much more than I did even about my own subjects. However much he tried, he could not help making me shy; but I was comforted that he liked me and admired many of my characteristics. He said I had guts. As for me, I was fond of him not only because of Diana, but also because of his special excellence, his quality, his extraordinary intelligence.

All Diana's fears and anxieties were now a reality. The thing she had dreaded for so many hours each day for so many years had, in fact, happened. I wondered how she could have the strength to live without her Duffie. Everything she had done was for him. A little while later a letter arrived from her on her way to Greece. Here is part of it:

This poor old smoking torch is passed on from hand to hand by these friends of gold and steel ... I suppose that the weary nomad evading, evading real emptiness will have to face it at Chantilly in April — early April. They'll assemble, these wondrous, surprising friends of Duff's & mine & light the candles & make a clamour for me. Will you be there? I told you I would write it all — this thing so obsessedly dreaded, because you are away & because as you said in your beautiful letter you knew Duff was very fond of you.

It was like this. We said for years we'd go to the W. Indies ... so with a formidable lot of pull — zestless really — we got the impossible — a suite on a ship called Colombe. *It sailed Jan. 30th & we left a very reduced Christmas party at Vaynol to board it at Southampton. No you, no David, no Simon — no Juliet — but it was happy enough — all Duff's presents were from Dior down to my work bag, & he seemed so happy & alert. In the shortness was the sadness, but in all everyone was happy but me, for I, of course, was agonized listening to Duff's cough — a bad one just inherited from a cold — estimating the colour of his dear face, the thickness or slimness of his ankles etc. These things always, but more especially since his illness in the Spring, were heavy on me as Christian's Burden.*

Southampton was cold; it was 11 p.m. ... luggage muddled, porters confused, tearing wind & rain; at last things sorted themselves and we boarded the ship to be greeted V.I.P.-wise; Shipping Line authorities,

pursers, captains ... a nice cabin, changed on arrival to the finest suite —
& Duff thro' the melee saying 'get rid of them all I feel rather sick'. I did
what was necessary & darted into a Loo where my bowels turned to
water, for the words were a knell. He said no, no, it was cold on the quay
— it would be alright. I beseeched him to chuck it all — it might be
recurrence of the spring's attack — who cared about the trip? Get off —
get off. 'No, no. No possible hotel in Southampton, luggage on board, too
late to change' (inelasticity of men). Then he was sick — we had not
started — and I saw in the result of vomiting no resemblance to the great
dread — yet still I begged. 'If it's another attack we'll be better on a boat
— quiet for three weeks.' Duff always had the sea in his heart. So I
resigned myself as the siren screamed and off we went S.E. into the
Atlantic — 'take a big sweep to avoid the bay' — & so into a child's
sleep for Duff & a drugged one for me.

Before leaving, always troubling, I had asked Dr Varay — a highly
thought of Doctor & friend — what to take as precaution & for crisis.
He had prescribed & I had bought — but his prescription added for my
benefit 'I do not expect any recurrence'. Thus equipped with the first aids I
went before sleeping to alert the ship's doctor. (I think he did his best, poor
man — it's all I can say, great doctors don't go to sea.)

For years, if you are like me, you have to beware of asking every 3
minutes how people are — if you love them. So I postponed as long as ever
I could from fear — fear of irritation — the fearful question. 'Not really
right,' Duff answered, & at noon it happened — a rush to the bathroom
& a bigger redder haemorrhage than he had before. 'Poor child,' he said,
'you said you couldn't go thro' it again.' I regretted then so often having
whined if Duff drunk so much as an extra glass of red wine. 'Please not,
I can't go thro' it again' (not that I think drink had much to do with it
all). I tore off to the Doctor — the ship was dressing itself up for the
Reveillon. He came & gave morphia as directed & injected the drug
(usual French patent, not really corresponding with prescription, it never
does) which I suppose was a coagulate of the blood. From this moment —

and contrary to expectation — what expectation — I became immensely calm & executive. I recognized this calm as a fatal sign, superstitiously, in fact, I think from the moment when I lost my way & found it at last to the Radiograph room I knew hope was over — hence the calm — it's hope that makes one hysterical. So in the Radio room I sent a message to Eden asking his influence at Madrid — for our first landing was at Vigo, a kind of Anglesey without the Irish link — another to John Julius to tell him his father was gravely ill & to follow Eden up — to which I got the darling typical reply 'Don't worry etc...' (I'd asked for it by fears of panic) — to Paris asking for a plane from SHAPE or the Embassy — and to Madrid asking for nurse & blood of Duff's kind & help generally.

Back in the cabin Duff white as a sheet was being sick every 2 hours — rather doped & desperately weak — his trouble, & I can hardly think of it now, was torturing thirst — he was allowed no water for the bleeding had to stop & I could only give him drops on my fingers, & he said once 'It's you, the others would give it me.' More sickness, more weakness & whiteness. There was the doctor, & a sort of jolly Bellocian old 'Infirmier' — jocund & an optimist. He was allowed to stay with me in this fine double cabin. New drugs were tried but the sickness continued. 'La mer est contre nous,' said the Doctor as the ship rolled, not in storm but in big swell. Duff never was sea-sick, but the sea's motion has an effect on stomachs as we know, & immobility is essential for staunching blood.

The day died — night grew — no one showed *anxiety. I don't suppose I did, except when I said to the old optimist,* 'J'ai peur, j'ai peur.' 'Peur de quoi?' *he asked, roundeyed with surprise.* 'Peur de la mort,' *I said. This was greeted by hoots of laughter.* 'Mais il n'y pas question, Madame.' *So that when about then in the night Duff said to me in a semi-doped way, 'Do they think I am going to die?' more calmly than he would have said 'Is dinner ready?' I said — & this is important because he had always said (never as a request to me for he knew it would have been perhaps useless — certainly destroyingly upsetting) that he would like to know when he was dying — I said, 'My darling, I have thought it always but I've just asked them and they've laughed me to scorn.' It was true ... true — & I think at that moment (I don't know for sure) if they had told me his end was so close I would have told him.*

In the cabin there were twin beds, & in the other half of this fine double cabin with open quadruple doors there was a bed sofa. The optimist begged me to sleep a little on this sofa while he kept watch awake sitting on the twin bed next to Duff's. I gave in knowing it to be useless, & got into a sort of painful coma to be brought round by the noise of the old brute snoring, stretched hill out on the bed & my darling Duff out of bed, not in his right mind, looking wildly round for me or water, too weak to stand. That was another stab in my mutilated heart. Do you remember that arrested-development maid? She said once in her macabre way when I told her that Freddie Fane, an old friend with a broken thigh, had got out of bed, fracture & all (incidentally so had Gerald du Maurier) 'Les mourants font toujours ça — ça semble qu'ils fuient la mort.' This phrase, like many such, had stuck & back it echoed to endorse my certainty & hopelessness.

Night — dawn, I suppose — morning — more things tried — artificial feeding — a little momentary restlessness — a pulse always rising — the optimist always finding it lower & stronger — more morphine to still movement. In the early hours the sickness stopped, but what was left? Not enough to colour his flesh or to turn his heart into beats; no hope of transfusions of another's blood — the sea still rolling — his breath shorter — no pain — no consciousness.

He faded out like daylight at 3.30 on the afternoon following the haemorrhage's start — New Year's Day at sea. I didn't see him die. They brought in a cylinder of oxygen with some mumble about 'cela c'est pour M. l'Ambassadeur; on ne le donne pas à tout le monde', and clapped a mouth piece up to his poor face which made his most difficult breathing worse. I stopped that quick. Nothing was any good, one could see; nor was another needle the size of a scure which they tried to force into his thigh for feeding the ¾ dead. *The three more doctors and 2 aids all leaning over my Duff looking deeply into his face — I couldn't look — I had never meant to.* I went into the open-doored bathroom and sat in a sort of apathy. I heard them whispering; I don't know for how long it was. The optimist came in & said, 'Venez, Madame.' 'Non, je ne viens pas s'il nest pas conscient. Vous me le dirai si il a un instant de conscience.' 'Mais voyons, il est encore vivant — un peu de courage.' *I couldn't naturally explain. It was not a* 'question de courage'. *I did not want to watch him* unconsciously die. *I greatly hope no one but strangers will watch my last breath. Duff's dying father said 'take the boy away'. Duff was 18. 'It's an unpleasant sight.' I heard no sound tho' I was within 3 yards or less. I dreaded the groans — no sound — he faded like the day & left me the night.*

I did not look at him dead. Does it all seem strange & weak to you? It didn't come under that category at all to me — I who had always anticipated screaming hysteria, off the roof into the sea — anyway the barbiturics found me like the overbombed — numb — but sure, unhesitant — saying to the boring optimist that Duff was to be wrapped in clean sheets, that I wanted his ring, that he should be laid on my bed, that his face should be covered, & the doors (4 fold) closed. Then came an endless stream, all on the whole helpful. The Captain's condolences but he cannot call before he has docked the ship. The Purser in Person with offers of help — we'll be docked in a few minutes — would I like anything? a cup of tea. No, I'd like some brandy. It came — a thimble — quickly followed by a bill, & a grown man saying he couldn't leave without his money — I saying I'd got no money, it was in the room where my dead husband was being prepared for the tomb. 'Mais c'est très ennuyeux pour moi, Madame.'

Then we are docked & the Consul, a nice little man called Lindsay, is there with the Ambassador's compliments — what can he do? He's taken already the liberty of ordering a coffin as the news had been radioed. It would be here shortly, meanwhile would I come to the hotel. His wife unfortunately couldn't speak English, but his niece would be my handmaiden who knew both languages. He'd lived 25 years in Vigo & had become a native but saw the Spaniards as he had seen them with Scotch eyes in his youth 'chaps who couldn't get a move on' not realizing he was one of them now. The optimist came to tell me what a good job he had done 'impeccable' repeated ad nauseam. I really ought to look — please — for his own pride. I couldn't explain — but alone I went in the loathed cabin & kissed what I felt was his brow & said 'Goodbye my darling, my darling' & met a very vulgar, helpfully vulgar Spanish coffin — black with any amount of silver bits & crucifixes. I was to get very fond of it only to have it scrapped without my permission by that horrible raqueteer undertaker of London.

Looking back & writing about it all makes me realize that never in my life have I felt more natural — perhaps it's not strange — but I'd imagined a grief stricken woman feeling embarrassed — or savage — or shy — none of these things & I have still this freedom — not that I'd ever much of a cage — then there is the freedom from anxiety & fear — & false hope & cancer & many lesser rubs — of course these liberations don't amount to much but on the credit side of this dreadful account something must be put.

Duff came first to Compostella & was put into this minute 'Dove'; a singularly beautiful pilot said 'I have to tell you the weather could not be worse'. The old Diana came into my throat & I hesitated asking questions about alternative routes — but we were off before the answers were found (there were no alternatives) & as usual the met. man was wrong & we rose high above the clouds into a child's idea of heaven — blue & gold with sun, & cloud carpeted — & dear Duff so peaceful beside me, so fearless.

So there on the runway were all the good dear friends ... & back they bore me ... & I was all right with a strong feeling that Duff was guiding my mind & smiles & Behaviour ... You cannot think, Cecil darling, what they have all been to me, meant to me when I think of the friendless, the D.P.s, the old paupers. I thought, too, really for the first time in my life (& we had long years of happy poverty) how wonderful it was to be able to charter a plane & to have £300 & say 'Come' — but friends cost nothing but love; you'd have been there if you'd been in England, I know — & I was born away to a sort of 2 days wake without the moaning ... A sort of shout of praise went up for Duff. He would have been so triumphantly pleased with it all; pleased with me too, I think — if people can know after death what is happening to the days & people they have so newly left. The crudest pain must be just such a case — that Duff should find me broken by his death — which he himself so little wanted ... Then they all took him to Belvoir which was a carefully thought out arrangement for both Duff & me. I never told him & I never asked Belvoir, but I knew when the day was here they would not refuse.

I did not go. I did not want to hear the clods fall or be the central tragic figure — or court & dodge photographers — but those who went — well I frogged too — Massigli head frog went — said it was wonderful; perhaps when you come back you will come with me & see where I'll lie at last. The chapel is to be admired 1840 — with a marble duchess rising to heaven in empire shroud amid her idealized stillborns; it was snow — covered when Duff was buried & as still as death itself — one man held one candle for the clergyman — & outside one can see the castle they tell me & a fruit tree sheds its petals. John Julius whose faith is that of a child's wrote to me that he went lately to see it & knew Papa was saying 'silly children, I'm not there' — a comforting ring. I think the dear boy sees his father sitting down with every one of his contemporaries dead in the last war plus all the rest that have left since — a White's group 'Let's have another, it can't hurt me now'.

The next day was St Margaret's memorial service — packed as for my wedding. I went, but hidden & couldn't see who was there but for Winston sobbing — & Bobbety who read the lesson, & Bob Boothby who made an oration — but people were moved by it & startled by the British Grenadiers which we got put into the voluntary.

Ali took the old torch most tenderly to Madrid, & then David[11] & Enid[12] carried it on & so to Rome & now to Athens. Then comes the fearful return & the rebuilding of a tail-end — emptying Chantilly — redisposing. I dare not look far or long — then too the numbness of shock & drama has gone — tho' the travel drag still obtains.

Much more to say but too tired now. Night has fallen we must be near Corinth. I wish I need not wake.

Fondest love,

Diana.

NEW YORK: JOHN MYERS

1954

I had contracted to do a lecture tour for a period of over six weeks which would take me throughout the States. This was a somewhat alarming project as it was something I had not before attempted.

The day before setting out I was last minute practising my lecture from the tape records I've made of it. Suddenly John Myers, an old friend, arrived in my room to give me a 'straight talk'. First he asked me to order breakfast for him from room service: grapefruit, eggs, kidneys, bacon, toast, coffee.

'You know I have your welfare very much at heart. I like you, and I feel I'm under a moral obligation to say what I have to say to you. No one wants to be the bearer of ill tidings; but this is really and truly something that, at the risk of being considered awful, I feel I've got to say.'

'Go ahead.'

---

[11] David Herbert.
[12] Enid Bagnold.

'Well, how much do you depend upon photography for your income? I don't mean in figures — but do you rely on it as the main source of your money so that you can live the way you do?'

'Yes, it is my main source of income.'

'Would you mind very much not living in the way you have all this time?'

'Yes. Why?'

'Well, I'm not just spreading gossip. This is factual, and it upset me very much when I heard it.'

'Go ahead. I can take it.'

'Oh, I know you're tough, but this is something that makes me feel quite sick to have to say. Do you mind if I help myself to a drink?' (Whisky — 11.30 a.m.)

'Tell.'

'I'll begin at the beginning. I had a dream about you the other night, and I know enough about Freudian theories to have it upset me considerably. Well, in this dream you fell down a great chute, and I wouldn't have minded that so much. But, the next day, I was with some person at *Harper's Bazaar*, and they didn't know I even knew you, and they were saying: "Oh, have you heard Cecil Beaton's on the skids over at *Vogue*? They say there his work is unpublishable. They don't give him any more pages to do. His attitude is absolutely of the thirties, and he's completely out of touch with life of today. There's only one old dame there — Mrs Chase — who upholds him; otherwise he'd have been out on his ear long ago."'

There was enough truth in this to make my mouth dry.

John went on: 'And they say the editors all hate to work with you — that you're temperamental and throw scenes. Nowadays, you know, everybody is saving their adrenalin and not getting upset so long as they get their pay cheque on a

Friday. Babs Simpson says it's just not worth while working with you. Now, how much would you mind having to give up the world of fashion? Having to live in a loft rather than in these rooms? How much do you want to hold on to what you've got? I mean, how much does it mean to you, living a life of luxury? I mean cutting down a lot. Massage is a very expensive item, for instance. You couldn't have massage.'

(Glumly): 'I can live without massage.'

'Then the ordering of room service — calling in for breakfasts, for example. That all costs money.'

'I could live without breakfast.'

'If you're going to concentrate only on the other things you do like writing and designing and painting then you'll have to give up *all* — but, my dear — *all* luxuries!'

I was not now listening to John so much as casting my mind back to others to whom this thing had happened. The little editors of *Vogue* loved to run around saying: 'Dior's on the rocks. Oh, he's dead and doesn't know it.' 'Dali's old hat.' 'Rawlings, the photographer, is out.' They love crashing their idols to the ground. Now, perhaps, it was my day: the day, like death, that one would rather not face.

There is all the difference in the world between wanting to quit photography, and photography quitting me. Perhaps, without realizing it, I had not been as interested in my photographic work of late. Perhaps I had hoped for time to develop more fully my other talents. Perhaps I had always known that the 'All About Eve' day would come when some other younger men would appear to make my work seem out-of-date. (Yet where were these younger men?) My reliable and understanding friend, Diane Vreeland, had explained things to me by saying, 'Now perhaps you're moving through a subterranean passage, and haven't yet come out to the light —

but you will, Cecil, you will! Mark my words!' But had I perhaps been caught unawares?

My stomach asserted itself as it only does at crises. When I came back into the sitting-room John looked as if he were going to burst into tears. He said he'd like another drink, then he asked if he too could use my bathroom. When he returned he asked: 'Now what do you want to do in life?'

'Go on developing as an artist.'

'But what do you see yourself doing?'

'I'd like to write for the theatre.'

'That's a full-time job, you know. Nothing is achieved without sacrifice. If you want to succeed as a writer you'll have to give all your energies — not just employ your left-over vitality after earning your living. If I were you, I'd keep off the band wagon. The values of the world of fashion are so fleeting and vulgar.'

I asked John if he thought the criticism was true?

'I didn't like your ballet designs for *Tintagel* at the New York City Centre. I think your best work was *Illuminations*. But your recent photographs really haven't meant a thing to me. They haven't carried any new imprint on them for five years. I've not been able to get their essence. Perhaps you haven't allowed yourself enough time to look at what's being done in modern painting and sculpture today. You haven't spent enough time studying and trying to get the feel of what is going on. You never stay in my gallery for longer than to give yourself a cursory glance around. You don't mind these home truths, do you?'

I told John that, far from resenting his frankness, I considered it a friendly, courageous action. For the rest of the day I was deeply preoccupied. Perhaps this shock had come at just the right moment — when I had time to think about it on the tour. Perhaps I would be able, on my return, to put on a superhuman spurt, and then retire of my own will on the crest of a high wave.

Later Greta came in to say *au revoir*. I read her a delightful article about herself, 'Incognita', from the *New Statesman*, in which her name, out of deference to her shyness, was not mentioned. She said, 'How sweet life can be if people behave like that to make it so.'

CHICAGO: IRENE CASTLE

January, 1954

Irene Castle, the dancer, is now sixty-one years old, only a decade older than I am, yet what a profound abyss of time separates her from me. As a day-schoolboy the pages of my notebooks were crammed with drawings of her in her flowing chiffon skirts, with her sensitive legs, bobbed hair and marmoset face. Before the First World War, she and her remarkable husband Vernon, with their entirely original ballroom dancing, had become the quintessence of the fresh and alluring. In the war that changed everything, Vernon had been killed flying, Irene had continued to dance, and her photographs inspired this precocious boy to euphoria. When first I met Irene there seemed to be an irrevocable age-gap so that I could only talk to her in a stilted way. Today I talk to Irene as a contemporary, although I try to make her reminisce about that time from which I was separated by only a short span.

Yes, she admitted, it had been extraordinary to wake up in Paris one morning and discover that, after the opening of last night's club, she and Vernon had become world-famous figures. Yes, it had been wonderful, having previously made her own clothes, to be able to order the best that Paris dressmakers could invent for her. Yes, she had known anyone one could mention from the Prince of Wales to all the great names of Europe and America. Yes, but it had been interesting, too, eventually to give it all up and settle down to other interests. And then, when Hollywood had decided to do a musical film about 'The Castles', with Fred Astaire as Vernon and Ginger Rogers as Irene, she had signed a contract to go out and advise about the clothes. Irene had motored from Chicago with the back of her car filled with albums and photographs of how she had appeared. It is a pity that these exquisite, timeless souvenirs were ignored.

The care and love of animals became Irene's great passion. She has fought vivisection in the face of the greatest hostility and ridicule, and put her well-earned money and enormous energies into an organization where ill-treated dogs, cats and pets could be cared for. At the moment four people work for her to help look after seventeen thousand dogs and cats; during the last years she has befriended three hundred thousand dogs. Each morning at seven she is up feeding the wild birds and her pet squirrels. On an average of at least once a week she is bitten by terrified dogs, but has never been stricken with any side ill-effects.

When I telephoned Irene that I was in Chicago on a lecture tour and had a free evening, she arranged to come in from her village outside the town with her fourth husband — a rather ineffective little German with a baby face — in order to spend six hours with me. We dined at six-thirty to be ready in time for a hockey match where Irene was on terms with everyone. She chewed gum, and conversed in her husky, rather rasping voice, as real chums with a policeman and his wife who, in turn, confided in me: 'You're with swell people tonight.' It seems that this cop helps Irene with tips when she is summoned before a magistrate on some animal case. Irene is convinced that this present rabies scare is a racket dreamed up by the laboratories in order to sell more vaccine. If an injection costs three dollars, and all the dogs in Chicago have to be vaccinated, that means a million dollars of serum is sold, so the manufacturers can afford to pay the Governor a good rake-off. Irene has said that she would gladly be bitten by a dog with rabies (in fact, she is sure she must have been many times before) in order to prove that this alarm, which has resulted in much cruelty to household pets, is false. But she is not a sentimental fanatic about animals; her attitude is the same as towards everything else — realistic and practical. She talks about 'the colour of, shall we call it, manure?' 'A squirrel with six pink pimples on its stomach — very pink.' In the restaurant: 'Do you want onion soup? It's included in the dinner — doesn't cost any more. I'm going to have pompano because we don't get that in our little village.'

She makes fun of the fact that she talks too much. Sometimes her bluntness surprises others. Although extremely kind and generous she knows the value of money and the importance of economy. ('Never waste money on an expensive hotel. Where does it get you once you leave it?') She has a real fellow-feeling (and no petty jealousy) for all performers on the stage and for her rivals. She is, in fact, a woman who loves the great prizes of the world but knows that they don't mean everything. She has no regrets for the glory that she enjoyed. She now lives in a country house without a servant so that she has to prepare her own breakfast; she is philosophical enough to welcome the changes. It seems to me that she is facing the ever-growing horrors of old age with courage, unbounded vitality, and the knowledge that, with her accustomed luck, she may succeed as a personality as effectively at the age of eighty as she did at eighteen.[13]

Today Irene has still the attractive face of a baby marmoset. The starlit eyes are small but astonishingly bright, with the upper lids slanting down the outer edges to give an expression of incredulous wonder. Her complexion, once so porcelain-smooth, is now lined with small crinkles, but the contours are remarkably the same, and her figure and 'carriage' are still colt-like — the back straight as a scimitar, long arms like an Arab, and a Greek athlete's legs ending in narrow ankles and pointed, bird-like feet. She still wears clothes of her own fashion, says she knows what is the best length for her skirt and sticks to it: the result is just as it should be.

I often feel that people who have succeeded in one aspect of life would have done equally well if their innate talent had been used in other directions. Of course some people are born with an extraordinary bump in the throat that causes them to emit wonderful sounds and become great singers; but they remain uninteresting, obnoxious creatures. Some cinema stars have little merit beyond their photogenic qualities. But it would appear that many 'celebrities' are in life even greater personages than the public imagines them. I am sure that Irene Castle would have created a stir in the world if she had never danced a step.

BEVERLY HILLS HOTEL

January 22nd, 1954

Back in the same hotel where I had had a happy time three or four years ago. Through the shutters one caught glimpses of

---

[13] Irene Castle died in 1969.

flowering trees, fresh leaves and palms. But suddenly I felt appallingly nostalgic and sad.

Ever since I first came to this place twenty years ago Greta has been, in my mind, the one person to elevate it to glory. Because she lived somewhere in these hills, even before I knew her, the suburban villas, the gas stations and fruit stalls had a certain magic: they were part of the place that, for me, she dominated. When I was here with Anita Loos in the twenties, Garbo's ghost haunted me; her name and magnetic face were to be seen everywhere overcoming the banality of the hoarding posters. Later, when I came back alone, she was the lure. And at last I met her. The encounter was wild and fantastic, yet I might never have seen her again. But after the war we did meet again, and the last time I came here I saw nobody but her. I felt Olympian while the lives of others were as pigmies.

And now I am here again (on my lecture tour), and she is far away, sad, impossibly pathetic with her small, plaintive voice on the other end of the wire in New York where it is cold. Here it is as if a death had taken place.

The film industry thrives: the local papers carry stories about starlets with names like Terry Moore. A new crowd has appeared with eager eyes, hungry smiles, and a rapid willingness to sell themselves in order to succeed. But the arch-goddess has gone. She will never come back. She could never come back; Hollywood wouldn't really want her now. She is ten years older, and that is the unforgivable.

The sun still shines, the orange trees simultaneously have blossoms and fruit on them, and the air is clean. Everything is as it was, but everything is missing — and Greta is the missing element.

NEW YORK: GRETA TAKES AN APARTMENT

After over ten years spent in impersonal New York hotels, Greta has, at last, made the decision to move into an apartment.

Alas, the event is not cloaked in smiles. She is anxious and over-tired rather than relieved. She will trust no decorator to guide her, has done the whole, rather large apartment on her own, and the result is a mess. As an actress she knows instinctively that the most effective results are achieved through boldness, simplicity and contrast. She has not learnt that the same applies to colour. The walls are of a piggy beige, the curtains have pink in them, the cushions are every range of red from squashed strawberry to dusty crimson and dirty rose. Some chairs are upholstered in striped 'old-rose' and buff, there is a Savonnerie pink carpet on the floor, and even her Renoirs, Bonnards, Rouaults, Soutines and Modiglianis, brought from Hollywood, do not come to her rescue.

The general muddle results from her being unable to make a definite stand about anything. When she asked my advice about one room (lavender walls, pink carpet, Italian wood-carvings on wall), I suggested she should get rid of the gilded cupids. Her expression of sadness and pain was hard to bear; I hated myself for being so brutal.

It is interesting that the girl from a poor quarter of Stockholm, who was sent away for the holidays to the country, as a charity child (where she first tasted chocolates) finds herself living on her earnings in such an expensive apartment. But this rather pretentious décor is quite wrong, and in no way expresses her taste. She is not the sort of lady who sits around on sofas with a fashionable coffee-table and an elaborate ashtray at the ready. Her dwelling should denote that its owner is totally unconventional, with an inborn understanding of quality and restraint.

But more serious than the unsuitability of her flat is, to me, the fact that she is not leading the sort of life she would better enjoy. For someone who is so near nature to become one of a unit in an impersonal block of flats is quite unthinkable. There is nearby nowhere for her to walk, no smell of trees or of grass. Little wonder that she is often filled with frustration, even despair.

Part VIII: On Home Ground, 1954-5

HOME THOUGHTS

In spite of the lecture tour the winter had not been financially successful: no stage jobs had come my way, and my *Vogue* work was severely criticized. I did no drawing at all — in fact, never brought my paint things out of the cupboard. It had been a pleasant enough visit, but once the ship on which I was sailing shot past the downtown skyscrapers of Manhattan my existence of the past four months slid painlessly and quickly into limbo.

At home a great number of elderly people, as well as hundreds of cattle at the Smithfield Market Fair, had died as a result of London's thickest, blackest fog. My mother had escaped being a mortal victim, but she was still in an extremely precarious condition. I know my relationship with my mother is one of the most important things in my life. Her illness had worried me so much during my time away, that my return to find her recovered to a large extent seemed almost an anti-climax. Yet there was an undercurrent of drama in the air, of suppressed emotion — even tears — so that the ploy of extracting the presents from my luggage was useful. There and then, in the hall at Pelham Place, with ostensibly only a cursory glance at my mother (lest she should look so ill that my eyes would betray my shock), I produced the straw tray, the teapot from Chinatown, the chocolates, the nylons, and the bottle of pink champagne with which we toasted her recovery.

Later I noticed that my mother appeared painfully white with dark eyes that had a puffy look; but she was by no means an old crock, and it was a tribute to her character that, at her great age, she had survived.

As my mother told me the story of her illness, pity was mixed with a gradual feeling of exasperation that so many things had gone wrong unnecessarily in my absence. My mother had fought for breath for three days before becoming desperate enough to send for the doctor. By this time her heart had been put to a terrifying strain. When two doctors appeared, they started fighting one another, then the servants fought each other, and various people had behaved tactlessly and made false economies. These seemed so poignant and unnecessary, so foolish and tragic, especially when I thought of my reckless extravagance while living in that turret with the miraculous views of New York stretching for miles beneath each window. Money had come to mean little to me. I couldn't resist taking people to meals at the most expensive restaurants, ordering theatre tickets, flowers and drinks, and I was enjoying myself so much in the open way that hotel life affords. It was with quite a conscious effort that I had to make myself realize the importance of family life and its human values.

It was quite hard to settle down calmly to a life so unlike that in the big cities of the States.

All the while I am with my mother, a hideous foreboding unsettles an otherwise rather calm spell which is, no doubt, induced by the knowledge that my business life is now being thoroughly looked after as it should have been all these years. Eileen Hose has proved to be the greatest blessing. A most delightful, sensitive companion, she is also cheerful, efficient and staunch: she could cope with any contingency. The change in the atmosphere that she has wrought at Pelham Place is quite remarkable. She brings the sunshine into the house; it is now a pleasure to be there.

On arrival at Broadchalke, Stacey, the gardener, told me it had been the hardest winter for fifty years. Like all our neighbours, we had had frozen pipes, burst cisterns; one hundred and forty gallons of water had come through my bedroom ceiling down the staircase to the hall. But now we were all enjoying the first days of spring: the birds in full throat, the daffodils doing a Wordsworth act in the grass; and indoors, protected from the winds and in the sun streaming through the windows, the forsythia was bursting into bud. This is a time of burgeoning. Let's hope there'll be a bit of burgeoning for me, and that after the hibernation the next months may induce a little inner growth!

REDDISH

Have been dipping once more into the Denton Welch Journals. Under the influence of that extraordinary youth, whose talented life was so painfully cut short by a quite unnecessary bicycle accident, I will try to write in detail, and in the way in which he is so expert, of how time passes when it is, perhaps, at its least eventful.

With a feeling of incompletion, but in a great hurry, I leave London, at the end of a busy week, for the country. Many things are yet to be done, but if I were to make even one more telephone call I would doubtless miss my train. Already I have left too little time for the taxi drive to Waterloo. It is a strain to 'cut it so fine' (my father's expression), even without the unexpected traffic jam in Parliament Square.

The taxi is filled with my baggage — empty flower and vegetable baskets — and a hamper. (People ask facetiously:

'Have you a cat in there?') As I leap from the cab with two minutes to go, I realize that Waterloo isn't the huge impersonal inferno of noise and hurry that I had imagined it. The porters have come to recognize me as being the eccentric traveller to Salisbury, wearing outsize hats, who is always late and laden with baskets, and their greetings make a pleasant addition to the ritual of departure. At last I have decided that economizing in small ways is apt to result in added irritation and physical exhaustion so, rather than sit surrounded by noisy children, talkative North-country housewives, ravenous, licentious soldiery, or heavy pipe-smokers, I now enjoy the luxury of a first-class non-smoker; thus, the journey is generally eventless, silently comfortable, and perhaps even solitary. I read the book, theatre and art reviews in the *New Statesman* and *Spectator*. I look at *Life* with a distaste for its heartless, clinical attitude to all and sundry — from a suicide's leap to a reportage on a great virtuoso. The foreign fashion magazines which have arrived during the week, and which I now flick through, seem particularly fantastic and artificial in contrast to the landscapes which rush past outside the train windows: the silver birch plantation, Brookwood Cemetery, Brooklands discarded racetrack, or the square, towered church and delightful village a few miles short of Basingstoke.

Soon my eyes begin to feel as if rimmed with fire: I close them. When I wake the meadows, the poplars and familiar landmarks tell me it is time to get down the baskets from the rack. Still punch drunk with slumber, I make my way, heavily laden, to the ticket turnstile (porters are scarce on Salisbury platform), and I notice that the people who come to meet friends from the train are a very different race from the Londoners we have left behind. It is not just that they are dressed in tweeds or flannels or in old country clothes; there is something engagingly different about their open-air voices and faces: they look neither nervy nor tired, their eyes are clear. They smile.

My mother is awaiting me in our shabby blue car. She has just done the weekend shopping in Salisbury, but has little news to impart for nothing much has happened since I left. If I am unlucky, she will regale me with an account of some minor disaster: rain through a roof, the mess made by a chimneysweep, the foolishness of the gardener, or the tantrums of the cook. But I make every effort not to be got down by the tidings, and try to impart the news of my busy urban days which, very abruptly, have begun to fade into unreality. Yes, I had been to see *Hippo Dancing*, a ridiculous play in which Robert Morley wasted his talent; I wasn't very interested in this fact even at the time, and now it certainly isn't of any importance. What else? My past activities have suddenly become facts. Without someone to throw back the ball to me, to stimulate further descriptions, my narrative gives a distorted picture of idleness and pleasure. Impossible to describe the lunch party at Pam Berry's which, in fact, had been quite hilarious with everyone shouting abuse at one another. It would be impossible to interest her with a list of those who had been there: Betty C, Mark Bonham C, Anthony H, Nancy Mitford, etc. It would also be silly to try to describe the particular intensity of that two days' long photograph session, starting with the pre-breakfast visit to buy enormous quantities of flowers at Covent Garden market, and ending lying on the floor in almost total collapse, after eight different women had come to pose among the baskets and buckets. In a desperate effort to entertain my mother I would start to recapitulate some of the other activities: the final proof-correcting with my publisher which went on for so many hours; the lunch with

270

that rock-like friend and support, Audrey Withers, the editor of the English *Vogue*. Without wishing it, I found I had embarked upon telling my mother of how, after all these years, my contract with American *Vogue* is over: that I have been sacked without even a 'thank you', let alone a golden handshake. Patchevitch's excuse is that I am not available often enough in New York. Although in some ways I am relieved, for their present editor suffocates my enthusiasms, I am now without any dependable source of income. But the saga dried up in my mouth. Why, oh why, had I ever touched upon it when it would only alarm my mother? Much better to skip my professional life and ask about the garden. What is Stacey, the gardener, busying himself with today? Has he started to dig the bed in front of the cottage? No, of course not. I notice that the avenues of trees from Wilton are beginning to burst into green; certainly there is a great difference in the countryside since last week. Spring is ready at hand; this sudden spurt of sun will work wonders...

With each return my house holds some surprise. There are letters, library books, or even a package awaiting me on the hall table; everything looks very clean and brushed and different. Perhaps in my thin London suit I feel the hall to be chilly, and it takes some time to heat up the rooms to my requisite temperature. The sherry decanter gives a welcome. I open the garden door and survey the scene on the terrace: the meadows are quiet, the rooks are cawing, the jackdaws have built in the chimney and the library fire is smoking. Ravenous for lunch — or is it mere greed? — I let myself go, for that is the mood, now that tension has relaxed.

I am incapable of mustering the energy even to make the telephone call to London about those vital things that should have been done before I left; a wonderful 'go-hang' slothfulness pervades. The Scots Agnes provides the necessary vitality with her bustle and smile and energy and kindness.

After lunch a heavy, protruding stomach precedes me up the garden, with secateurs and basket, to cut prize flowers. The procedure is a great source of contentment and relaxation. This lovely luxury is followed by another: an abandonment to sleep. Not a rushed forty winks: a real 'hogging it', with clothes off, and a hot-water bottle which has been placed by Agnes in the turned-down bed. Oh, the joy of sleeping until one begins to half-wake, and then to feel that one can go on dozing or sleeping, that one may rest until one is numb with silliness and warmth and a deep sense of recuperation.

Eventually, hours later, one comes downstairs feeling a totally different human being. Everything is changed about oneself: one's skin, one's vision, one's mind. The country clothes one has put on help the change, but the transformation is also organic: it's like a rebirth. What to do with this new life? Nothing. Why not enjoy it — savour it to the full? So the quiet evening is spent with scrapbooks or art books, turning out old magazines, smoking a cigar, or doodling while one listens to the wireless. It is like a pleasant convalescence after illness.

One is never idle for long in the country. The dash to Salisbury in time to be at the market before the plants of the Women's Institute are sold, the thatcher to be implored to come to the rescue, the sods of turf or the peat ordered, the 'cottage for sale' to be seen — so much to do without even contact with the neighbours who, nevertheless, are very often at the back of one's mind. Their antics assert themselves with insistence while one is weeding; in fact, weeding is a great test of one's peace of mind. If one has something upsetting to concentrate upon, it is best to give up weeding for the day.

Of late, I have become very like farmer Bundy and his family: they spend most of their time working and very little at play. I feel sometimes like a monk, and this existence is apt to have the effect of making me feel extremely old. But I know that this quiet dedication is the right sort of life; it is healthy and natural, and goes with the grain. New York is a stimulating drug; it is terrific for the time being, but more than three months wreaks havoc with the life of the spirit.

Here, the bird song, the balmy air, the long nights of sleep and the slower tempo of day are cushions to the senses and, at the same time, a more lasting foundation on which to build one's strength and capabilities for the future.

AGNES

It is a great joy to have about the house someone who is as great a character as our ancient Scots Agnes. She is good, cleanliving, and Victorian. She lives with my mother and me, acting as house and parlour maid. The only trouble is that although she appears to be healthy and strong, she is not. During the war she was working in a munitions factory when a bomb fell. She was blown the length of the factory floor; for weeks she was written off as a total loss, but eventually she came back to life — though thenceforward suffering from horrific bouts of asthma. Through many of these attacks my mother has nursed her with loving care. Eventually my mother decided that Agnes should be transported from London to the country. Here, in the clean air of Wiltshire, her condition has improved and, having been brought up as a country girl she relishes the delights of Broadchalke. She has a way with all animals, tends the household pets in their illnesses, and makes ready friends with the villagers.

In her own way Agnes is an artist. She enjoys wearing the rather grotesque, long-skirted, plum-coloured alpaca uniforms that I have designed for her, and she looks delightfully Miss Mitfordian with her crisp white hair as she goes out to select carefully the ivy or magnolia leaves, polishes them, and places them among the green apples on the marble top of the dining-table. Never before has the table acquired this glass-like polish; she puts more elbow grease into her cleaning than anyone of half her age!

Agnes tells us of her childhood's excitements: how her father owned a horse that was a 'freak-a-nature', and how some neighbours (the daughters were eighty-five years old and the mother a hundred-and-six) were so old-fashioned that they were dressed like 'ghosts'. Then Agnes goes on to tell of her arrival from Scotland in London. 'The first film I saw was *Viennese Nights*. Oh, I loved it so much I couldn't leave the cinema when it was over. It was lovely! There was Strauss's old mother and she died and there was a moon. They had a night sky painted, and right in the middle of it there was a great round moon. Oh, I wish I wasn't so sentimental!'

But Agnes did not become sentimental about Reddish House. One morning she came to my bedroom and, turning to the window and looking up the paddock where the old white horse grazes, told me she didn't know why, but she wanted to leave us. There was no reason she could think of for going, and we had all been kind to her, but suddenly she felt disenchanted with the place; it had lost its magic for her. It was not a question of Agnes getting on badly with Mrs Murdoch, the cook; she had settled that score decisively some time ago. When first she came to us, Mrs Murdoch bullied Agnes unmercifully. 'Get out of my kitchen! You know you're not allowed in here while I'm preparing haddock savoury. Go and dust your pantry — you should be ashamed of yourself living in such a pig-sty! You aren't fit to work under a first-class chef like myself; the least you can do is to make yourself scarce!' Agnes bore the punishment with saintlike patience, until one day she had enough; Mrs Murdoch humiliated Agnes once too often. Suddenly Agnes saw electric sparks of purple like those that flash from tramwires at evening. Summoning all her Scotch strength, Agnes pulled herself up to her full four feet eight inches and, with clenched fists, let fly. After a straight left followed by a right, and again another left aimed between the eyes, Mrs Murdoch lay unconscious on the stone floor. When the cook eventually regained consciousness, she and Agnes had become good friends.

So why did Agnes now wish to abandon us? No matter how loud we were in our cries of disbelief, horror and appeal, Agnes was determined to go. And go she did — without further explanation. We never heard a further word from her.

BROADCHALKE: A BADDISH PATCH

It's been a baddish patch. I thought I'd enjoy being quietly here in the country. I was at the end of any specific job, so here was the opportunity I've often longed for, of being able to read, and visit houses and places, and perhaps have a few intimates to stay. But it doesn't seem to have turned out that way. Perhaps being in such close contact with my mother, for many weeks on end, has proven rather a strain. We don't have much to talk about or discuss, and we are likely to get on one another's nerves. (Different generation trouble.) Friends I wanted to stay couldn't come, those in the neighbourhood whom I'd have liked to drop in for a meal weren't available or were ill, and I found myself already rather chafing and stale when I was overcome by a sudden bilious attack. There is nothing like an upset stomach to undermine one's whole existence. I became morbid and introspective, full of fears of what life will be when, or if, one gets much older. Already I feel appallingly aged and decrepit.

JEFFERY & BOARDER

July, 1955

Mr Jeffery of Jeffery & Boarder, photographic experts, has died aged eighty-three — very sad. But little at the time of his death did we, who had all our technical work entrusted to this worthy and remarkable Victorian firm, realize just how sad it was going to be for us. Naturally we thought the well-established and unique business would continue, but no preparations had been made for what might happen after his death. Mr Herbert, his partner, sixty-five and stunned by shock, comes out of the dark-room for the first time in forty years, feels he cannot take on the responsibility of running the organization, and within two weeks the entire staff of twenty are given notice, the equipment is sold for a song, and the goodwill of the business disappears into thin air.

J & B was a firm of craftsmen. The work was old-fashioned, but it had a quality that is lacking today. If an hour had to be spent obtaining a good enlargement from a particular negative, then an hour was spent; no expense or time was spared. The prints were developed in an acid (almidol) that no one else uses today. Each time a batch of prints came up the results were quite a revelation.

Jeffery & Boarder's Mrs Driver who, for more years than I like to admit, has filed all my negatives and dealt with our orders, has been an important personage in my life although I have only known her through the telephone. Now today she comes from Ealing to meet me in the flesh and discuss this terrible disintegration. She sits with a cup of tea on her lap as she tells me that Mr Herbert, the partner, who has been making these beautiful silver and black prints all his life, is now looking for a job.

'He wants to become a postman.'

'But isn't that foolish?' I ask. 'Isn't that very selfish?'

Oh, Mrs Driver agrees. 'So many people are stranded and put out of a job. Lots of firms will have to go out of business. Dorothy Wilding has had us do all her enlargements for Her Majesty The Queen, and Douglas Glass his *Sunday Times* portraits. And there's a man who's been relying on us for forty years: a man who used to take photographs of bulls, and he took them anywhere — against a shed or a haystack or farm buildings — and Mr Jeffery used to paint out the background for him. It was a very tricky thing to do, but *The Field* insisted on a plain white background. Well, of course, you can't always place a bull against a plain white background, and as Mr Jeffery was the only man who could do this work, the poor photographer has had to retire and *The Field* is frantic!'

For myself I feel as if I had broken a limb, and will have to try to move with my arm or leg in plaster. It is a great shock to my self-confidence. I used to know that Mr Jeffery would produce something good even from a poor negative. Now the struggle for better than the-run-of-the-mill will continue with frustration and despair.

CHURCHILL'S GOODBYE FAMILY PARTY

The invitations did not suggest it was to be a 'Goodbye to No. 10' party, although all friends knew that this, in fact, was the chief reason for forgathering. The cards informed us that 'Sir Winston was "At Home" to celebrate the anniversary of Lady Churchill's birthday'. Indeed it was her birthday, and all family friends and supporters and every old crony who had been bidden were determined not to miss this very particular celebration. I was impressed at being sent a card which, I am sure, was inspired by a reminder of my existence from a mutual friend, the beautiful lady, Rhoda Birley, with whom I dined before the festivity. For many years I have been friends with at least some members of the Churchill clan, but, since they have so many acquaintances, I was surprised to find myself among the chosen.

Rhoda is very Irish and very vague. This evening she seemed to be in another world. She was a man short for dinner, and said her day had been a nightmare — everything wrong. She had cooked the dinner herself (she is a painter, but also an artist in the kitchen), and thrown the dessert over her head. Guests: Jock Colville, for a considerable time the Private Secretary of Churchill, and his redoubtable mother, Lady Cynthia of prison reform; the Hamish Hamiltons; Tortor Gilmour, gaunt, of ivory bones; gentle and smiling Lady Lascelles, wife of the late King's Private Secretary, who bought from my father our house in Hyde Park Gardens where we lived before difficulties caught up with us all. An unusual, yet pleasant enough party. The men lingered in the dining-room talking about Burgess and Maclean so that we were late arriving at Downing Street, where the large and lofty rooms were already crowded.

The public servants (or are they old Churchill servants? — I doubt it) seemed much more familiar and friendly than at most social gatherings. They beamed, and their eyes twinkled a welcome, for they knew and liked almost all the guests, and the announcer at the top of the staircase did not need to ask many names before sending forth, in stentorian tones, the latest arrivals into the *mêlée*.

A buzz of excited conversation and pleasant laughter. A flooding of light. An impression of flowers. All the years rolled by. To think that this gathering was being given by someone whose face already went back into history. It was part of the Boer War, a face, still young and calf-like, that showed such intelligent anger among the other bland leaders of the First World War. It became the smiling face that knew defeat, that scowled in eclipse, and came out into the brilliance again to guide us during the last terrible years. At a time when Churchill could promise us nothing good but ultimate victory, he was the rallying point. Without him we might have been defeated. For a long lifetime now we have taken for granted this figure in our midst. Almost as familiar is the face of his wife: her Grecian profile, the deep -set, pale-blue eyes, have changed little with the years. She was always gaunt and elegant: in her bridal dress, in 1914 'tailor-mades', and in the ubiquitous bandanna kerchief of the last war. These two faces have together travelled through many epochs in our personal history. Tonight was a private goodbye.

Churchill stood alone by the door, immaculate in his sagging evening dress — very pink and rose-buddy. Although still stunningly like his image carved in memory, he appeared smaller than one remembered. A cigar was held in tapering pink fingers, and he wore a look of acute amusement in his eyes. Between spasms of newly-arriving guests he would sit down on a chair with his legs planted well apart, a hand on each knee, resting.

Lady Churchill was dressed in black lace with orchids at the waist, and her eyes were focused to other distances.

Nevertheless, she could still throw out a few *mondanites*, and answered some stupidity of mine by saying it was not surprising that they had made the rooms look 'lived-in' considering that this had been their home now for so long. It was said that Lady Churchill was tonight suffering agonies from phlebitis; but there is still fire and dash in the consort of the old warrior.

These noble rooms of good Georgian proportions have been poorly decorated by the Office of Works. The imitation silk curtains, of meagre quality, are not full enough, have shrunk, and hang five inches from the floor. Sofas are upholstered in timid, pukey pea-greens, almonds and beiges. Yet the effect tonight was splendid, the English portraits making an effective background, the fine chandeliers of Bristol glass sparkingly clear. Friends and well-wishers had sent so many flowers that every ledge and table was adorned with offerings of different shapes and sizes. There were luxurious baskets with sprays of peach blossom, roses and orchids: others were more humble precursors of spring with early daffodils. The personal touch was supplied by portraits of the family by Orpen and Birley, some refined, good taste 'still-lives' in muted colours and bevelled frames by that most sensitive and beautiful painter, William Nicolson, and rows of framed snapshots of the family.

But the guests provided the chief interest of the evening. Proust said that it is possible to get a vivid impression of the quality of a party by reading only a few of the names published in a newspaper. One look at this assemblage and one could tell that this was of a fine vintage, mellow and restrained. By the omissions one could tell as much as by those present. These people were not necessarily of the aristocracy, nor of politics; few of them were involved seriously in the arts — though literature was represented; but the gathering represented a quality that is above distinctions; that, unmindful of what the world thinks, has its own code of merit. Neither did beauty, or rare good looks, play a preponderant role — no one was invited for their renown. In this household Royalty is certainly highly respected; but this was a private occasion, an occasion apart, and the presence of Royalty, which always creates a tension, would be contrary to the effect desired. So no Royal personage was invited, but relations, friends, and the confederates who went back into the very earliest years were relaxing together in affection and friendship.

Churchill's doctor was among the favoured; but none of his professional allies were invited, unless they happened to be friends too. Ghosts of former Governments abounded: reminders of Asquith in Lady Violet Bonham Carter, with Etruscan profile and scared donkey's eyes, tonight surprisingly *décolletée* in bright pink satin — surprising because, with her great intelligence and intellectual interests, she has seldom shown an interest in chiffons; and Cynthia Asquith, looking sadly stolid instead of the pre-Raphaelite sprite that she always will be remembered as. Still recognizable as having been a great Edwardian beauty was old Pamela Lytton, curved and bent, but pink and white in black lace. It is said that the young Churchill admired her above others, and there was a question of an engagement. How astonished she would have been if I, a complete stranger, had gone up to her and asked why, when she went to that Empire Day Ball given by F. E. Smith and Lord Winterton in 1911, dressed as Pavlova as 'The Swan', she had worn a long skirt instead of showing her legs in a tutu! How could she guess that this interloper enjoyed gleaning such pieces of useless information as a precocious schoolchild from the society magazines? I remembered also the early photographs of Anita Leslie, a descendant of the Leslie clan, as a tall, shy child. Now she was looking just as surprised as ever with her raised eyebrows, but she had suddenly become mature — a matron. How impersonal and beastly is the disguise of old age! It reduces the individuality of the most vivid personalities: even Margaret, Lady Birkenhead, with aquiline features and bright, bird-like eyes, whom one imagined would always challenge the years, now looks rather sad and perturbed in old age. Margaret was one of my first upholders, and she occupies a large place in my heart. She always judged people by her own standards, never accepted ready-made opinions or acknowledged reputations decided by others. Gipsy-like, unconventional, utterly unsnobbish, she wore very lightly the burdens of her husband's high office; tonight she brought to the gathering her own craggy bonhomie and the aura of the great F.E.

I doubt if white-haired, but ageless and indefatigable Sylvia Henley, Venetia Montague's sister, a tremendous Churchill prop, ever looked much different — but then I've only known her for twenty years. Apart from the immediate family there were masses of Romillys, and naturally Mitfords. There, with red bobbed hair, was Molly Long, known as 'Marmalade Moll'; she exudes the friendliness and sympathy of a firelit tea in winter, and her voice is like the crunching of toast.

Many important relics of the last war were on view. Sir Archibald Sinclair, who used to be so handsome in a romantic Victorian mould, has now become diminished of stature and the fiery black has turned to cinders. His wife, by his side, is now twice his size — an enormous grey-haired matron. Another figure from the past: that horrid old snob, Professor Lindemann, now risen to be Lord somebody. Faces known by caricature and political cartoons acquired an extra dignity this evening as they came out of retirement. Lord Ivor Spencer

Churchill always presents a most remarkable appearance, aristocratic and refined, with the pursed, cherubic features of his American mother, Madame Balsan, famous for the Boldini and Helleu portraits, and his expression that denotes that he, quicker than anyone, realizes the sadness and amusement of the fact that he will never appear grown-up. Clarissa and Anthony Eden — successors to this house — were conspicuous by their absence in Manchester.

This was no occasion for an exchange of darts, for political, social or any other warfare. People stood about, drinking a glass of champagne and displaying their nicest moods. Although happy at receiving this cheerful hospitality they knew that, although nothing has been announced, the resignation of the Prime Minister is imminent. The Churchills had left Chequers for the last time this weekend, the Queen comes to dine here on Tuesday, and it is assumed that the resignation will be given next day. So this was the end of an epoch, and everyone present realized it. There was much unmentioned sadness.

We wandered into the small dining-room where the host cut the birthday cake. Juliet Duff suggested that Winston should make a speech. 'My days of speech-making are almost over,' he said. 'Someone else can do it,' and he pointed to Lord Goddard. 'Why not he who sends bad men to the gallows?'

Randolph was emotionally upset and carrying on a feud against the world; one's heart went out to him in his suffering. Later he led me up to sit and talk with his father while Diana Cooper was having her half-hour with the great man. I was extremely diffident of encroaching as, with certain people whom I most admire, I would rather run a hundred miles than be forced vis-à-vis. I found that the two were talking about modern painting and Winston raged against his portrait by

Graham Sutherland. 'These modern chaps! You're in their power. They make some drawings, and then go away and do their damnedest: they like to make a fool of you. I *hate* this thing! And I wouldn't be surprised if no one got the opportunity of looking at it after my day. It's a horrible portrait — a horror and vile in colour!'

The first time I had ever met Churchill was at a party Venetia Montague had given for his birthday at a time when he was still in eclipse after the Dardanelles decision. Supper was served for about a dozen of us around a large table; there was iced champagne, hot oysters, a very special dish that I believe Venetia had had sent in from the Embassy Club, and a great reverence for the great 'star' of the evening. I became paralysed with fright, and was incapable of speech except to confide my terror to another young man present named George Burgess.

Then again, before the war, in New York when I was living and photographing in the towers of the Waldorf Astoria, the Churchill family arrived *en masse* on the floor below me. There was much *va-et-vient* at all times of the day and night, and each member of the family except the father was given impromptu photographic sittings. I found the man generally sitting apart and glowering at us all, too formidable to approach; I felt that every minute of his time was too precious to be wasted on such a frivolity. He was seeing a lot of Bernard Baruch, and there were big deals with magazines and newspapers. He left his rooms but seldom, the representatives of the outside world coming to Mahomet to pay their court. But one day Churchill broke his rule and went out to some engagement. We heard that he had been knocked down by a taxi-cab on Park Avenue. His condition for a while caused anxiety. It is spooky to think that by such a small margin he might not have survived to bring us through the conflict to come.

Tonight I peered at Churchill at the end of his long and glorious career. His pale eyelashes were blinking, his thin wisps of delicate white hair were combed neatly back, and I noticed the very peculiar, flat end to his bulbous nose which appeared as if cut off straight with a knife. Churchill sat hunched up, his shirt-front rose in a high big roll, and his waistcoat seemed almost 'Empire' in cut. He sucked on the end of a long cigar without pretence of smoking it. He made a few jokes that showed that the old spirit had not deserted him and our laughter was a little exaggerated with relief; but his delivery is so high in Gibbonian style, with long pauses for effect, that every remark is given added pith when delivered in such a grandiose manner — or conversely, when thrown away in his own inimitable offhand style. Churchill, aged eighty-one, looked fit — a very, very healthy baby — but he was somewhat deaf and hated being shouted at by kind friends who were gallantly doing their best to amuse him.

Winston does not enjoy having to accept the inevitability of old age. He said, rather sadly, that if he were to loose the reins of responsibility, and leave the fate of the country in the hands of others, he would, at any rate, have leisure for his painting. But, although he feels groggy some of the time, he knows that in fits and starts he is more alert and experienced than anyone else.

I left the gathering with Diana. She was very sad. Trying to comfort her, I made some ridiculous remarks about the Churchills going out on a high wave. Diana listened hardly at all to my imbecilities: she was deep in her own thoughts. Duff had been such a friend ... his whole life — and their life together — so closely linked with Winston ... Diana was inconsolable.

A NOTE TO THE READER

If you have enjoyed Cecil Beaton's Memoir enough to leave a review on **Amazon** and **Goodreads**, then we would be truly grateful.

Sapere Books is an exciting new publisher of brilliant fiction and popular history.

To find out more about our latest releases and our monthly bargain books visit our website: **saperebooks.com**

49404788R00171

Made in the USA
Columbia, SC
20 January 2019